M000199476

04

OUR CRY FOR LIFE

OUR CRY FOR LIFE

Feminist Theology from Latin America

María Pilar Aquino

Translated from the Spanish
by Dinah Livingstone

Wipf and Stock Publishers
EUGENE, OREGON

First published as *Nuestro clamor por la vida: teología latinoamericana desde la perspectiva de la mujer* by Editorial Departamento Ecuménico de Investigaciones (DEI), Apartado 390-2070, Sabanilla, San José, Costa Rica. © 1992 by María Pilar Aquino

Wipf and Stock Publishers
199 West 8th Avenue, Suite 3
Eugene, Oregon 97401

Our Cry for Life
By Aquino, María Pilar
Copyright©1993 Orbis Books
ISBN: 1-59244-101-7
Publication date: November, 2002
Previously published by Orbis Books, 1993.

Contents

v

PART 2
WOMEN AS DOERS OF THEOLOGY

Acknowledgments

This book would not have been possible without the help of various persons during the many phases of its development. In some way, each of these persons enabled me to develop the basic confidence necessary to start and finish what seemed to be only a dream. I am very grateful to Elsa Tamez and Enrique Dussel for encouraging me in my theological work over the years and particularly for motivating this project since its beginning. It was like a blessing from God to meet with Elsa to discuss, criticize, and correct my work, and even to laugh a little, sometimes in foreign lands. I have great esteem for the Pontifical University of Salamanca with its Faculty of Theology and the Superior Pastoral Institute (Madrid) that offered their support while I was doing my doctorate.

My thanks also to Marie Alexis Navarro, IHM, and Sister Kathleen Mary McCarthy, CSJ, for their support. I am very grateful to Bridget Clare McKeever, SSL, who was always there to clarify my doubts. And I should emphasize the valuable collaboration of María Clara L. Bingemer, whose assistance, suggestions, and affection made my job much easier. During the most difficult times, the help, availability, and affection of John Diercksmeier and Elizabeth Hernández were fundamental. Beyond mere technical assistance, they showed me the strength of solidarity. I want to express my great admiration and affection for Casiano Floristán, director of my doctoral studies; he has inspired my personal and professional life with his wisdom, commitment, kindness, and the extraordinary intensity with which he embraces the events of daily life. The presence of Juan José Tamayo-Acosta is without a doubt a key part in my work. His theoretical clarity and great sensitivity to women's issues, especially those of oppressed women, afforded me new ways to view numerous vital issues. I also want to underline the valuable contribution of Sister Karen Wilhemy, CSJ, Rev. Jerome A. Bouska, and my dear friend Rev. Edward Donovan, whose generosity made this project possible. My gratitude to Allan F. Deck, SJ, and the Association of Catholic Hispanic Theologians in the United States for the trust they have always shown me. Likewise, I am thankful for the help I received from Rev. Antonio Salas, Carmina Virgili, María

vii

Josefa García Callado, Margarita Pintos, Amparo Martínez, Leonor Aída Concha, Carmen Lora, Maruja González B.; and my sisters, Bertha, Evelia, Livier, Araceli, and the many other women who have helped me along the way. I should also make special mention of DEI; in particular, Raquel R. Rodríguez, Pablo Richard, and Franz Hinkelammert, who have nourished and strengthened the fundamental choices of my life. My appreciation to Mónica Errejón and Silvia Conde of the Society of Helpers for me helping to understand better my experience of faith. I also want to mention the influence that Rev. Jorge Domínguez, OFM, had on my theological vocation. To him my warmest regards. Finally, the greatest words of love to my father, Clemente, and my mother, Efigenia, who, in their daily struggles for the survival of our large family, showed us all the meaning of hope, endurance, and solidarity. All of these persons in one way or another freely lent me their light.

Introduction

In recent years there has been a serious effort to establish the role of women in history, church, and theology. The region of Latin America and the Caribbean is no exception. Women have emerged in various fields of human activity, with a growing participation in the liberating processes taking place. Present-day popular social movements and the various Christian communities, particularly the base communities, recognize the presence of many women. This is one of the factors in Latin America today that offers great hope and challenges Latin American liberation theology, the church, and society in general.

In this book, my reflection concentrates primarily on Latin American women's experiences of oppression and liberation as I investigate the special features of theology done from the perspective of women in Latin America. It is important to point out from the beginning that this cannot be seen as a task dissociated from the expectations, questions, and immense suffering of the great majority of our peoples. It is a task based on their efforts to transform their present oppression, pain, and inhuman conditions of life into liberation, true joy, and human integrity for women and men from the perspective of Christian faith.

Although women's theological work is set within the broad context of liberation theology, I will try to clarify the particular contributions made by women both to the historical processes of change and to the epistemology of liberation theology, where until recently women were given scant attention, either as a theme for reflection or as doers of theology. So women's theological reflection is set within liberation theology in general, but acquires its own special features because of where it is coming from: poor and oppressed women. Daily these women experience the combined effects of oppression deriving from the Ibero-Portuguese colonial legacy, the *machista* patriarchal system, and the present structure of capitalism. Because they are women, they suffer inhuman domination, racist subjugation, growing impoverishment, and systematic exclusion. Theology done by women wants to contribute to changing this situation. How women propose to do so, their instruments, the itin-

1

erary they propose, their limitations, and challenges are matters for this inquiry.

Since the end of the 1970s, women have been working on this theology, although their work became clearer and more widespread in the middle of the 1980s. Today the theological perspective of women needs to be deepened in order to achieve greater methodological consistency. Thus one of the purposes of this book is to increase the dialogue in the Christian communities between men and women, among women themselves, and between women and the Latin American theological communities. In addition to correcting our mistakes and omissions, we need above all to clarify together the way to move toward the fullness of life that is anticipated in Jesus Christ, activated in the struggle of the poor and oppressed, and destined by God for the whole of creation. In Latin America we are going through very difficult times as we approach the twenty-first century. Yet they are times in which we see more clearly the primary human and Christian options of our peoples: for *life*. It is imperative to reaffirm our hope, strengthen the promotion of life, nourish spiritual energy, and widen the spaces in which the popular sectors can operate. Theology done by women stands with these urgent tasks.

My choice of subject was influenced by a sense of solidarity and faith shared with other women, by a desire to contribute, theologically, to the search for new theoretical and practical solutions to our problems—solutions that embody a liberating vision and lead to new realities in society and the church. The theological perspective of women is fruitful for understanding the liberation process as a whole as well as women's liberation in particular; however, there is a distinct need to stress and make visible the perspective of women.

Likewise, I am convinced that Latin American liberation theology from the perspective of women is a necessary response to God's present activity in the life of poor and oppressed women. The steps they are taking toward their own liberation, driven by the power of the Spirit, are in line with this new experience. The theological task of women clarifies, encourages, criticizes, and activates this liberating activity in the light of the gospel. In fact, we are seeing today the emergence of a new self-awareness in women, a new way of understanding and speaking about revelation, daily life, and the larger political reality, the relations between men and women, and our own spiritual pilgrimage *as women*.

I hope to show that theology done by Latin American women has special features that distinguish it from the theology done by men and women in other latitudes. This does not mean, however, that we distance ourselves from our common commitment to liberation. On the contrary, it highlights our originality and particular identity. It invites male theologians to overcome their androcentric systems and it stresses our links with other feminists. No liberating theology can set itself up in opposition to other women, and our theological work must emphasize our solidarity with the liberating experiences and hopes of men and other women. We share a hermeneutic position that bases the process of knowledge and consequently our understanding of faith on *actual human life* as it is lived by both men and women.

I want to point out from the start that my study is not trying to present a compilation of theology done by Latin American women. Neither is it a collection of what liberation theologians have said about women nor is it an evaluation of epistemological status in terms of first-world feminist liberation theology. Rather, it is an attempt to grasp the re-creating work of the Spirit that activates the strength, word, memory, and liberating struggles of women. Hence, I point out certain presuppositions in the work of Latin American women theologians, and establish certain criteria to evaluate critically our contributions as theologians. I have made a conscious effort to extract the maximum meaning and implicit or explicit content in the categories and theoretical structures present in the theological viewpoint of women.

At the beginning of this project I suspected that not everything that is happening in Latin America is being written about. Women's experiences in the church and politics today go far beyond what we can discover in recent publications, including the primary sources I use here. Current publications omit three fundamental matters: first, the character of knowledge as process, from which the absence of women has only recently been noted; second, the Latin American historical situation, which forces people to associate women's interests (as poor women from a subjugated race) with the cause of the people as a whole; and third, the difficult working conditions for third-world women doing theology. In our context theological activity customarily brings with it a heavy load of practical pastoral work. In Latin America we do not have an exclusive university environment or the material means to allow us to research and write in abundance and with rigor, even less so in the case of lay women theologians, who are the majority. Yet women's theological intuitions interwoven with our experience of life, feminist analytic science, and Bible rereading nourish hope and theological reflections.

It easily can be seen that my primary sources are the contributions of Latin American women themselves. In the process of writing this book I have given plenty of space to the theological intuitions and formulations discussed in the Christian communities to which women belong. Much valuable criticism of my work, traditional theology, liberation theology, and our attempts to name ourselves grew within informal conversations, suggestions, and concerns shared with other Latin American women theologians. They contributed significantly to the vision in this book.

One of the most significant features of the Latin American experience is the importance given to meeting others and to personal relations. Among women, meetings give rise to solidarity, friendship, mutual enrichment, discussion in depth, and greater clarity about our whole liberating vision. Moreover, personal relations strengthen the mutual support network, encourage theological and pastoral creativity, and enable us to arrive at the minimum consensus necessary for our work in different regions. The community reflections and the meetings I have participated in over the last twelve years with women from Latin America and the Caribbean and poor Latin women in North America are the background to the convictions and hopes reflected in this book. Its object is to reaffirm our faith, activate our self-esteem, heal our wounds, and give comfort on the road toward the realities that are the reason for our hope.

The book is divided into two parts. The first part tries systematically to expound the historical and ecclesial genesis of theology done by women. The context of our theological viewpoint is liberation theology, which underpins it. I examine the special features of theology done by women that distinguishes it from other theologies, and how women's theology advances liberation theology by widening its analytic and hermeneutic scope.

The second part of the book looks at the methodological characteristics and specific content of theology done by women. This is the longer and more important part. It is reflection—what we women say about our experience of faith, its implications, and the demands and consequences for the future in theology, in rereading the Bible, and in church and society.

Two things remain to be said. The first is to stress again our *collaboration* with liberation theologians. This study aims to strengthen discussion, dialogue, and communication between men and women. We are aware that men are also interested in overcoming gender inequalities. Informal meetings with male theologians, friendly informal conversations, and equal sharing in meetings, such as those organized by the Ecumenical Association of Third World Theologians (EATWOT), nourish the vision of a new earth and lead to new discourse promoting our mutual liberation. Second, I want to stress the *collective* character of my study. It is not just collective because I have made use of the works by many women, but because we share dreams and sorrows in daily life. The concerns, doubts, searches, and discoveries of countless women and countless community and group reflections have shaped this work; it could not have been done without them.

The works I have consulted appeared originally in several languages. In order to avoid overloading the text with quotations in foreign languages, I have taken the liberty of translating them. Biblical quotations follow *The New Jerusalem Bible*.

PART 1

WOMEN AND THEOLOGY: GENESIS AND STATE OF THE QUESTION

1

The Irruption of History
into Women's Life and Consciousness

Recent theology done from the perspective of women in Latin America is set within the broad context of liberation theology. In fact, without this reference point it would have been much more difficult for women to contribute to the church and theology in Latin America and the Caribbean. In order to understand the power and significance of women's contributions, we first need to consider certain key features characterizing theological reflection in Latin America today.[1] Only then can we identify what is peculiar to the work done from the perspective of women, both in theology and in their efforts to create new ways of living together in the church and society.

The Way of Speaking about God

Theology is a discipline that exists specifically to articulate the language of faith. It refers to an experience of living rather than to a speculative exposition of abstract truths. It starts from experience and reflects on God's self-communication in the history of the world. The understanding of faith is a never-ending effort to reach the ultimate meaning of life, history, and the fate of the world and humanity. Theology does this in the light of God's revelation insofar as it is accessible within the limits of human knowledge. As Gustavo Gutiérrez notes,

It is appropriate to keep in mind from the very outset that theological thought about God is *thought about a mystery*. I mention this because it influences an attitude to be adopted in the effort to talk about God. I mean an attitude of respect that is incom-

9

patible with the kind of God-talk that is sure, at times arrogantly sure, that it knows everything there is to know about God.[2]

In liberation theology this attitude points directly to the method that distinguishes its way of doing theology. It can be summed up thus: "God is first contemplated when we do God's will and allow God to reign; only after that do we think about God. To use familiar categories: contemplation and practice together make up a *first act*; theologizing is a *second act*."[3] That is, contemplation and practice, silence and word, prayer and commitment are fundamental and inseparable dimensions for any understanding of faith seeking to give an account of the original experience of the liberating process in Latin America today.

Rather than reducing revelation to a body of rigid certainties, liberation theology realizes that divine revelation cannot be imprisoned, much less manipulated, to prevent or resist the intrinsic transforming power of the Spirit. It cannot go against the lives of the continent's impoverished masses. It has to keep an open mind to God's ineffable absolute mystery, which erupts as love, liberating power, and hope among the poor and oppressed of the earth, among the outsiders in society and the church. Liberation theology does not think about faith in the abstract, but only as it carries out God's original plan. This is to draw human creatures (men and women) toward God, so that they may share in the divine being. Therefore theology's task is to point out what human action is directed *toward*, *whither* it must go in order to be really obedient in faith and to be a fulfillment of the world and humanity.[4] And experience of *whither* faith is going must explain another element: *whence* it is speaking from, where it sets out on its road (its method), *what* it is that makes it proceed in a certain way and not another. This *whence* and *what* give any understanding of faith its particularity, forcing it to face the questions arising from its own reality.[5] They also enable it to work out *how* (by what method) to seek and find valid answers for its own historical situation. These are some of the central questions to which liberation theology is trying to respond: What does it mean to be a Christian in a world of poor people struggling for liberation? In what language can those who have been denied human wholeness be told that they are daughters and sons of God? How can the fullness of life in God be proclaimed to those who live at the edge of survival? What does it mean to be a woman in a continent conquered and then colonized by aggressive patriarchal capitalism?

The answers to these questions depend on the context and consciously taken position of those asking them, and they depend on the theoretical and practical tools available. The standpoint from which faith is understood (the primary experience, the first act) is a structural dimension giving consistency to the second word, *theology* properly speaking, as a human word (*logos*) about God (*theos*), as an understanding of faith and not just rational speculation. They are two structural dimensions of a single movement, which is deepened through action itself. "Our theologies," María Clara Bingemer observes, "recognize that the most important thing is not their theological discourse and the words they use, but the liberation that has to take place, in the process of which theology has a part to play and a specific identity."[6] Thus liberation theology's central concern is not to become a self-sufficient discipline, but rather to contribute to the liberation of oppressed peoples. It concerns women and men who have taken on the task of constructing new—more equal and more human—ways of living together.

The Primacy of Practice in Liberation Theology

From the first, liberation theology affirmed the primacy of historical action.[7] There are two reasons for this priority. The first is the recovery of the biblical notion of *doing the truth*, which means that "truth is not simply something that can be known or talked about but something that must also be acted upon and realized in deeds."[8] Thus theology cannot acquire the character of right thinking or right speaking without also doing right. The uniqueness of biblical faith is this close union between truth and fulfillment: "Promise and fulfillment," says Raúl Vidales, "are the two components of the truth that divine revelation proclaims to us. Something is truth if it is promised and then carried out so that it thereby acquires duration and solidity. God is truthful because he does what he promises, thus giving credence to our confidence and adherence."[9] These dimensions, Vidales writes, "are the dynamic elements of faith as a historical praxis of liberation; at the very same time they constitute the primordial field of locus of liberation hermeneutics."[10]

The second reason has to do with the context in which liberation theology arose, that is, the questions asked by countless believers about their faith, men and women involved in the social and popular movements for the liberation of the poor and oppressed. Theology maintains a vital and permanent relationship with historical action; it illuminates it and accompanies it. At the same time theology is challenged and enriched by action in a fruitful way to enable it to contribute to the transformation of the unjust reality. Thus thinking about faith means thinking from and about action for liberation.

Faith confronts a reality in which systems of oppression and injustice[11] operate in all spheres of life: destruction of basic survival systems, destruction of the ecosystems of nature and the earth, and deterioration in social ways of coping and interhuman relationships.[12] Oppression by imperialist capitalism converges with other forms of inequality and domination such as racism and sexism. Theology stresses the importance of action, because it is the poor and oppressed themselves who have initiated a brave struggle against their oppression and who choose to defend life in all its manifestations. Here the practical commitment of the oppressed to the construction of a new world acquires a triple significance: it *denounces* the existence of evils as going against God's original plan, which is fullness of life; it *transforms* the situation by making the poor and oppressed actors (subjects) in their own history; it *proclaims in advance* what is the true hope of the poor, that is, the coming of a re-created humanity in a new world on a new earth.

Ultimately, says Gutiérrez, Christian interest in becoming present in history derives from "the conviction of the radical incompatibility of evangelical demands with an unjust and alienating society. They [the poor] felt keenly that they cannot claim to be Christians without a commitment to liberation."[13] On this practical basis liberation theology reflects on the whole Christian message as well as on the church's identity and mission. This starting point is what forced liberation theology to structure itself in a particular and original way, different from traditional theology.[14] This is why it is called a *new way* of doing theology, reflecting on the faith and understanding it from the starting point of praxis. Praxis is not just a matter for theological reflection; it is faith's verification principle. It is this theology's hermeneutic viewpoint and, as such, becomes the structural horizon for theological knowledge. Praxis acquires an epistemological value as well as an ethical value.

Liberation theology has gone on to describe the activities actually taking place. These are the various doings of the popular sectors in pastoral, ecclesio-political, or strictly political spheres.[15] However, during the last few years this perspective has substantially widened to include other important dimensions, from which liberation theology was previously absent. The importance of public and private daily life is stressed; for example, the social division of work between the sexes, the existence of stereotypes affirming the superiority of men to women, the unequal relationship between men and women legitimated by a supposed *natural order* of social functions, the importance of sexuality and interpersonal relationships, in which the poor woman, in particular, is the victim of profound sexual discrimination.[16] These aspects had been discounted through an understanding of reality giving priority only to global social phenomena; daily life and the relationship between men and women were regarded as of secondary importance.[17] This view polarized the political and the public spheres of human activity to the detriment of the private sphere, and thus life was not taken as a whole but split in two. This meant that theology failed to offer any fruitful criticism of private daily life, which is the basis of people's actual experience of living. The incorporation of these previously neglected elements is closely linked to the emergence of a new active participant in history and theology: *women*. Their commitment, activities, and reflections contribute enormous wealth to liberation theology, enabling it to broaden its horizon, method, and content.[18]

From a Despoiled and Dominated Continent: A Brief History

For a critical understanding of the importance of women's presence today, their particular demands in the liberation process, and their contributions to theology, we must turn to history. The recovery of their past is a central dimension in people's ability to understand their own situation, take control of it, become aware of its limitations and possibilities, and thus share in the building of their own future.[19] On the other hand, as Carmen Lora notes, there is a tendency to analyze the reality of women's oppression as an accepted unilateral process, which almost consents to its own oppression.[20] However the history of Latin American women's struggles and resistance against different forms of destruction shows the contrary.

Latin America, like other third-world continents, has undergone the dramatic experience of being conquered and colonized by European powers. Although discrimination against women has a long tradition in society and the church,[21] for the women of Latin America and the Caribbean it reached violent dimensions through the conquest. Women were not only mistreated with the conquered people as a whole but were considered even more inferior because they were women. In the conquistadors' logic the basic argument ran thus: the indigenous are "as inferior to the Spaniards as children are to adults and women to men."[22] The sixteenth century was using the same argument as Aristotle to justify the subjection of those considered to be barbarians with limited mind and will. As Leopoldo Zea notes, the conquistadors were speaking of "slaves, women, children, those belonging to barbarian peoples; women who were in this situation through the natural limitation of their reason; and children whose reason needed to develop."[23] The claim that conquered peoples lacked full human stature profoundly affected women. Even though the pre-Columbian cultures had a patriarchal structure, with some exceptions in the Southern Cone, women shared in practically all walks of life, including military affairs, government, decisions about their own bodies, and the administration of property.[24] Hence the strongly segregationist structure imposed by the conquistadors had enormous impact.

We may distinguish three aspects concerning women in this period.[25]

First, indigenous women, sharing in the conquest of the whole people and the consequences of a cruel and unequal war, were particularly ill-treated, because at the beginning the creation of *mestizos*—mixed-race offspring—took place through rape and sexual abuse. A short indigenous account is illuminating:

> This is the way the Mexicans died, the *tlatelolca*. They left their city deserted . . . and we had nothing to eat and we ate nothing. And all night long it rained on us. . . . This was when people began to leave the town and when they left they went in rags and the women's buttocks were almost naked. And from all sides Christians chased them. They pulled open their skirts, they handled them all over, their ears, their breasts, their hair . . . and they also took them by force, they chose those women with white skin, those with fair skin, those with fair bodies. And at the time of the attack some women covered their faces with mud and put on rags.[26]

Second, the women did not just acquiesce. They resisted and joined, often in leadership positions, in the defense of their lands. This rebel presence made women aware of their own contributions to the struggle against the invader. They did not surrender their part in the history of their people.[27] The fact that the *official* view of history has hidden the presence of women in the many daily tasks of resistance and defense does not mean they were not there. On the contrary, it points to another deprivation. Women have been deprived of a *voice*, which defines us as human because it enables us to describe our own lives. The efforts being made today to recover the voice of women "belie the stereotype of cowardice, servility and passivity in the women of our race."[28] This image was propagated by androcentric colonial literature but does not represent reality or include women's voices.

Third, the search for a just and equal social order includes the dimension of race. If this dimension was used as a weapon of domination by the conqueror, it was also and has continued to be a central factor in resistance and struggle by women for their own rights as indigenous people and as women. Of course Latin America is not a homogenous whole, and cultural roots vary from region to region. But this reality, instead of being a source of disagreement, can become a force of solidarity, because we share a common past of colonization that has marginalized us, a common struggle for survival and liberation in the present, a common effort to create a different future, and a common search for our own identity as women. These elements help us see that "it is possible to go along a road of solidarity among those of us who come from different races on the continent."[29]

Against the will and the interests of the colonizing powers the struggles for independence started growing from the beginning of the nineteenth century. This period saw the organized explosion of the continued resistance of whole peoples against colonial domination. Certainly, women took part in these processes, in many cases as protagonists, even though official history has muffled their voices and experience. Nevertheless, although the struggles for independence claimed to be constructing a democratic society released from colonial domination, in reality, as Leonardo Boff observes, they did not have the effect of liberation, "since external exploitation continued through the economic neo-colonialism of the industrialized nations coupled with internal exploitation by the oligarchies and bourgeoisie, associated with the interests of multi-national capital."[30] Domination by Spain and Portugal was replaced by other great powers, such as England, France, Germany, and the United States. This change did not bring about the disappearance of unequal relations between men and women or the disappearance of patriarchal power over women. On the contrary, new forms of oppression gave rise to new demands and new forms of struggle associated with the industrialization process.

In predominantly agrarian societies, the nuclear family (made up of father, mother and children) has a fundamental role. It joins the public and private world, because it has productive and reproductive functions as well as economic, social, political, and cultural ones. The focal point of the relationship lies in the head of the family, the father (or paterfamilias). In this kind of organization the father of the family guarantees order, controls and distributes the work among family members, and makes the decisions about human reproduction and the resulting parental relationships. He also decides upon the forms of relationship between the sexes and the formation (or not) of new family units. Even though the majority of Latin Americans were never the direct owners of their instruments of production (these were in the hands of the great landowners, who were the heirs of the colonists), the family model centered on the father still predominated.

The relationship between the sexes in the nuclear family model is unequal, because men have power over women. The subordinate position occupied by women derives from the control exercised by men over sexuality, reproduction, and women's work. This control carries over from and at the same time reflects existing social relationships.[31] Nevertheless, I do not mean to suggest that women do not share in some way in society or have great importance in the nuclear family. I simply want to point out that it is the head of the family, the man, who controls women's activities. In the Latin American context this type of social organization makes women's oppression even worse (whether the women are mestizo, indigenous, or black), because as well as doing their share in working for a daily living together with the male workers on the great estates, they also have exclusive responsibility for the children and housework,[32] an arrangement that merely emphasizes the power of the male sex over the female.

The coming of industrialization generates different forms of social organization and different kinds of oppression for women. Although industrialization is not proceeding at an equal pace throughout the continent, the phenomenon appears to be common: the appearance of a public space that embraces the world of economics, politics, culture, and so on, and that is separate from the private space in which biological reproductive functions, interpersonal relations, and domestic tasks take place. "Women entering waged productive work," says Lora, "or sharing in their husbands' condition, experience the changes produced by industrialization and the new forms of oppression and exploitation this implies."[33] Nevertheless, women are very soon forced to return to their "natural" domestic labors, their reproductive function in the family, and their "special duties" in the home.[34] Thus a separation arises between the public and private domain. The public domain becomes the sphere controlled by men (productive work for wages, politics, economics, and so on) and the private domain is again assigned to women. Their "special domain" is the domestic one, and they are supposed to see themselves as only wife and mother, always dependent upon the man. Thus women's subordinate position persists in both domains. This process is accompanied by a redefinition of the masculine and the feminine, according to which it is necessary to separate these two domains because of biological differences. It becomes "natural" for the feminine to correspond to reproduction and the private sphere, and the masculine to correspond to production and the outside world. In this vision the daily domestic world does not compete with the masculine. Worse, women do not share in the decision-making in either sphere; that is to say, they are not recognized as persons with their own rights, capable of making decisions about their own lives or being responsible for their own sexuality.

This situation gives rise to heavy discrimination against women in the popular sectors in Latin America. The continual deterioration of living standards, the pressure to gain a minimum level of subsistence for the whole family, the awareness of their lack of rights to education and civil rights, the discrimination suffered for being women, and the need to defend their own dignity force women to undertake an organized struggle to demand work, land, and civil rights, without giving up the domestic tasks left exclusively to them.[35] Women's efforts have resulted in the gaining of certain civil rights such as the vote, education, relatively acceptable hours of work, and others. But the attainment of these rights has not done away with women's oppression or their unequal relationship to men. Nor has it alleviated the oppressive conditions of the mass of women.

Two facts stand out in this context. First, neither the independence struggles nor women's gains in the field of civil rights (the vote, work, and so forth), nor their access to education and other previously forbidden territories have been sufficient to overcome discrimination against them. Here the sexual division of labor, which helps explain the multiple character of women's oppression through their double work load, requires us to inquire more deeply why this situation persists and seek ways to overcome it.

Second, in our countries so-called industrialization and development projects have had the effect of plunging the continent and the Caribbean into inhuman conditions. More acute forms of impoverishment arise among the oppressed masses, and likewise, the structures perpetuating women's subordinate position proliferate. The ever-growing realization that Latin America is not only poor and oppressed, but purposely kept in conditions of increasing impoverishment by the great neo-colonial powers and national dominant sectors leads us to reject the existing situation. This rejection is translated into the long and powerful process of liberation that has arisen since the end of the 1960s. This is the emergence of a popular movement, the irruption of the poor and oppressed onto the stage of history. The presence of women will make itself felt once again until their demands have a voice.

The Emergence of Women as Active Participants in History and Theology

The most important development in recent decades in Latin America has been the emergence of what we call the *popular movement.* This term is used to define, as Pablo Richard points out, "simply all the organizations, activities and other expressions by which the poor and the oppressed manifest their struggle for liberation and which demonstrate that the people are on the move."[36] This movement is made up of the masses identifying themselves as creators (subjects or doers) of their own history. It is expressed in the various popular social movements converging toward the radical transformation of society and the defense of life in all its aspects. In a context of growing frustration with the model of imperialist capitalism, which not only hinders the life of the poor but makes it impossible, the need arises to struggle for liberation. Here countless Christian women and men have found a place where they can live their faith in a committed and liberating way.[37] They have adopted many practices whose aim is to overcome the various social inequalities and to make the people become the ones who change things. They become a real social and political force intent on constructing a popular, democratic, and equal life.

The most important thing about this collective action to improve their lot (for example, defense of the land; defense of human rights; demand for services such as health, transport, housing, and so forth; formation of popular trade unions; neighborhood associations; rural cooperatives; mothers' clubs; popular kitchens; the self-affirmation of indigenous and Afro-American people; literacy campaigns; alternative popular media; Christian base communities; production cooperatives; and more) is that from being a faceless, anonymous mass, the various sectors of the poor and oppressed become political and social actors with their own awareness, organization, and mobilization. They achieve an awareness of their own dignity, rights, their own strength and capacity to take their fate into their own hands.[38] The dynamism of this process, allowing for its regional variations, is presented by Maruja González and Itziar Lozano under eight points, which I summarize here:[39]

— advancement and consolidation of local and regional peasant organizations;

— rise of ethnic movements, such as the indigenous and Afro-American movements;

— strong, organized presence of broad popular urban sectors;

— emergence of the workers' movement with various levels of development and organization;

— radicalization of the student movement and sectors of the middle classes linked to the popular struggles;

— development and presence of the popular Christian movement;

— presence of women as protagonists, both in broad groupings and in movements exclusively formed by women;

— incorporation of intellectuals into the popular struggles.

For a better understanding of the protagonists in the popular movement we should not view this list as a description of separate social groups; that is, as if there were no students among the urban popular sectors, or peasants in the indigenous movement, or women in peasant organizations, or Christians in all sectors. The list merely points out the specific struggles of different social sectors. It shows how heterogeneous and complex the popular struggle is. Rather, as explained by Ana Sojo, the popular movement "is constituted by all those who occupy a subordinate position in the various constellations of power in society."[40] So we are talking about a social force that is aware of its own interests, that processes its own experience and accumulates the memory of its struggles. It organizes and conducts its own specific struggles. It is a broad process made up of many different popular social movements, driven to the defense of the life of the poor and oppressed. Here the participation of women is a striking and novel factor.[41] Their active presence and conscious participation has made it necessary to reflect on the special nature of women's liberation and oppression, and likewise on the specific character of their demands for the creation of an egalitarian alternative society.

In this process there is no area in the struggle to defend life from which women are absent. They are present in the daily struggles for survival and in the collective manifestation of opposition to every kind of oppressive system (which may be governments allied to North American domination, organizations, and trade unions with a strong streak of *machismo*, or even sexist pastoral projects). Here I want to stress the importance of daily struggles, because often a perspective that gives priority to large social changes tends to undervalue the daily struggles undertaken by women in the popular sectors to obtain immediate vital needs such as bread for themselves and their dependants (usually old people, children and the sick). These daily struggles for survival unfortunately are seen as having little or no historical effect on social change. Thus, it is necessary to reclaim for the liberation project *all* forms of struggle for life engaged in by women. They show up the capitalist system's inability to respond to the vital needs of the poor and provide basic human rights for women. When we set these daily struggles within the broad context of the struggle for life as a whole, we recognize them as women's struggles to claim their right to life and full humanity.[42] We should not be surprised, then, that in Latin America motherhood is often not felt as a source of oppression—in that it ties women exclusively to their procreative role—but rather as a source of struggle, because being a mother becomes a fundamental reason to make changes in the domestic sphere and family relationships within the broader social context of alternative forms of social organization.[43]

Following Lora, we may say that,

It is the search for new survival strategies, in the face of increasing poverty, that has enabled women in the popular classes over the last ten years to accumulate a very rich experience of organization with important potential for liberation. New dimensions, such as friendship, organization and the defense of life, the attempt to create — men and women together — a new society, the value of the participation of each person, are elements which are active today in the women's base organizations.[44]

In this context it is necessary to point out certain features. The attempts by women in the popular sectors to create new forms of living together — in interpersonal relations, in civil society, and in the church — implies a radical change in the ways that women see themselves; they must distance themselves critically from what others say about them and their destiny.[45] Going outside the domestic sphere as the exclusive domain for female being and doing has forced women to reformulate questions about their own situation and the conditions necessary for them to be recognized as subjects in their own right with full human status. This is why we speak about the irruption of history into the lives of women. What does this mean? Ivone Gebara says,

> When we speak of the irruption of history into the lives of women — and especially the theological expression of their faith — we do not mean the entrance of women into history; they have always been present. What we have in mind is something qualitatively different and new, that is, the irruption of historical consciousness into the lives of millions and millions of women, leading them to the liberation struggle by means of an active participation in different fronts from which they had previously been absent.[46]

Knowing the reality of oppression makes women aware of the need for change, so that they might have real access to control over their own lives and full participation in society and politics. Gaining this awareness through particular commitments helps women understand themselves in relation to oppression, to become conscious of it, and transform it. It is a sort of encounter with themselves in which they reappropriate the right, refused until very recently, to share in the forging of their own lives.

There is a close link between women's liberation and the liberation of the poor, but the liberation of the poor cannot be fully achieved without women's liberation. "Entering into history in fact means becoming aware of history, entering into a broader meaning, in which women are also creators or increasingly want to be forgers of history."[47] So women want their faces to be among those seeking liberation, they want this social body's face to have female features, because they know there can be no new and equal society without a solution to the oppression they suffer as women and without the necessary changes to the structures used to justify their subordinate position. Becoming conscious of this reality means a break with both men's and women's traditional ways of thinking about the processes of social change, because up till now these processes have been thought of only from the androcentric point of view.

Another important aspect to consider in the context of the emergence of the popular movement is women's growing awareness of the double oppression they suffer. This has been a very important aspect in the theological work done by Latin American women. Women's double oppression resides in their *double workload.* That is to say, besides waged work in generally more disadvantaged conditions than men, many women also continue to be solely responsible for domestic tasks at home. This is the basis of "the great injustice and exploitation women suffer because they have to do a double working day, inside and outside the home."[48] Thus women suffer a double oppression, as workers and as women. This situation has been fully debated by feminist movements within the social sciences, especially in the analysis of the relationship between the capitalist system and domestic work.[49] Women's double working day helps to distinguish the multiple loads that fall upon women but it is not sufficient to explain why the sexual division of labor persists along with those structures that legitimate women's subordinate and inferior position. The problem is not the existence of housework as such, but that family and domestic work is assigned to women as their exclusive responsibility.

Obviously there is a division of social roles by sex. Capitalism benefits from this sexual division of labor, because, among other things, the very existence of unpaid work—housework—lowers the price for the reproduction of the work force, legitimates the classification of women as a second-class work force (because women's primary work is domestic), and produces a segmentation in the labor market that justifies the fact that women receive lower wages or specialize in low-status work. Thus women become a reserve work force. So capitalism uses the sexual division of labor to its own advantage and, at the same time, increases the exploitation and discrimination against poor women in Latin America and the Third World in general. This is not to claim that women's oppression derives exclusively from the present socio-economic system. Women's subordinate position under capitalism must be set within the context of other factors that result in women's inequality.

As well as the double working day, women's growing involvement in social and popular struggles and in solidarity tasks has often led them to engage in another area of struggle: conflict with their male companions. As Lora indicates, "There is a well-known difficulty facing many working class women who, facing police repression of their attempts to mobilize in order to get water, health services, price decreases and other necessities, come home to face criticism and sometimes violence from their male companions."[50] That is, they face oppression at home as well as in society. These experiences have made women in Latin America realize that they are oppressed both because they are poor and because they are women. Two structures of domination combine in their exploitation: the capitalist system's exclusive structure and a system of domination that justifies the subordination of women by men. These structures coexist.

Although there is no agreement among analysts on a precise term to describe the structure that promotes and justifies women's oppression, in general the term used is *patriarchy* (or the *patriarchal system/structure*). Latin American theological literature produced by women more often uses the term *machismo* (or *machista structure*) to describe this reality.[51] *Machismo* does not derive or have its origins in capitalism, although it converges and combines with it in mutual reinforcement. But it can also combine with socialist structures in which unequal relationships persist between men and women, if there is insufficient criticism of women's double work load, the sexual division of labor, and inequalities between the sexes in general. Creating new and more equal ways for human beings to live together means not subordinating the causes and the struggles of one group to others.[52] In Latin America we cannot sustain a hierarchy of evils, in which women's oppression is "only" a minor evil or a circumstantial phenomenon.

Since the beginning of the 1980s the presence of women in the popular movement (and in the church of the poor, as we shall see) demands recognition of their role as history makers, that is, as active participants in social transformations and in the decisions about the fate of the world, history, and humanity. Although it is linked to other struggles, claiming this right acquires special importance because often women's rights with all their implications are not incorporated into the liberation process as a whole, even by other sectors of the people themselves, indeed not even by other women. That is to say, the role of women—with its massive potential for transformation—is recognized as a power to be made use of in claiming better living conditions for the poor, who are an oppressed social class. But the same recognition is not given to women's own rights *as women*. There is a sort of mental block—produced by an androcentric *machista* culture—against the acceptance of women's own interests as women.

For Elsa Tamez, regarding women as active participants is fundamental in speaking about the construction of a new and equal society formed by new women and new men.[53] The basic principle underlying these considerations has political implications because women's power, resistance, knowledge, experience, and capacity for struggle strengthen popular processes. But it also has profound anthropological implications because it demands and propounds a new way of thinking about women, not just as a strategic force in processes of social change, but as historical actors, that is, persons with their own consciousness of their interests and struggles in history.[54] Throughout the years countless women, either in the political or pastoral field, have had to make great sacrifices in their efforts to demand recognition—what we call the "double quota." They have had to demonstrate their capacity for work by redoubling their efforts to be efficient both inside and outside the home, with obvious physical and psychological costs. Men have never seen the double quota as their problem, because they have benefited from it at women's expense. According to the male-centered tradition, the daily work of taking care of the family falls to women *by nature*. Consequently, women have always had the harder part. From women's point of view, however, it has become necessary to combat the stereotype created for women by an ancestral *machista* mentality. There is a need to combat paternalistic attitudes that put down women in their activities because they are women. However, fighting the stereotype has not produced the desired effect; it merely has reinforced sexist attitudes.[55] Many women have torn themselves apart and reached the limits of their resistance and hope in the hope to change these attitudes. The struggle is not yet over.

On the other hand, a majority of women on many fronts in society and the church have shown their power and ability. As Gebara notes:

Women dare to talk about themselves, about social and political organization or disorganization. They have the freedom to reflect, agree or disagree and then their consciousness, lulled by the clatter of plates and pans, begins to awaken. It finds words and feels the urge to reorganize this world differently.[56]

Women are claiming their indisputable place as active members in the popular struggle. Their contribution to the struggles to create a new society benefits themselves, of course, but also benefits others who are struggling and yearning for the liberation of the oppressed. In this sense, problems affecting women are not just women's matters. They involve women and men equally, because every gain in the struggle for new ways of living together is a victory against oppression—of the poor through their poverty and of women both as poor and as women. Therefore the struggle against all forms of *machista* exclusion is very important, whether in ideologico-cultural expression or in sexist politico-social structures. In Latin America, a conscious struggle against *machismo* must be the work of women and men in a common effort.

Today, the importance of women as a social sector is recognized within the broad process of the liberation of the poor and oppressed of Latin America and the Caribbean. As we shall see, liberation theology is paying more and more attention to the challenges arising from women. Women are forcefully breaking in and bringing a new perspective and new vital force to theology itself, furthering the faith's own self-awareness and the building of new social and ecclesial realities. To the extent that women recover their own word, become aware of their own strength, and speak in their own accents of their experience of the faith, they are actively participating in history and theology, offering a unique perspective from which to consider all the contents of the faith.

2

Latin American Women's Discovery of Causality

One of the fundamental characteristics of liberation theology is its incorporation of socio-analytic tools as an intrinsic part of its own method.[1] Although theology maintains its own status—its internal regime as the discipline that articulates the language of faith—it resorts to the analytic sciences, particularly the socio-historical sciences, because its primary interest is not, as we saw in the previous chapter, the creation of a self-sufficient inward-looking discourse, but an efficacious contribution to the liberation of the poor and oppressed from the standpoint of Christian faith. Liberation theology is conscious that its content, as Leonardo Boff stresses, "depends for its subject matter on culture, society, and historical situations. These, after all, are what challenge it, thereby imposing a direction of its reflections."[2] It is a mediated discourse, as all Christian theology to date has been. It takes as the core of its reflection the practical liberation of the oppressed, so it resorts to the critical instrument that best enables it to analyze the causes of impoverishment and oppression with the object of transforming them and producing alternatives that will be of radical benefit to the Latin American peoples.

A noted novelty in Latin America is the whole people's growing awareness of the *causes* of poverty and wretchedness that grinds them down. Side by side with this awareness of causes, the obvious question is what must be done to eliminate the inequalities in the present situation. As Gustavo Gutiérrez has indicated, what is new in the present situation is primarily that the people "are beginning to grasp the causes of their situation of injustice and are seeking to release themselves from it. Likewise new and important is the role which faith in the God who liberates is playing in the process."[3]

Here, in the effort to discover causes, call them by their names, and deal with them, is where we link with analytic science. The contributions made by women to the analysis of the particular situation will throw new light on the critical body of work done by liberation theology.

Changes in Ways of Understanding from the Perspective of Women

Before I turn to the systematic analytic corpus, I should point out that the perception of the deep inequality suffered by women has been growing. More and more evidence has been gathered of the subordinate position that women have occupied throughout the history of humanity. Therefore we can say that the inequality between men and women is the most prolonged, scandalous and hidden of existing inequalities. A long history of women's subordination, reification, and "blanking" has tried to eliminate all possibility for women to fulfil themselves as actors in their own right.[4] But the most important thing now is the new awareness that these shackles that have bound women for so long need not bind them forever. Change is possible. New models of living together can be created that enable women and men to exercise their mutual responsibility in history. Here we may note the point made by Ivone Gebara about Latin American women's growing self-awareness:

> In connection with history, one can speak of the causality of things. The condition of women is the result of an evolution: it has been different, and it can be different. Their present state can be partly explained on the basis of historic causes. The discovery of the causes of the oppression of the poor and, among them, of the oppression of women, has changed women's understanding of themselves as persons individually and corporately. Woman is not marked for an unchangeable fate, nor is she the object of alien wills that shape her existence. Despite the conditions inherent in human existence, she can conquer spaces in which to express her word and her being.[5]

What is happening is a substantial change in women's own understanding of themselves; they see themselves as active subjects—not passive objects—in history. In an androcentric world women were in some way indefinite (which is not the same as not defined, as indefiniteness is itself a sort of definition), because they intrinsically did not form part of this world. As women become aware of the causes of their subordinate position and audibly claim a voice and their own life, they force a change to occur in the understanding of reality and introduce a new and different meaning for humanity and its destiny. This awareness provokes a profound reorganization of the ways of understanding the whole of existence to include previously omitted elements. This awareness is not just a psychological state; it is an intellectual process concerned with the special way in which women understand themselves in their situations and their experiences. It is also concerned with how they understand reality, starting from their own self-awareness and their own reality as women. In this context it is interesting that Gebara uses the term *creativity* to indicate this change in women's awareness. She points out that among other things women are adopting a new attitude toward the family, hierarchically organized under the control of the man. This awareness helps women to initiate new and more equal relationships and even to change certain aspects of the male role. It makes them realize the value of domestic work, never recognized as having worth, and struggle to have it truly recognized and valued.[6] So we speak of the entry of new elements into the understanding of reality, the relationship between men and women in both the personal and social dimension, the existence of ancestral stereotypes defining male and female tasks, the social division of labor between the sexes, the broadening of the political dimension from the public to the private, the three-fold struggles of class, sex, and race, and the importance of daily life. These elements were present before, of course, but they were not articulated correctly with respect to women. These aspects not only have an important political value for the present and future, but also a fundamental cognitive value for the understanding of faith.

Gebara notes that,

the discovery of causality within women's experience bears the characteristic marks of the particular way in which they perceive and approach the problems of life. No one single cause is absolutized but, rather, the causes are multiple. This way of looking at matters is obedient to their perception, as women, in its complexity, diversity, and mystery.[7]

This characteristic may well not be exclusive to women, but it does appear in them particularly strongly because their contact with the real world embraces the many dimensions of life, from the nitty gritty of daily life, including the satisfaction or lack of satisfaction of vital needs, their intrinsic relationship with systems of life support, their deep empathy with the earth, their emphasis on a *sentient* grasp of reality, to the broad dimensions of the social and political.[8] It is a multilateral and articulated contact with the world, whereas men's relation with reality seems to be more one-sided and dissociated.

The perception of the many dimensions of life does not mean compartmentalizing them. Different spheres of life cannot be made autonomous and explained independently. The multiple dimensions of life with which women are involved conform to reality as it is. This is not made up of the sum of its elements but by all the elements in relation with one another. Therefore women's attention to life's various problems does not accord relevance only to the economic aspects, leaving out politics; it does not set a priority on the political while leaving out the dimension of sexuality; it does not concentrate on sexuality while leaving out the religious and cultural. Neither does it contemplate only the epic moments of social change while relegating daily life to the sidelines. It does not look only to the change in the socio-economic structures as the recipe for women's liberation. It absorbs reality in all its diversity, complexity, and relatedness.

These observations enable us to understand better the special way in which women analyze their own situation. They are elements that must be incorporated systematically into the whole body of liberation theology by men and women; they directly affect understanding of the specific and the total liberation process. On the epistemological plane, the analytical tools provided by the social sciences give liberation theology the instruments it needs to discern the causes of oppression of the Latin American masses.[9] Tamayo-Acosta points out that

> the human sciences, and especially the social sciences, offer theology a diagnostic of reality, show the causes and roots of the oppression experienced by Latin American people, reveal the structural dynamisms and processes, show the functioning and tendencies of the systems and alternatives to it, and point out the organizational channels the masses have available to fulfil their aspirations. Moreover the social sciences are an instrument enabling theology to pinpoint more precisely the challenges pre-

sented by the social reality to the proclamation of the gospel and therefore to theological reflection (G. Gutiérrez). Finally they give theology more historical lucidity, more tools for criticism and analysis (R. Vidales).[10]

Consequently, liberation theology speaks of the development of the dominant capitalist empires at the expense of underdevelopment in the dominated countries, dependence on the economic power centers, unequal relationships between the center and the periphery, and of systematically necrophilic capitalism. But this analysis of reality still lacks understanding of the many mechanisms that operate in the oppression of women.

Far from despising the epistemological advances already gained by liberation theology, critical reflection from the perspective of women's oppression-liberation assumes them, and in turn contributes to these gains by widening the field of reflection. The following remarks point out other elements besides those mentioned in the previous chapter. These are important in describing the heterogeneous nature of the actors in the popular struggle. In particular they are useful in describing women's situations and the alternatives offered to women in their struggles for liberation. Choosing these tools for analysis rather than others means we are adopting a methodological position for our theology. From the broad field of critical feminist investigation in the social sciences on the unequal and subordinate position of women, women's theology gives priority to those elements most relevant to its own primary concern: the liberation of poor and oppressed women as a fundamentally important part of the process of total liberation.

The Political Character of Biology in the Subordination of Women

There have been various attempts to explain the causes of the unequal and subordinate position of women. Nevertheless, in spite of the efforts of the previous decade, we cannot yet speak of the creation of a consistent theoretical body of work which gives an account of this situation.[11] Lora indicates that

there has often been a tendency to explain it as a dependent and subordinate effect of other forms of domination: fundamentally of economic exploitation. From this viewpoint the struggle against women's oppression was described as being like other forms of oppression—racial oppression, for example—and entirely subordinate to the class struggle. On the other hand, this line provoked a reaction from feminists toward using absolute reference points in their analysis, such as patriarchy, which became a causal explanation of all the oppression suffered by women.[12]

Historically, the social situation of women has been determined by their biological functions, in particular their role in human reproduction. This natural biological fact also constitutes a social phenomenon when it operates in a specific form of social organization. Indeed, it is this social regulation of reproduction and fertility that has led to the creation of social roles for the sexes, creating a hierarchy in which women occupy the lower rank. Women take on the housewife role—wife and mother—or else take on the inevitable double workload. The secondary role occupied by women is made worse when their biological condition interacts with other forms of inequality, such as class and race. "In sum," Ana Sojo remarks, "biology has been made to justify women's inferiority to men, to give women particular characteristics that sanctify their relegation to the domestic spheres, with motherhood having a central place in these conceptions."[13]

Here I must point out the close link that exists between the political and the biological. It might be thought that these dimensions are autonomous and separate. In fact, the condition of women is inseparable from the social organization in which they find themselves. Thus the inequality between men and women can be explained by the type of social relations established between them, without any necessary reference to their respective anatomies. In Latin America poor men suffer hunger, deprivation, and violence as women and children do. The unique problem of women is the particular mode of social, political, and family organization that makes them second-class citizens and converts their biological power to have children into a source of oppressive power used against them.[14] Biological differences should not create an unequal relationship between the sexes, but such a relationship exists, and the male-dominated society justifies this inequality in terms of biological differences. Poor men—who are themselves oppressed—share equally in this system of repressing women. The poor are not exempt from *machismo*, and paradoxically, many women also subscribe to it. Women's biological condition is used as the bulwark of a social system that oppresses them. So biology is political. It is important to stress, with Sojo, that "the capacity to conceive and give birth does not imply, as a biological fact, that women should be charged with the care of children—or that only women should have to do the housework. The way in which biology enters social relations is political not biological."[15]

These considerations do not imply that motherhood is of secondary importance, even as a source of strength and struggle for survival. The problem lies in the politico-ideological treatment of women's power to bear children, not in the power itself. Here I may note two fundamental points. On the one hand, human motherhood cannot be considered as simply one biological experience among others—like eating, which is also a social matter. Neither can it be reduced to an instinct—as happens in non-rational species. As Fryné Santisteban says, "We must look at motherhood as a total human experience in which feelings, affection and the capacity to relate to others and oneself are the principal ingredients."[16] This alludes to something that is intrinsic to women as women and should be a source of liberation and humanism, not of condemnation. On the other hand, we must not create a romantic mystique of femininity, which exalts women and puts them on a pedestal as wife and mother. This is clearly a *machista* mechanism, which tends to overrate women's sublime nature as wife and mother in order to conceal their exclusion from real decision-making and keep them within the private domestic sphere.

This is merely an ideological expression of the problem I referred to earlier, that from an androcentric viewpoint women are constituted by nature to be mothers, and so their whole life (interests, desires, aspirations, and concerns) revolves around their role as mothers. Motherhood becomes the only way to fulfil themselves as women. What is wrong here is that this model becomes the unique criterion for women's identity.[17] We must combat the idealization of the maternal function because the idealization is intrinsically oppressive. Santisteban notes that this idealization "deprives the woman-mother of her complexity and human particularity, because in making her a symbol it dehumanizes her and thereby justifies the denial of her needs and her actual situation as a woman and as a mother."[18] Therefore, in the creation of alternative forms of social organization, motherhood and the biological condition of women cannot be used as arguments to justify women's subordinate role.

These observations show the need to resort to other analytic categories to help identify the structural dynamism and the roots of the multiple oppression of women. Simply referring to patriarchy on its own to explain men's domination over women or saying that women's oppression is a secondary effect of economic exploitation by present-day imperialist capitalism does not seem adequate to describe the present situation of women.[19] We must analyze women's situation in a way that accounts as well as possible for the multiplicity of women's experiences and the special characteristics of their oppression as poor persons and as women, not forgetting the aspect of race.

The Creation of Social Gender

Women's biological condition has served to legitimate an unequal model of social and family relationships. One way of talking about this is in terms of the sex-gender system.[20] This system seeks to give an account of women's unequal situation in order to remedy it. Maruja González indicates that "the difference between sex and gender is highly important for the feminist struggle. The concept of gender has not only made a contribution to the social sciences but also, fundamentally, to feminism."[21] This system attempts to explain how models of relationships and social behavior have been constructed upon the biological difference to justify the superiority of one sex to another. Sex as a biological fact becomes a social fact through the creation of gender stereotypes conferring an identity upon either sex. Gender is the social form adopted by the sexes whenever they are ascribed specific values, functions, and norms, or what are also rather clumsily called social roles. The sex-gender system forms men's and women's identities and the relationship between them upon the basis of certain norms of behavior considered "proper" to each sex. Thus the significance of the biological difference depends upon the values and meanings ascribed to it and derives from the social construction of the so-called "masculine" and the "feminine" at a particular historical moment.

The complexity increases when the differences, which in principle should relate to differences between the sexes intrinsic to the human species, are identified with gender stereotypes used to legitimate "masculine" superiority and an unequal relationship between men and women. Sojo stresses that

in its fetishized form when gender is treated as the same as sex, the relationship between the sexes is presented as natural and the differences between men and women as strictly biological in character. Therefore they are given an aura of natural inevitability and in the present sex-gender system, with its male domination, the biological difference covers up the creation of gender differences and is used as the basis for an oppressive system.[22]

Thus it is believed that women's subordination is natural because it is based on the natural "fact" of women's inferiority.

On the basis of the sex-gender system legitimating men's superiority, there is an androcentric tendency to dissociate parts that really should be taken together as a nonhierarchical whole. It is certainly true that throughout history there have been gender stereotypes emphasizing to a greater or lesser extent that being a woman implies sensitivity and tenderness, emotion, passivity, submission, intuition, the incomprehensible, and the mysterious, whereas being a man implies rationality and aggressiveness, action, clarity, logic, force, and power.[23] Once the stereotype has been established, it has to be observed, and the relationship between the sexes becomes hierarchical and unequal because women a priori have a subordinate role. To a less biased vision, this androcentric dissociation is pernicious, both for men and women, because both are amputated in their personalities. But I believe that the dehumanizing consequences are always worse for the ones who occupy the subordinate position, in this case women, especially women who are also poor.

An unequal system maintains the stereotypes and demands ways of behaving prescribed by the culture, religion, and society for each sex according to gender identity. For example, in everyday life men are expected to forego behavior that is cooperative and generous; they are not expected to display qualities of receptivity, intuition, and tenderness, which are ascribed to women, even when, as is often the case, this goes against their own inclinations. At the same time women are expected to surrender their strength, initiative, intelligence, and competitiveness, even though these are qualities both men and women can develop. However, I must stress that although these gender stereotypes are machista and androcentric constructions, women also contribute to their persistence and reproduction, sometimes even willingly. Therefore an enormous amount of work will be required to restore wholeness to both women and men's humanity. And, of course, in the present context of clear oppression of women there is a special need to encourage women to express themselves so that their contribution may really be, as María Josefa García Callado puts it, "a substance and not a shadow, a word and not an echo."[24] Biological sex is not the original creator of a natural inequality between women and men. It is used by interested parties to legitimate an unequal relationship in personal and social affairs. It is becoming more and more urgent to analyze the sex-gender system as it operates in the context of our societies, a context that cannot be dissociated from the patriarchal capitalism dominating Latin America. The churches and theology have a fundamental role in either maintaining or else criticizing and transforming these systems.

The sex-gender system is linked to another matter mentioned in the preceding chapter: the division of labor, which depends on the separation of the public and private spheres. Women are relegated to the private sphere, which is basically concerned with children and housework. Men are assigned to the public sphere, which is related to production and the political arena. Sojo notes that this division is the source of their unequal power,

> because with the social division of labor women are assigned to the domestic spheres as natural for them; they are only allowed to enter the public spheres under discriminatory conditions, which are expressed, among other things, in wage differentials and jobs that are subordinate to male authority. This division of labor maintains the unequal power structure because it prevents women having access to certain areas of human development through the operation of gender in the division of labor.[25]

Women are always at a disadvantage, and it is easy to see why women who are also poor and oppressed suffer intolerable burdens.

Because of their biology women are relegated to the private sphere where they carry out their reproductive tasks, but this ignores the fact that *reproduction* is a matter for both the public and the private sphere. "In the domestic sphere," says Sojo,

> educational tasks and socialization processes take place as well as material reproductive functions. In symbolic terms, the private, the domestic, is seen as the special place for the individual and personal, as opposed to the public, which is seen as the domain of politics. Thus the public sphere is valued as resulting from social interactions, whereas the domestic is isolated from

the political and surrounded by a halo of naturalness. Linked to a sex-gender system of male domination, the domestic sphere is seen as women's natural place and becomes cut off from politics. It is the sphere where presumed female characteristics prevail, also considered natural, and the disposition of power becomes a biological matter.[26]

The sexual division of labor, accompanied by a definition of the masculine and the feminine, gives rise to a profoundly unequal order. In the economy only waged work is regarded as work, thus excluding domestic work. In matters of property, although women from the dominant classes are also excluded, nevertheless they do enjoy the privileges of their class and race and benefit from the work of poor indigenous, black, and mestizo women. In politics the domestic space is privatized and not accorded its intrinsic political character, because it is regarded as the natural sphere for women to operate in and is thus cut off from the public arena. In cultural matters predominance is given to the rational and logical, to science and production; the world of intuition, feeling, intelligence, and popular ways of seeing that does not exclusively favor speculative reason is undervalued. Irrationality is considered characteristic of the "feminine" stereotype. In the anthropological (and hence theological) sphere, there is a dualism between woman-man, body-soul, matter-spirit, evil-good, and so on,[27] as well as a negative view of sexuality in which women appear as the source of all evil.

Sojo points out that the existence of separate spheres in society need not be criticized and questioned in itself but only to the extent that it introduces unequal relationships between people.[28] It is important to defend a private sphere, which is necessary for personal recreation, and a public sphere, which is necessary for creativity. But they must be set within a new model of relationships of equality and respect, in which women and men can develop their own talents and experience their human wholeness in mutual solidarity and communion with their fellow humans, the earth, and God.

Finally, this line of reflection criticizes our understanding of the masculine and the feminine and invites us to reformulate it in the Latin American context. It is easy for both men and women to try to integrate our feminine and masculine sides while leaving other sources of inequality intact, such as the sexual division of labor, the separation of spheres, and the social assignment of tasks by sex.

Without this context, the feminine and the masculine not only contribute little to the real liberation of women, but have no critical effect on real lives.

The Three-dimensional Character of the Struggle

Concentration on the great liberation processes of the poor or on movements that do not have deep roots among the masses may tend to weaken the multiple claims for their rights made by the women of oppressed peoples, claims arising out of their poverty, their subordinate race, and their womanhood. It may also happen that even while affirming the great liberating principles, some may not apply them to the dimensions of class, race and sex. The analysis made by women from the context of oppression, poverty, and the struggle for liberation necessarily tends to articulate these aspects because women are convinced that the new society they want can be built only if these are taken into account. No one of these aspects must be given priority over the others.

In order to understand the link among these three dimensions we must look at the position occupied by women in society as a whole, because our social position largely determines our interests, needs, and struggles. Here the racial and sexual aspects are fundamental, because a society that is unequal in terms of class is also unequal in race and sex relations. An approach that concentrates on women's biological characteristics as an oppressive condition they all share tends to be misleading because it assumes that the interests of women in all social classes are equal. All women are said to be equally oppressed because they all suffer gender discrimination. This position neglects two important aspects: the specific struggles of poor women among the oppressed people in their daily struggle for their children and their own survival, and the claim by indigenous, black, or mestizo women to be subjects with full rights. Rosemary Radford Ruether stresses this aspect:

Women of the upper class and race easily fall into an abstract analysis of woman's oppressed status that ignores their own class and race privileges. When this happens, their movement fails to connect with that of women of oppressed groups. Their movement becomes a white upper-class movement, which fails to go beyond the demand for privileges commensurate with those enjoyed by males of their group, oblivious to the unjust racist and class context of these privileges.[29]

Liberation theology is aware that women collectively share a common oppressed condition but their position in unequal and opposed social sectors and the differences in their daily lives cannot be ignored. The struggles of women belonging to oppressed peoples and dominated races are concerned with the satisfaction of daily survival needs—work, bread, health, roof, clothing, education, and so on—or recognition, self-esteem, integrity, sharing in decision-making, and others. These needs are not so urgent and intense for women who live leisured lives, nor are they so important for men who enjoy greater well-being at women's expense. According to Sojo:

> We can say that discrimination against women has specific features according to which class they are in. There are particular forms of discrimination affecting each. The bourgeois woman may be an object or the victim of domestic violence, but she is not economically exploited. She also benefits from the exploitation of the female work force. The woman in the petty bourgeois class may be the victim of sexual aggression, she suffers wage discrimination in comparison with men, she is manipulated by the mass media, and exploited as a member of her class. Working class and peasant women are both exploited economically and endure all the other forms of gender discrimination suffered by women as a whole.[30]

Thus women's demands depend to some extent on their social position and the needs they experience in their daily lives. Women belonging to oppressed peoples cannot divorce their struggle as women from their situation of poverty or their membership in a dominated race.[31]

It is therefore clear that the three-dimensional character of the struggles for liberation by women in Latin America—and in other latitudes, for example, poor and outcast black and Latina women in North America—cannot be reduced to a single issue. Processes of social change that do not include the three dimensions do not fully understand liberation in a way that meets the needs of the people concerned. "The elimination of classes in society is a *necessary* but not *sufficient* condition for the elimination of sexism and racism."[32]

The Centrality of Daily Life

Until very recently analysis has laid greater stress on the direct changes in the socio-economic-political structure than on the other, also structural, dimension of daily life. The same thing happens with daily life as with the other dimensions. That is, they have always been there, as part of reality, molding particular ways of living together, and sustaining particular kinds of relationships, but their meaning and their relationship to the struggles of the oppressed for liberation have not been grasped. The emergence of women has been largely responsible for the discovery of daily life issues as crucial to the struggle. Although it is often regarded as autonomous, daily life is in fact at the center of history, invading all aspects of life.[33] Therefore it can produce and reproduce oppressive and unequal relationships, or it can be the source of equal and liberating ones. Daily life does not mean just the individual rhythms of domestic life but, as Sojo indicates, it refers to

> the totality of activities by individuals relating to reproduction, which in turn make the reproduction of society possible. It includes activities of appropriating the world that continually take place — systematically, permanently, repeatedly — in relation to the different stages of an individual's life. ... Day to day relationships are both the basis and the image of the totality of social relations.[34]

Daily life is closely linked to the problems mentioned earlier: the division of labor by sexes; the split between the public and private spheres; and the creation of the sex-gender system, which affirms male superiority. If daily life has to do with the whole of life, with the public *and* the private, we may expect to find the real basis legitimating the subordinate condition of women here.

> This inequality of power has caused a double reductionism: the domestic, exiled to the domain of the individual has been depoliticized, whereas the political is limited to the public area, ignoring the political significance both of the domestic and of the public arena in its discrimination against women. Among other things this fetishism makes possible the covering up of the power relationships operating in the domestic sphere.[35]

There are unequal relationships with women in the subordinate position operating in both spheres, but it is the domestic sphere that more clearly reveals male power.

The relationships established in private are similar to the relationships sanctioned in public, where women are also at a disadvantage. These social relationships are then enveloped in a veil of so-called "naturalness." If ways of living together, values and behavior are first learned at home, when the home models unequal relationships between men and women, it becomes the crucial place for the perpetuation of hierarchical models. Daily relationships become the basis and image of all social relations. This is why analysts stress that daily life permeates the public as well as the private spheres, because the activities carried out in both spheres "imply a level of dailiness, daily actions that confer upon this oppression, day after day, an air of naturalness."[36] This is why women stress the need to change the way things are done in daily life in order to construct equal models of interhuman relationships. These observations do not mean the struggle should be conducted only on the domestic field. They are simply trying to point out the need not to isolate or split off processes developing in society from interpersonal relations in the domestic and private sphere. The area of struggle for women must incorporate both. The point is to broaden the horizon so that daily life is also seen as an area of struggle for liberation and thus ceases to be cut off from the rest of life.

Likewise, daily life is connected with thoughts about the nuclear family, which has to be considered in any attempt to develop new and equal forms of relationships or in maintaining oppressive ones. In many cases people engaged in social and popular movements do not know how to link the two areas. They may lead separate and parallel lives, a liberating life in public and an oppressive one in private. As Raúl Vidales says, "The macro-world enters in, is engendered, and is perpetuated from generation to generation through, among other factors, everyday life."[37] In the family we learn our earliest ways of behaving—living together, religious and cultural values, solidarity, and ways to confront social conflicts. When the family is hierarchical and unequal, its members learn these forms of relationship. Thus the family is not the source of new attitudes when the women within it occupy a position of systematic inferiority. Even when the relationships among classes become more equal, if the political apparatus is run in a democratic and popular manner and at the same time an unequal order continues within families, they go on producing structural sources of conflict.

Within Latin American liberation processes daily life has to do with the unequal relations between classes, but here we are mainly concerned with the relating between men and women. According to Elsa Tamez, the subject of women is highly and secretly polemical within the popular movement. "It is painful to air it because we all are affected by it very personally. We are all either male or female, a polarity that is not present between rich and poor. ... We are facing an impasse that we must overcome."[38] Both women and men may share in the various tasks in the struggle for liberation of the oppressed, but at the same time the men may be hanging on to their privileges. Daily life is a real problem. This problem must be addressed, because here lies the basis for a possible new society.

Finally, daily life shows us how to understand liberation and therefore becomes an analytic category for understanding social practices and the processes of oppression-liberation. A theology that tries to accompany and make explicit the liberating aspirations of the poor and oppressed must look here. For as Tamez says,

> There is a truth here that we cannot overlook and that we who seek a new order of life must embrace: the foretastes of utopia are experienced in everyday life, and it is in everyday life that we begin to build this utopia (Vidales). There is no place else. And everyday life in the private sphere is the focal point for re-establishing a new relationship that will have its effect in the public sphere.[39]

Taking these points seriously means that we all—men and women—must adopt an attitude of realism, honestly recognizing the dark corner into which poor women have been pushed, especially indigenous, black, and mestizo women. Once we recognize this reality, we must make a theoretical and practical commitment to the final eradication of the causes of this oppression. We have a lot to do.

3

Women in the Church of the Poor

The emergence of the church of the poor at the heart of the liberating processes in Latin America is the most important sign of the church's renewal on the continent, especially during recent decades. Its basis is the people's new liberation movement. It is related to the Christian masses' new awareness: they regard themselves as the people of God and the subjects of the church's transformation and experience of faith. The word renewal suggests particular action for change, modifying a status quo or particular situation toward another that is regarded as new and better. Renewal substantially alters what has existed up till now in the church without losing its specific identity, because the "new" belongs to its very nature.[1] Large-scale participation by the poor in the church's activity, described in the documents of Medellín and Puebla, makes possible this new way of being for the church in Latin America. This is not the rise of a new church but rather a new way of being the church, called the church of the poor. It has been born of the renewal of the church "within the popular movements as a response of faith by the poor and oppressed to God's liberating action in history."[2]

It is well known that the idea of the church of the poor was present at Vatican II. Although the idea was not equally welcomed by all, it was assumed that the church must be in the service of the poor, following Christ, who was poor.[3] It was in Latin America that this insight bore the most fruit, though there are still many challenges to be faced. These have to do with the complex development of Latin American processes and the configuration of the masses as historical participants. Speaking of the church of the poor means, among other things, speaking of a fundamental change in the way the church sees itself. Historically the church has been organized and developed its mission following the model of the dominant minorities in the society. These were the people it primarily

42

addressed. But the church of the poor sees itself as the sacrament of liberation for the oppressed masses and is structured on the basis of equal participation by all its members. The ecclesiological actor is not the hierarchical male body but the people: women and men in their resistance and their heroic struggles, who live and nourish their faith in popular communities, and push the church toward being a discipleship of equals.[4]

The emergence of the church of the poor, especially in its most important form in the church base communities, shows a strong presence of women, who were previously silenced and suppressed in the church's many daily activities. It is an indisputable fact, says María Clara Bingemer, that

> women carry on their shoulders a large part of the actual work of the church. In the base community and the parish, in the schools, movements and pastoral work, women, both nuns and laywomen, are present as coordinators, catechists, enablers, giving of their best, their time, their warmth, their strength, their guts, their lives, even their blood. . . . In the church and in society women are struggling to conquer a space for themselves, affirming their incontestable leadership in the base communities, registering their presence in the popular movement, carrying out nearly all the important catechetical work, and entering at last into the field of work on theology and spirituality.[5]

The active presence of women means that we can now speak of the emergence of women as new ecclesiological active subjects in the church of the poor. Before looking at women's contributions to the renewal of the church, I should point out that although the context here is the Roman Catholic church, many activities and reflections converge with the experiences and perspectives of other Christian women who also see their faith as a commitment to new ecclesial structures in line with the church of the poor.

The Conquistadors' Mission and Logic

Latin American women's experience of faith is indelibly marked by colonial history, which has shaped their historical resistance and given birth to their struggles for emancipation. A conquered and doubly colonized continent has its own peculiarities, which decisively influence both the knowledge and ways of seeing reality and the ecclesial, theological, and political proposals for change. Rereading the past is different when it is done from the standpoint of the sufferer rather than from that of those who imposed the suffering. From the perspective of women, patriarchal Christianity, imposed on Latin America by the conquest, both demonstrated a high level of racism against the indigenous people and combined this with a sexist attitude toward women. It cannot be denied, as Gebara and Bingemer point out, that "During the first generation of the conquest there was a great deal of religious violence, and the indigenous religious culture was destroyed in the name of the purity and truth of Christianity."[6] As well as imposing the patriarchal European Christianity of the sixteenth century, colonial Christianity in Latin America made plain its intention to eliminate women from the public spheres, to which at that time they had access. It was also determined to suppress every cult of the mother goddess common among the indigenous peoples.

The conquest of Latin America was carried out by Spain and Portugal, both by their nobles and their clergy, combining the sword and the cross as two sides of the same coin. "The language of the conquest clearly demonstrates the warlike and combative nature of Iberian Catholicism, which was viewed by its practitioners as the only way to salvation for humankind. ... This enterprise of 'salvation' was as important as conquering new lands for the glory of the Spanish and Portuguese crowns."[7] This great enterprise of conquest had two aims: one military, to obtain power, territory, wealth, and increase the number of the king's subjects; the other spiritual, to draw the indigenous people to the Christian faith and increase the number of adherents to Christianity. They were not opposed or parallel aims but, as Fernando Mires makes clear, "there was an interconnection between them, a mutual assistance which engendered phenomena of social symbiosis very important both legally and politically."[8] The evangelization of the continent and the Caribbean developed in this complex blend of conquest and colonization. The two processes jointly had profound effects on the forms of social relations, family organization, art, moral values, ways of thinking, and religion and spirituality of the ancestral Latin American peoples and cultures.[9] There has been little exploration of the impact and consequences of these processes in women's lives, but, as Carmen Lora observes, "there are indications that the morality and customs imparted by the church's representatives imposed new forms of submission upon women with respect to previous cultural patterns."[10]

In fact, the church's missionary activity in its earliest forms was considered as inherent to the conquest itself, because often the missionaries came with the conquistadors and legitimated their inhuman practices, as we see in this atrocious account by Bartholomé de las Casas:

> The grim Spaniards went about with fierce dogs seeking and hunting the Indian men and women. Seeing she could not flee from the dogs and to prevent them tearing her to pieces as they were doing to others, a sick Indian woman took a rope, tied her one-year-old child to her foot and hung herself on a rafter. No sooner had she done this than the dogs arrived and tore the child to pieces. But before he died, a friar baptized him.[11]

According to this story the friar baptized the child but did not stop the dogs! Only later did the missionaries begin to understand evangelization not just as something other than aggressive conquest but even contrary to it, a rupture from it, especially after Las Casas made his denunciations and defended the Indians.[12] This conflict generated two different ways of understanding the task of preaching the gospel and the church's presence in Latin America. The first model is associated with the spheres of power in which the church is subordinate to the state, and Catholicism in its turn gives the state its symbolic universe of legitimacy. The other is the prophetic and liberating model associated with the cause of the indigenous peoples.[13] Women played an important part in the persistence and continuity of this second model, which today has become the church of the poor.

It is interesting to observe, as Mires stresses, the *obviousness* with which the historians of the time ignore the domination of women, which was nearly always worse than that of Indian men. In this period neither the Iberian state nor the church offered a space for the defense of women, except when genocide threatened to diminish the work force.[14] Then women were preserved for reproductive work. This *obviousness* indicates the level of fetishism reached by the sexism of the age. For historians the silencing of women was obvious, because their inferiority was "natural." Certain aspects of the situation of women related to the church's behavior.

First, women were used as a work force, particularly in the mines and in agriculture, as we hear in this account:

And the care that was taken of them was to send the men to the mines to dig for gold, which is intolerable labor, and the women they placed on the estates, which are farms, to dig the soil and cultivate the land, which is work for very strong and tough men. They gave neither men nor women anything to eat but grass and food that did not sustain them. They drew off the milk from the breasts of women who had given birth and thus all their babies quickly died. And because the husbands were separated from them and never saw their wives, all childbearing ceased among them.[15]

This situation brought about a profound change in the ways in which women understood their role in the indigenous family and society, which were based on economic and family self-sufficiency under a communal regime. The church opposed the forced labor of women, but primarily because such opposition was necessary to guarantee the reproduction of the work force and provide attention to the domestic sphere, which was considered women's work by nature.

Second, indigenous women suffered sexual exploitation, says Mires,

which was so notorious that it is hard to credit why so many historians say nothing about it. The strict prohibitions and rigid Spanish sexual morality were quickly relaxed in the Indias, where at least in the initial stages of the conquest there was real sexual anarchy. ... A Muslim type of patriarchy well known to the Spaniards was imposed in America upon the Catholic-monogamous type of patriarchy. The "harem" was in practice a semi-official institution, to the point where a chronicler referred to the "Mohommed's paradise" established by the Spaniards. For the Indian women, of course, this Paradise was hell.[16]

For women the conquest meant dehumanization; they were shared out just as the lands and animals were shared, with absolute silence from the church. Such distributions were bound to devastate the indigenous socio-economic family organization and the part women played in it in production and transmission of the socio-cultural inheritance. Among the kinds of distribution the following were found: distributions by means of marriage, by which the Iberian gained direct access to land property; distribution of women for domestic service, which was prolonged in worse conditions once the Spanish women arrived, because then the Indians and mestizas became slaves or concubines; distribution of women as gifts given by the indigenous chief to the conquistador, in which case the indigenous patriarchy converged with the Spanish medieval patriarchy; distribution of women by rape and as simple war booty.[17] In none of these cases did the church raise its voice to defend women. Neither did it do so against the extreme conditions of exploitation and inhumanity imposed upon black women who arrived on the Latin American continent, having been snatched out of Africa. Indians, black, and mestizo women were always on the bottom rung of the human ladder. In the end, the unequal social stratification, typical of Iberian society in the sixteenth century, was transplanted to Latin America, together with the rigid division of sexual roles in accordance with the medieval European structure. The Europeans never asked the indigenous people how they had organized themselves for centuries or how they wished to organize themselves in this new situation. They simply imposed their own models. They did not even inquire whether these were better. Thus the church impregnated the whole of colonial society, including both public and private daily life, sexuality and women's activities. One way of controlling daily life was the regeneration of the masculine and feminine stereotypes for women and men recently incorporated into Christianity. In accordance with this split the foundations were laid in Latin America to "grant" the private domestic sphere to women and the public social sphere to men.[18]

Latin American women shared the conditions of oppression and exploitation imposed upon the conquered peoples, and they also had other burdens laid on them because of their sex and race. But there was one essential aspect of the women who went before us that helps to explain the potential of women today. It was primarily the women, with their mature wisdom seasoned in memory by suffering and hope, who selected and kept what was best in the gospel message together with the best elements in their own ancestral cultural symbolic world. Here we see the role of historical memory in women's lives. When the Society of Jesus opposed the religious ordination of Indians and mestizos at the end of the sixteenth century, the argument was that "in this villa there are not many Spaniards or Creoles, they are all mestizos, children of Spanish men and Indian women. These are usually unfit to be ministers of the church because they keep up many customs of the mothers who bore them."[19] As Ignacio Ellacuría says, "The conquistadors never concealed their intention of reducing all religious competition to nothing."[20] But it seems clear that Latin American women "had the capacity to distinguish the message from the cultural baggage that accompanied it and they created mechanisms of cultural resistance, which preserved many ancestral values and also incorporated central elements of the gospel message."[21] This version, with its more communal and liberating character, is what we believe has bloomed in the life of poor and oppressed women who understand their faith in the context of the church of the poor. They have kept their ancestral logic of the primacy of life above the logic of death, which belongs to every conquest, whether in the sixteenth or the twentieth century.

Women's Emergence as Actors/Subjects in the Church

It is not exaggerating to say that women from the popular sectors have welcomed and made their own the Latin American church's deepest identity, if we understand its mission in line with *Evangelii Nuntiandi*: "Evangelizing is the church's deepest identity. It exists to evangelize" (no. 14). A major characteristic of the Latin American church is the quantity and quality of involvement by women in its various activities: proclaiming the gospel, witness, celebration, action to transform the world and forge unity.[22] Although women have also done a good deal of practical pastoral work in the church, up till recently they were not recognized as active participants, as church-makers and preachers of the gospel. Tereza Cavalcanti mentions this problem:

Before the church base communities made their presence felt in the church in Latin America, women were already there working without being noticed, praying, calling others to join together and organize. . . . From the beginning they were active in the daily work, but were not very visible. They emerged from solitude for the sake of solidarity, driven by a stubborn confidence in life and love. Slowly these women are losing their anonymity and appearing as an important contingent in the community. This has meant that the church is beginning to discover its own female face.[23]

Recognizing women as new actors in the church has meant making a fundamental change in hermeneutics. First, it is no longer just the people—with a male or androcentric connotation—who are the focal point of the church's activity, but also women, who comprise an ecclesial and social force in themselves, linked to other activists. Second, there is no longer a question of speaking for women or instead of them, reducing women themselves to mute and passive objects or simply recipients of the church's activity. Women are creating their own awareness, they are interpreting their own words, and making the church's mission present in their own way as women. So we are confronting a new and challenging process with considerable historical consequences for the church and theology.

An important factor favoring the emergence of women in the church was, without doubt, the preferential option for the poor officially and collectively adopted by the Latin American church in the episcopal conferences of Medellín (1968) and Puebla (1979). This option marks the church's solidarity with the causes of the impoverished masses and defends their lives; it clearly embraces the cause of oppressed women. The option is expressed in the Final Document of Puebla in the footnote to number 1135: "The poor do not lack simply material goods. They also miss, on the level of human dignity, full participation in sociopolitical life. ... In this category women in these social sectors have a very special place because they are doubly oppressed and marginalized." It would have been better if this option for women had been incorporated into the body of the document and not just stated in a footnote. Nevertheless, it is important to recognize that it is not just the church opting for the poor, including poor women, but that there is also a movement in the other direction—women are opting for this church and making their own mark on it through their ways of living and reflecting on the faith, pastoral work, liturgy, spirituality, theology, the community, and so forth.

The church is enriched by the contributions of women and women are finding a larger scope in which to reformulate and define their Christian identity. In the traditional model of the church, which is hierarchical, verticalist, authoritarian, and clerical, women occupy a secondary position and are usually relegated to a passive role. But when, as is happening in Latin America, the church undergoes a renewal process in solidarity with the struggles of the poor and oppressed, women find scope in which to act as participants with their own creativity, because this renewal tends, of its own accord, to create more equal, participatory and communitarian structures.[24] Here bishops, priests, monks, nuns, theologians, and laity see a community without gross inequalities and themselves as God's people through their common baptismal calling.

Like every Christian community, the church of the poor is organized around certain key beliefs that give it its peculiar character. The description we offer does not claim to cover the whole complex dynamism of the church in Latin America. It merely points out certain fields of action in which women participate and where their voices are heard with increasing frequency.[25]

Preaching the Gospel

Basically, preaching the gospel covers women's activities connected with the proclamation of the word. Women are assuming the responsibility for the catechesis of children, young people, and adults, preparing them for the sacraments, preaching the word, visiting the old and sick, accompanying the dead and their families in services and prayers, urging people to solidarity, giving spiritual support to people in their daily lives in the church community, and preaching a gospel of liberation during the liturgical year. They celebrate saints' days and days celebrating the people's martyrs, produce popular biblical and theological material, write articles, conduct retreats, and strengthen the spirituality of the poor.

Celebration

In recent years there has been a renewal in the ways of celebrating the faith in Christian communities. The presence of women has encouraged the creation of a new symbolism and a new language associated with the renewal of life, down-to-earth experience and commitment to the struggle for justice. Women's own liturgical creativity, which had been largely suppressed by the coldness of Western rituals with a strong androcentric accent, has been awakened. A new language linked to the ancestral cultures is making its appearance in the people's celebrations, as we can often see in community meetings. Women are arranging the liturgy and introducing new symbols with a female character into celebrations, prayer, poetry and song, the calling to memory of the martyrs and those who have put themselves forward in the struggle for justice, in musical compositions, plays, popular theater, and representations of life connected with biblical experience.

Transforming Action in the World

In this sphere women Christians engage in many important activities. Initiatives to organize for social change may start from women only or mixed groups, but the presence of women is always fundamental. These activities include promotion and defense of vital rights; participation in social and popular movements such as trade unions, broad fronts, solidarity marches; membership in associations of domestic workers, washer women, sewing women, corn-grinders; organization of mothers' clubs, nurseries or popular schools, health groups for women and children; literacy teaching; collective work to build houses or settlements; land takeovers; work with prostitutes and drug addicts; work in solidarity committees; care for prisoners; organization to support the unemployed; creation of neighborhood committees; membership in indigenous and peasant land movements; organization of community pharmacies and groups for the use of natural medicines; setting up cooperatives; representation of the community before political or civil authorities; and more.

Coordination for Unity

Women do the important work of animating and coordinating the communities in the church of the poor. Although they are still discriminated against in the priesthood, administration of the sacraments and decision-making, as full members of God's people women play a key role in community unity. It is not rare to see women deeply committed to the life of the church as members of teams coordinating the communities or acting as a link among farms, villages, and regions in order to ensure unity and communion. On many occasions it is women who raise their voice to call some communities to solidarity with others. Women feel responsible for the church's mission and the spread of Christ's gospel, without this implying any non-recognition of the traditional ministries of the church.

Women's wide participation in Latin American ecclesial life, which I have barely sketched here, helps to rebuild the church from within. Women's presence is evidence of a change in the church's nature, because they contribute to the creative reformulation of traditional ways of understanding and doing. This affects preaching and action, administrative structures, symbolic liturgical expression, and ways of illustrating the church's unity. Women are definitely emerging as new actors in the church. However, this process is not taking place without conflicts, because there still exist sectors in the church not only opposed to the recognition of women as active participants, but to the renewal of the church at all. Even with these tensions, the spirit, the courage, and the vital strength women are bringing to the church of the poor are visible throughout the length and breadth of the continent and the Caribbean. This phenomenon calls to mind what Karl Rahner said about the new possibilities the historical moment offers the church for renewal, as long as it does not suffocate the presence of the Spirit:

> We live in an age in which it is absolutely necessary to be ready to go to the utmost extremes of boldness in our attitude towards the new and the untried, to that point at which it would be, beyond all dispute, simply inconceivable for one who accepts Christian teaching and has a Christian conscience at all to go any further. In practice the only admissible "tutiorism" in the life of the Church today is the tutiorism which consists in taking risks.[26]

Women Are Giving the Church a New Face

The essential face of the church of the poor is seen in the ecclesial base communities. Their dynamism is showing the new way of being the church in Latin America, because they are making possible the vital and creative participation of all the traditionally marginalized sectors in the church: the poor, the indigenous, blacks, and women.[27] From the theological, historical, and social points of view, this means that the church is finding the principle of its structure, organization, and mission within the poor and the marginalized and sees what it is and does in the world from their standpoint. As Leonardo Boff says:

> People, especially the poor, are organizing themselves in order to live their faith in a communal way. They are not repeating the past nor are they reforming present structures. A new future is dawning, something unforeseen during the past centuries of ecclesial rule. We are dealing with a true ecclesiogenesis, that is, the genesis of a Church that is born of the faith of the people.[28]

Important in this process is the omnipresence of women in the creation and development of the ecclesial base communities. They constitute the bulk of the communities,[29] so if the fundamental theological datum is that the Spirit of Jesus is in the poor and re-creating the whole of the church from their standpoint,[30] it would be nonsense not to recognize that it is this same Spirit acting strongly in women. Women offer certain insights often not imagined from an androcentric perspective.

A New Way of Living the Church

At their deepest level the ecclesial base communities offer women their primary experience of faith, hope, and communion. Rather than a movement or group to which they belong through cultural or traditional inertia, the community means a new way of experiencing the reality of the church. Cavalcanti observes that the community

> constitutes a new space for liberation and consciousness-raising, fed by the reading of events in the light of the Bible, by the practice of solidarity and the celebration of life in terms of faith. The Gospel again becomes surprising good news. It makes women leave behind an attitude of fear and lack of confidence in order to ally themselves with the suffering and oppressed in a liberation process.[31]

This experience affects individual lives, the reality of the people, and God's word. It inspires confidence that God is with those who carry out Jesus' egalitarian practice and provides the certainty that such actions are taken in the power of the Spirit.

In the ecclesial base communities women reclaim their right to be the church and regarded as creative participants in it. In fact, the majority of participants in the communities agree that "it is women who take the first step and push the community forward, they are the most active, they give the community life and strengthen the new church."[32] In the community the church becomes a *happening* where women's word and commitment reinvent it. Women encourage and support others—men and women, children and old people, healthy and sick—to "hear the word of God, believe in it, and vow together to follow Jesus Christ, inspired by the Holy Spirit."[33] Because of their communitarian structure the church base communities give women the real possibility of more equal participation. In many cases the women are the representatives of their local communities, "who are responsible for order and presiding over the celebrations and the sacramental aspects of the community,"[34] especially in more remote country districts. The evangelical communion, which is the rule in the church base communities, coordinates services and ministries and ensures that the community is run on the basis of common discipleship and not rigid ecclesiastical divisions.[35] Nevertheless, although women share in most services, there are contradictions when it comes to describing and recognizing this daily work in theological and pastoral reflection or when the community is being publicly represented at larger meetings, because then women's participation is often silenced. "Certainly women work more than they appear to," observes Cavalcanti. This fact forces us to recognize that sexual discrimination and certain forms of *machismo* survive even in the church base communities.[36]

As a new way of living the church, the ecclesial base communities offer a new ministerial structure in which pastors play a true diaconal role of service, animation, and defense. At the same time new ministries arise in the communities and are taken on by women and men so that both contribute to serving the various needs of the community. The single criterion is the priority of life. But women push more for the renewal of the ways in which the ministries are carried out, as Cavalcanti observes:

> The church base communities point towards a church that is totally ministerial where the services are a team effort with the participation of the community in every ministry serving the church as a whole. For example, if women are the majority in catechesis, in biblical circles and every kind of service that prepares and builds the community, it is odd that they are set aside when the work flourishes and is transfigured into the sacraments. We recognize that this question is not yet ripe and should be analyzed seriously in the future. Nevertheless this cannot prevent us calling attention to a problem that can no longer be hidden.[37]

Without any doubt this question is fundamental for the present and future of the church of the poor. The serious problem from women's point of view is that although the traditionally oppressed and marginalized, the poor, the indigenous, blacks, and women *in fact* participate in the church of the poor, *men* who are poor, indigenous, or black have the possibility of entry to *all* levels of the church—the sacraments, the priesthood, and decision-making—but these are at present closed to women. While the church of the poor offers greater possibilities for overcoming racism and classism, it is obvious that it ought also to offer greater possibilities for overcoming sexism, which cannot be overcome in the Christendom model. Only thus can it maintain genuine communion, participation, and equality in the Christian community.[38]

The Power of Convocation

The church base communities have a surprising capacity for convocation. They do so to the extent that their members take on the concerns of the masses and celebrate in faith every transforming practice that anticipates a new world. This power of convocation appears with greater emphasis when women keep the memory of martyrs present as a source of courage and hope, or when some community success evokes the original biblical liberating experience and brings about new ways of working together for those who suffer the most.[39] For women in particular in the church base communities the Bible has a fundamental role. Reading the gospel and connecting it with their own lives generate attitudes of solidarity that aim to transform the church and society. As Cavalcanti points out,

> There is a general awareness that Bible reading involves a critical spirit, denunciations, and claiming of rights. And this brings persecution, death threats, distrust by many, both within and outside the church. But this does not make the women abandon their prophetic position. On the contrary, they make the biblical language their own and read the facts of their lives in the light of faith.[40]

In their hands the Bible becomes a comrade in their struggle against oppression and the subordinate condition they suffer as women. Paradoxically, even when the biblical world displays a patriarchal character, precisely because the Bible is being read in intimate contact with the reality of their situation as poor and as women, the critical consciousness awakened by their reading leads them to identify the various forms of *machismo* existing in present-day society, in the church and in the Bible itself. "Then there are denunciations and protests against sexual discrimination, not always recognized by society or even by members of the church base communities themselves."[41] In the community the women not only identify the causes and mechanisms causing the people's impoverishment but also the causes and mechanisms of their subordination as women.

A genuine perspective of solidarity and equal participation gives rise in the church base communities to an awareness of the grave problems suffered by women and encourages them to take the necessary action to uproot *machismo*. In the church base communities women denounce the many injustices that have been committed against them for centuries and summon women and men to struggle collectively to eradicate the ancient evil. According to Cavalcanti, this experience in the church base communities has two important consequences. First, "sexual discrimination meets growing resistance, beginning with the women themselves and then from men who are becoming aware that in the struggle for liberation *machismo* is a nonsense and only slows up the process."[42] Second, a collective protest grows against the open sexual discrimination in the church's own organization, where the clergy look anxiously upon the work done by women's organizations and the hierarchy fails to offer women any increased participation in the ministry.[43]

Christian faith is not a separate area experienced by women independently of their identity as women or detached from their culture. When women denounce their subordination in society and the church and propose new kinds of relations in society and the church from their experience in the church base community, they are demonstrating the liberating aspect of Christian faith and its power to summon people to support the just causes of the oppressed. Through their faith women struggle for a new social order in accordance with their religious and cultural values. They struggle to make possible new relationships in society and the church in which they can fulfil themselves as subjects with full rights in both public and private spheres. They seek relationships in which their identity is not subsumed or discounted in models that claim to be participatory but which in fact do not integrate their aspirations and interests as believers, as poor, and as women.[44]

Seeds of the New Creation

The communities' internal dynamism nourishes the women and enables them to engage in various activities concerned with the construction of a sharing and equal society. However, because changes do not come of their own accord or as a result of abstract discussions, women must engage in political action to fight for their rights. In women's struggles the field of political action covers both the public and private spheres. These experiences acquire a character that anticipates the New Creation, because their aim is to overcome inequalities. Many gains — even painful and partial ones — express the conviction that a new order is possible without oppression and without exploitation of human beings or of the earth. So "women's struggle in the church base communities for a new society is sowing seed, as a member of the mothers' club rightly put it. Sowing requires both initiative and patience. Initiative requires courage. Patience is the basis of organization, discipline, and power to resist."[45] As this mothers' club member observes, this attitude is very different from the unfortunate Thomistic view that active virtue belongs to the masculine sex and passive virtue to the feminine, using the same metaphor of the seed to refer to reproduction and the "natural" division of labor between men and women, to the women's disadvantage.[46]

Looking to the future requires us to stand firmly in the present but at the same time to recover our own past, the ancestral wisdom of whole peoples, and the infinity of women who preceded us in the struggle for a more just world.[47] In the church base communities women look back at their own past, the hidden history of those who were condemned on earth. They recall women's forbidden words, not only in order to recover their own identity but also to rebuild their hope and give meaning to today's expectations. Cavalcanti rightly underlines women's fundamental role in the preservation of the collective historical memory as a bond that unites them, an aid to resistance as an activating force in present struggles.[48] Memory stretches back in time in a long line of collective solidarity, in which we recognize the poor and oppressed women in their resistance and common struggles. Neither the conquest nor the double colonization, neither present-day imperialist patriarchal capitalism nor sexist clericalism have succeeded in wiping from the face of the earth the living memory of countless women who have kept alive the best of the ancestral cultures and the intrinsically liberating character of the gospel. This is the source of our courage and strength; it is the living demonstration of women's self-awareness.[49]

In the church base communities there is no place for the competitive egoism of macho patriarchal cultures. The guiding principle in the communities is solidarity shared from below. So the ways of living together in society and the church that they give rise to are participatory, equal and not exclusive. Solidarity is experienced within the community and also stretches its hands outward. It is experienced in both the public and private spheres, both the social and the intimate. It embraces hard work and also that other dimension denied to the poor and oppressed: the right to leisure, entertainment, play, enjoyment and rest. In a hierarchical society—classist, racist, and sexist—only a minority enjoy the benefits of leisure and the freedom to create, at the expense of others' labor and women's oppression. When the call to solidarity arises in the church base communities, the call to struggle coming from women's initiatives,[50] the tasks have a global quality because they aim to solve the evils afflicting women, men, and the earth. Calls from men do not always propose the eradication of evils afflicting women.

In women's activities in the base communities we see the huge capacity for resistance by the poor. Indeed, what is hoped for is seen to be possible. Countless testimonies demonstrate "women's resistance capacity in moments of extreme difficulty, which enables them to face hunger, tiredness, distance, migrations, contempt and violence, prejudices, and the temptation to throw it all in"[51] when others weaken and men waver. Women of the people have a profound sense of what is lasting, because they know that life has priority. With their capacity for resistance and their mature wisdom they incorporate into the processes of change the dimension of permanence, hope and anticipatory forms of the New Creation.

Fruitful Space for Courage and Compassion

In the church base communities Christian faith has truly reached the possible frontiers where the church's credibility is tested. As a result of their option for the liberation of the poor and oppressed, countless women have known the horrors of torture, persecution, and martyrdom. Because of their option for life, women have exposed themselves to the violence of an unjust social order, sacrificing their own lives. They also give birth to and bring up those who shed their blood for the people's cause.[52] Women share the struggles and hopes of the masses, and above all, they share what has been the tragic destiny of the poor and those in solidarity with them: persecution and martyrdom.[53]

The context of the church in Latin America is a context of conflict. That is why individuals need what Karl Rahner calls *supreme courage* in order to stand with those without power, the outcast, and impoverished, even when this stance means loss of security, prestige, and even one's own life.[54] Faith is not something possessed once and for all. It is not a legacy of timid fancies exempt from responsibility. It is a happening that nourishes a daily commitment to restore the rights to life and voice to those deprived of them. So the communities become a good place for women to share and express themselves; they become, according to Cavalcanti, a

> fertile ground from which women draw faith, love, tenacity, and hope and then plow it back in. The strength that comes from the community makes many of them think of the church as a space belonging to them, where they feel secure and strong to face the most varied challenges.[55]

Communities distill the faith whose distinctive mark is daring and supreme courage.

Daring and courage are all the more necessary as the women's own lives are constantly threatened because they have committed themselves to the church or popular social movements. One of the most humiliating and horrible experiences suffered by countless women is rape. Elsa Tamez has denounced this reality on several occasions. She points out that in some Central American countries,

> Poor women or those in solidarity with the poor (indigenous and mestizos) are frequently raped by members of the armed forces in both countries — Guatemala and El Salvador. . . . All these women are victims of a general situation of repression in the whole region . . . and because they are persons with female bodies they suffer worse and are humiliated more. The soldiers' machismo shows at its most grotesque in certain countries with a high degree of irrationality, like Guatemala and El Salvador, because they mingle torture, blood, and semen.[56]

This reality recalls the sordid and disturbing account of the rape of the women in Loma (Judges 19), a text that Tamez uses to criticize the reality today, because today too women and men "consider, take counsel, and speak" as the inhabitants of Canaan once did.

To the strength, daring, and courage of the women in the church base communities another biblical quality is added: _compassion._ Compassion relates directly to the analogy between women and the divine mystery. God is identified and compared with the love of a mother who feels for the child of her womb. According to Cavalcanti, *compassion* means "feeling with, suffering together, opening up to communion with the other . . . and the community encourages women to leave their narrow domestic world and discover that others have similar concerns to theirs. Here we are talking about solidarity."[57] Of course it is women's participation in the church of the poor that makes the realization of these qualities possible. In another context many of these experiences remained isolated and subjective. This is not the case in the base communities where women demonstrate their own strength and courage by taking on the struggle for their own and their comrades' lives.

Celebration of Living Faith

Celebration of the faith is a fundamental element of the church base communities. The community has become the primary channel for the public expression of the faith of the poor; that is, of the special way in which the oppressed and outcast experience God in their struggles and resistance. Here it is not a question of fulfilling certain religious prescriptions, which confirm membership in a great religious institution. This is a communal manifestation — in liturgy, symbol, and prayer — of the experience of faith in accordance with the way in which the poor feel they are the church. It is not surprising to find that it is the communities themselves, and mainly women, who organize the celebrations in a creative and vital way.[58] In spite of their multiple oppression the people still have a talent for enjoyment and festival. In the celebrations they recall the promises of a full life; the community expresses their experience of transcendence; the celebrations are where the people give meaning to the mystery of their existence; and the celebrations confirm the people's own culture and thereby increase their cohesion and identity.

The form of the celebrations varies widely in every region of Latin America and the Caribbean. But some elements appear to be common. To the celebration of the eucharist — central in every church base community — are added representations of biblical history with situations today, song, poetry, dance, processions, and more. The community's creativity makes a lively synthesis between art and cult, simplicity and beauty, variety and coherence. But above all it recovers the true Christian meaning of the liturgical celebration by placing the gospel message in the context of the problems the people are experiencing today. Thus the celebrations encourage solidarity and the simple sharing of goods. They are sources of liberating hope and incentives to personal and social transformation. No participant—child, old person, or woman—feels like a mere spectator; all have an active part.

The celebration becomes an articulated system of symbolic practices, where through gestures, signs, symbols, rites, and songs (signifiers), the community expresses its own experience of the Christian mystery. A vital, permanent and dynamic connection is established between the symbol and what is symbolized.[59] As the community members experience God's compassion, mercy, and goodness in their lives, they gain the strength to transform and re-create the exiting order. Popular creativity creates a space of resistance and opposition to the different forms of cultural domination emanating from the imperialist power centers, which generally have an anti-popular, ethnocentric, racist, and sexist character.

Women's leading role in the celebrations is contributing a fundamental element to the community, where they express themselves as members of the people and as women. There is a markedly female tone in popular celebration.[60] Popular celebration is marked by a vision of the cosmos that is more female than male. There are constant references to the earth, nature, natural cycles with their creative, destructive, and re-creative rhythms, and links with gestation, pregnancy, labor, and birth. The people's religious and Christian experience predominantly keeps the language of symbol, analogy, poetry, existential realities, the best of human feelings, the intuitive, and the connecting. Reality and symbol are understood by the mind and heart. Past, present and future are fused, inner and outer, body and mind, sameness and difference a single, unsplit reality. In popular celebration there is often an absence of piecemeal, hierarchical, ordering, Western logic, which belongs more to the patriarchal cultures with their abstract, conceptual, and ahistorical language. The presence of women in the celebrations of faith removes the cold reasoning of orthodox official Catholicism and replaces it with the language of symbol, in which human experience and mystery converge, characteristics which come closer to women's experience.[61]

Finally, the participation of women in the celebration of faith demands the church's renewal in its ministerial structures so that women can share fully in the ordained ministry with full power to celebrate the eucharist. As Pablo Richard suggests, although "we know that this is something for the future, we must move in this direction in faith, hoping for the harvest of new times."[62]

4

The Understanding of Faith from the Perspective of Women

Liberation theology is a critical reflection on all historical activity combatting forms of oppression, impoverishment, death, and inhumanity suffered by people because of unjust structures. It begins with the particular struggles of the oppressed in their efforts to construct more equal and participatory forms of life. Social inequalities must be abolished and the full humanity of women and men recognized; there must be a decent life for all. This means that liberation theology must incorporate and make explicit the historical and spiritual experiences of women, their specific struggles, and their proposals; women suffer not only from economic exploitation and socio-political and cultural oppression, but also from ancestral androcentric racist and sexist structures in society, the church, and theology.[1] It is only recently that this idea has become explicit in Latin American theological reflection.

Although the theological treatment of women's problems and their solutions is not a matter exclusively for women, it is they who have taken the initiative to break the bonds of silence and make their voices heard within theology. Women have reclaimed a right they have been denied in the past—the right to reflect on their own experience of faith and to articulate their own understanding of the Christian experience, with a view toward change and liberation. This is certainly a new phenomenon in Latin American liberation theology—as it is in the church in general—and it is evidence of a change in women's self-awareness. Ivone Gebara observes that "Women's attainment of historical self-awareness and their readiness to act on it is one of the cultural revolutions of our time. Hence it is also a theological revolution struggling to happen in spite of difficulties of all kinds."[2]

62

It was not till the end of the seventies and beginning of the eighties that the importance of women as active subjects in theological reflection began to be seen. Elsa Tamez called attention to the situation of women, who up till then had been passed over, and the perspective of women began to be expressed. It showed the pernicious split between practice and theory on the part of the popular movement and the church of the poor. Both accepted women's fulfillment in theory, but not in practice: "The aspirations and contributions of the female subject, also part of the broad collective subject (meaning men and women of the oppressed classes, races, and cultures) had not been adopted or systematized or put to use."[3]

This shortcoming, which deprives women of their right to make history or theology, comes partly from an inadequate understanding of women's oppression-liberation. In a society rent by scandalous divisions of class and race, some women's movements, influenced by first-world feminist currents, fought for women's liberation as a struggle in itself. This view was rejected by many women in the popular sectors because they could not set aside their more pressing demands stemming from race and class struggle. Many theologians—including other women—were skeptical about the demands made by women engaged in movements for social change. To put it plainly, they thought that matters relating to women's liberation were a deviation from the principal conflict, the class struggle. Further, within the liberation processes of the church of the poor it was believed that women's emancipation would follow from the global liberation of society and renewal of the church. This viewpoint saw women's emancipation as secondary, and resulted in a split between liberation theology and women's aspirations and expectations.[4] Certainly, even with the class struggle resolved, no society can consider itself equal if it maintains inequalities of race or sex.

Nevertheless, thanks to liberation theology's self-critical and dynamic character, women found space within it for reflection on their own Christian experience, in dialogue with other men and women who were gradually discovering the systematically sexist and androcentric emphasis in their own theology and the church. If liberation theology constitutes the expression of the faith of the poor and oppressed, it must necessarily open itself to the experience of faith of the oppressed women of Latin America and the Caribbean.

Women and Liberation Theology

The need to formulate a type of reflection taking into account the struggles, resistance, and aspirations of women begins with the massive and growing fact of women's oppression. Women increasingly participate in popular social movements and the church. Liberation theology derives its vitality from these social and church experiences of a search for change. These are its *primary act*. In fact, it is difficult to conceive of Christian reflection responding to women's interests that is outside the context of liberation theology.

Liberation theology is a theory describing the experience of God of those who are struggling for the life of the poor and oppressed. As well as consciously taking on faith's political implications, liberation theology is concerned with its efficacy in dealing with reality. Because of Christian revelation's historical dimension and because it takes God's manifestation in current reality absolutely seriously, in order to correspond in faith to this manifestation,[5] it also must also denounce those who crucify the vast mass of humanity. It clarifies through rigorous analysis the oppressive elements and structures present not only in society but also in the church, theology, scripture itself, and the church's traditions. The aim is to eradicate suffering and transform it into justice and liberation. Liberation theology remains open to the questions of the poor and oppressed, and together with them it elaborates answers to encourage them on their way in the light of the gospel. In this process the people experience their faith in a new way and articulate it in a fresh manner, so that they themselves become doers of theology—theology's primary subject.

However, liberation theology has a fundamental lack: the absence of reflection on the historical and spiritual experiences of women and their efforts to transform the systems destroying their lives and their human integrity. Failure to be aware of this lack was a contradiction, because liberation theology assumed the principle of total liberation and fullness of life for the poor and oppressed, among whom women stand out for their neediness. As critical reflection, liberation theology ought to make a serious analysis of mechanisms operating to the detriment of the lives of the people and identify those that oppress women both as poor and as women. Gradually liberation theology has become more open to these matters.

If liberation theology wants to be the interpretation of the word of the poor and consciously assumes as its horizon the interests, hopes, and struggles of the oppressed, it ought to promote women's self-expression. As Julio de Santa Ana observes, it became necessary to correct the "excessively male bias in liberation theology until the beginning of this decade."[6] Liberation theology was running the risk of becoming merely rhetorical by abstracting itself from the particular faces of the people it was about, including women. The ideological gap, which left out or relegated to a secondary level the sexist, *machista*, and patriarchal elements in society, the church, and theology, was brought to light by the presence of women doing theology. They aspired to be the makers of their own word, as they were of the Latin American historical experience. Their demand deepened the hermeneutics of liberation theology and widened its epistemological field. It is not exaggerating to recognize that women, as new doers of theology and a new locus for hermeneutics, have come not merely to reform but to re-create liberation theology, just as black and indigenous people do.[7] This is why we can speak of a new stage in Latin American theology and a new way of doing theology.

Discovery of the androcentric character of liberation theology introduced modifications into its content and its ways of understanding reality and the experience of faith. It was made clear that it was no longer a matter of speaking *about* women as if they were an object of reflection set apart from the doers of liberation theology. Neither was it a discourse *for* women as if they had passively to wait for others to define their destiny. Neither was it a case of speaking *on behalf of* women, as if they were incapable of intelligence and too mentally limited to articulate their own wisdom and justification of the faith. Neither was it a matter of speaking *in the name of* women. Women are the makers of their own theory, worked out from the point of view of their own consciousness and experience. Women want to reappropriate history and to work out their own theological perspectives, in order to clarify ways to eradicate their ancestral sufferings and to inspire processes that promote fullness of life and encourage the march toward a new earth where men and women share equally and realize together their full humanity.

Although this is a situation that is improving, the absence of women from theology, either as doers of theology or as the content of theological reflection, is another expression of their subordinate condition.[8] Women's invisibility in theology is not accidental; it is in accordance with the way theology has been done for centuries.[9] So it is not surprising that women see theology as a sexist profession. They have been excluded simply because of their sex, because they are women.[10] To the extent that theology excludes women, it becomes a partial and abstract discourse, based unilaterally on the masculine and ignoring humanity's intrinsic equality.

This absence of women in theology has, as I have indicated, been pointed out to liberation theologians.[11] The reasons explaining this absence also explain this theology's progressive opening up to women. The first reason is what I call *historical urgency*. As the new theology identified with the suffering of the Latin American masses, it was bound to articulate a word of solidarity and compassion, a cry for justice for this suffering and crucified people, in order to promote their liberation. Liberation theology was not born in the illustrious academic centers, which base their work on clear and distinct premises. Instead, it originated in an oppressed world as a response to God's primary word crying out in the people's massive suffering, as a response of human and Christian compassion for the masses condemned to death before their time. In this context liberation theology understood that its proposals should include all social sectors.

A second reason was theologians' *lack of awareness* of women's oppression and struggles. Neither male nor female theologians consciously set out to exclude women's reality. By pointing out this lack I do not mean to blame them but to signal the need for increased self-awareness in theology. The situation of women simply was not incorporated as a necessary factor for understanding oppression, because it was concealed under the veil of *naturalness*. Neither women nor their situation was seen as important for the understanding and interpretation of reality as a whole. This had to do with epistemological processes and not with subjective guilt, although a minimum of goodwill was always needed to broach the situation of women.

A third reason has already been mentioned: the *machista* and androcentric nature of theology up to the present. Most liberation theologians were educated under these structures, although fortunately many are beginning to free themselves from their presuppositions.

Women's incorporation into liberation theology is a perspective from which to interpret the world, history, the church, and Christian faith. It is an attempt to overcome the partial nature of the andro-centric viewpoint and to expose the experiences and knowledge of women striving for a new social order and a church that benefits both women and men. Feminist liberation theology is, therefore, a *fundamental theology*. So I do not speak of a *theology of women*. Neither are women a *theme* for reflection like any other. "We want to speak," says Elsa Tamez, "of a theology from women's perspec-tive, that is, from the point of view of women's oppression, that attempts to change their situation."[12] This perspective is liberation theology itself. By incorporating the perspective of women it aspires to be a way of understanding faith, rooted in the particular, through which women and men can fulfill themselves in accordance with the gospel of equality.

Women Doing Theology: Word in Context

Latin American women realize that not all theology or every way of living in the church is favorable to their own creativity and self-esteem. They suspect that not every construction of theological knowledge promotes their fulfillment as subjects with full rights. Liberation theology and the church of the poor are devoted to lib-eration, justice, and a full life to the poor and oppressed, which is why they provide women with space in which to operate. In them women gather sufficient courage to transform their so-called weak-ness into strength. They offer a framework within which to study, explain, and describe what is and what has been women's historical experience under structures that supported male superiority, and also to work out what it would be like to live the faith in a new way without inequalities.

In theology in general women's past is distinguished by silence and invisibility.[13] What makes it worse is that this theology has claimed objectivity and universality. Until very recently the theme of women was dealt with in reflection upon Mary and in theological anthropology. In neither case was it a discourse elaborated from the viewpoint of women's own understanding of faith. María Clara Bingemer sums this up:

The theme of women did not appear separately in treatises, courses, or books of theology. It was subsumed under the treatise on theological anthropology, which reflected on the human being in *his* condition as God's image and creature. Women, diluted and hidden even by the language itself, were included under the ambiguous global and androcentric term: man. The category *man* claimed to designate the whole human species: men and women. But unconsciously the form of this term influenced the content, and the object of reflection really became man as the male rather than the whole of humanity: men and women.[14]

The situation is not different when we speak of women as producers of theology. "There had been no concern to define or make explicit the sex of the authors of theological texts and professors of theology. It was *assumed* that this was a task for men."[15]

To a large extent this phenomenon has its roots in the dualistic anthropology upon which theology in general has been built.[16] But of course it is also connected with the lifestyle of churchmen and theologians—the producers of theology—which is remote from ordinary daily life with its sexual division of labor. Socialized to segregate public and private realms, they have not been involved in tasks usually done by women. Impelled to conform to a rigidly male stereotype, they do not incorporate into their reflection on faith the human dimensions of desire, emotion, or affection. Thus, Bingemer observes:

> During all this time theology was not enriched by female thinking and speaking, with its own particular way of being and expressing itself. Women's feelings, reflections, and tone of voice were absent. This impoverished theology, the church, and humanity. And women suffered like the woman in the parable in Luke 15:8–10. She kept looking for the lost coin, which she was completely certain existed and was not willing to give up.[17]

In Latin America today women no longer wait for others to define their experience of life and faith. They have decided to define themselves. They want to express in their own words their particular way of experiencing revelation and living the faith as a liberating force. In the midst of a reality in which women are doubly and triply oppressed, doing liberation theology from women's viewpoint is not a luxury but a necessity and a right to be claimed. It is a necessity because Christian women are convinced that faith has something to say about their situation. God of the gospel message or a large part of the church community cannot remain impervious to their sufferings. They need to reclaim a right that has been taken away and denied for centuries in the history of the church and theology: articulating their understanding of the faith from where they stand as impoverished and oppressed women struggling for liberation. With their experience of the faith in the popular struggle[18] they are reappropriating their right to speak for themselves. They do their theology in their own context as Latin American Christian women.[19]

Women

We want to explore our own identity as women, rediscovering ourselves as human persons capable of integrating our differences, mutuality, and particularity. We want to tell our own history and speak about our condition as women and our expectations. We want to dialogue with men and with other women to recover the elements of our own originality. In spite of the imposition of stereotypes, which do not correspond to what we want or how we see themselves, women resist being what culture, religion, and *machista* ideology have defined us to be. We do not want to be something different from what we are, because we recognize that these external definitions do not correspond to what we deeply seek. There is a tension between what is *expected* of women and what we really want to be. Women seek alternative models for involving ourselves in action, and we rebel against the structures that limit, oppress, and deny our fulfillment. We seek new ways of cooperation, solidarity, and living. In spite of the persistence of Western, white models, women of Latin America and the Caribbean want to control our own calling as women who are Indian, black, mestizo, or white, in solidarity with those who are striving for human fulfillment as a whole. This is a project still to be fulfilled and a dimension that exclusivist Western culture has not been able to realize.

Latin Americans

Latin American women share with our people a common condition of dependence and oppression. Our lives cannot be understood without this vital connection with the popular social movements of transformation, which are also trying to construct a new history. As Latin Americans we share with others the expectation of a future not yet fully revealed but already present in germ from its American Indian origins. The goal of the people's movement is to fulfill Latin Americans' destiny. Together with other comrades in the struggle, Latin American women cannot give up what is our own—our history, our particular cultural expression, our desire for equal and participatory social relations. While systems exist that oppress the masses, subordinate women, marginalize non-white races, and exploit the earth to make a profit from it, Latin American women will continue to resist and continue our rebellion in a thousand ways. Our enormous capacity to give priority to life is not a legacy of violent Iberian and current North American colonization. On the contrary, it is part of the legacy of the ancestral peoples, the disinherited, the condemned of the earth, who have nurtured solidarity as a means of survival and as a profound attitude toward other human beings. This is a form of solidarity unknown to the colonists and their *machista* systems but one which women have kept alive for centuries.

Christians

For Latin American women being Christian is not, as Nelly Ritchie points out, exclusively a *religious* matter:

> It is a cosmic vision. It is indicative of the motives and basis of our struggle and of our efforts. As the Incarnate Word, Jesus Christ is God's revealed word. We fight against any use of this to disguise reality. Instead we promote a dialogical and transformative word that uncovers this reality.[20]

For Latin American women being Christian is partly a cultural tradition and inheritance. But above all it is a vocation, a special way of living and experiencing the world as the place where God works and, with motherly care, re-creates life from apparent dryness and desert. This is the horizon from which Latin American women experience the mystery in the depths of our being. Vitally linked to the earth, our people, ancestral traditions, customs, and hopes through our faith, Latin American women have experienced the power of the Spirit. We are taking our first steps to assume our history and also be its protagonists; we want to gain a name, to pass from invisible to visible, from object to subject.[21] Nevertheless, however painful it is to recognize it, throughout the five hundred years of its presence in Latin America, the church, which is meant to utter the voice of the Spirit, has mostly failed to understand the Spirit's manifestation in the lives of women. It has done little to bring women out of our silence and darkness. The church must now repay this debt to women with justice and generosity. In spite of this exclusion, Latin American women love the church. We believe we are the church. Our love is imbued with tenderness, patience, perseverance, and good doses of rebelliousness and audacity.

When Latin American women do theology, the intent is not to eliminate cooperation in solidarity with men nor to undermine current theological discourse. "Our struggle," Elsa Tamez declares, "which must be passionate, is against machistic ideology, the victims of which are not only men but also the many women who are accomplices as well as victims. We also struggle against the whole oppressive system of war which kills thousands of innocent people, many of them poor."[22] We do not want to produce a parallel theological discourse that ignores our particularity. We want to try out a new language, a new understanding of faith, which will empower our common capacity to be fully women and men with enriching differences. We are doing a new practical and intellectual exercise, which is not yet complete but which promises to be the way in which theology can become really Christian.

> Latin American women, along with their partners, want to recreate cultural, ecclesial, and theological history, cultivating it with new hands, new seeds, new care, and new weapons in order to produce new fruits, new everyday relations, new ways of practicing our faith within the church, and new theological discourse. In summary, we hope to give rise to the sixth sun, under the protection of our Lord Jesus Christ. And, as men and women we want to be healed and to heal each other, the so-called "open veins" of Latin America.[23]

Theology Done by Women and Traditional Theology

None of the most recent works on the present situation in Latin American liberation theology omits women's contributions to theology or fails to mention contributions from the black and indigenous perspectives.[24] For Bingemer these three are the *new protagonists* or "sectors oppressed over the centuries for their color, race, and sex. ... They are indispensable for understanding the present state of liberation theology and for glimpsing its future, because they bring new questions to theology, a new method, and a new type of discourse."[25] Women theologians have pointed out certain aspects characterizing traditional theology from the viewpoint of Latin American women.[26] I shall take a look at this critique because in order to understand what is special about the new, we first need to identify the elements that help or hinder women doing theology.

This analysis is not exhaustive. It is simply an indication of those aspects that make possible the creation of something new in theology and therefore its transformation. By pointing out the ways in which traditional theological discourse has operated, we shall be in a better position to distinguish the epistemological and methodological ways women have chosen to do theology. The creative theological capacity found in Latin American women's reflections on faith does not start from nothing. In doing theology women must show a serious knowledge of the general and specific theological and exegetic disciplines; therefore their discourse is consciously set in the context of throwing new light on other ways of doing theology. They also need to set out more systematically those aspects they are interested in transcending or radically modifying.

The first aspect to stress is the *logocentric* character of traditional theology as compared with the theology done by women, which concentrates more on practice and context. The central role of *logos* as the special tool for giving an account of faith in traditional theology, observes Tamez, means that "the only, or rather, the best way to approach reality is through rational discourse, that is, through Western systematic logic. Other forms of expressing real life in play, in poetry, or painting, are regarded as less serious, or even as lesser forms."[27] No real theological status is given to other ways of understanding and explaining the faith, like wisdom literature or the narrative oral testimonial tradition, even though they are regarded as important matters for reflection. They are also appropriate ways of thinking about and expressing the ancient and perennial truths of the Christian faith as they are experienced in the resistance processes and the struggle for life.[28] It is not that women deny or reject the rational in the construction of theological discourse; if they did they would merely be encouraging the classic androcentric view of women as irrational. It is rather that they are putting *logos* and its function in a different place, a place in which men are not its only possessors and it is not the single universal tool of theology as understanding and knowledge of faith.[29]

Precisely because of its logocentric character, traditional theology often became polarized as knowing for the sake of knowing. It became reasoning, clarifying, and defining truths; any other human approach to the truth was regarded as false and inconsistent, thereby excluding the possibility of other forms of knowledge. The most serious problem with this procedure was that theology, enveloped in a web of speculation, closed off the road toward what was *real* in reality and thus cut itself off from existing oppression and from the fact that divine revelation existed in historical reality. It turned out that this word was the *logos* only of Western, capitalist, white, male culture. It became an elitist discourse, excluding other words that did not faithfully repeat its own or speak its language, such as women's words. It established a mono-logue between men, and not a dialogue between women and men as the whole of humanity. It was concerned with attaining creditable theoretical-scientific status.[30] It did not consider people in particular, especially not poor people or women, and failed to give them the necessary tools for a real understanding of the faith in its support for their struggles for life, survival, and liberation.

A second aspect, which follows from the previous one, is the *impositional* character of traditional theology. It was linked to Western culture throughout the long history of Christendom and became a constituent part of the colonial imposition—at first Iberian and now European and North American in Latin America. As third-world theologians point out: "Traditional theology has not involved itself in the real drama of a people's life, or spoken in the religious and cultural idioms and expressions of the masses in a meaningful way. It has remained highly academic, speculative, and individualistic, without regard for the societal and structural aspects of sin."[31] Neither has it been aware of women's permanent subordination or questioned their marginalization on grounds of race. So traditional theology does not seem able to contribute to the solutions women in the Third World and elsewhere are seeking. This theology concedes in its own teaching the *naturalness* of women's subordinate condition and consecrates the unequal stereotypes of the masculine and the feminine as desired by God, thereby endorsing women's oppressive destiny. Overcoming this impositional aspect will be possible only when the poor and outcast, especially women, are able to deliver their own word of faith to the world.

A third aspect of traditional theology is the *conquering and colonial logic* it has displayed for centuries, as opposed to the logic of solidarity and mutuality characterizing the way the oppressed and women feel and think. There is a general tendency in this theology to ignore the age-old evils suffered by the masses, because they are not the evils listed in its conception of what humanity should be. In truth,

> Though this traditional theology has provided an impetus for personal spirituality and for tremendous missionary expansion, it has been incapable of responding to the social problems of the First World and to the challenges of the Third World. For the Third World, this theology has been alienated and alienating. It has not provided the motivation for opposing the evils of racism, sexism, capitalism, colonialism, and neocolonialism. It has failed to understand our religious, indigenous cultures, and traditions, and to relate to them in a respectful way.[32]

Traditional theology has legitimated the denial of women's alterity, an alterity that Latin American *machismo* has subjugated both on the personal and the structural level. Oppressed women have had to create their own subterranean systems of common solidarity, or rather it might appear that they have acted in complicity with the earth and history to conserve their own memory of struggle and resistance, symbols, and actions that keep alive their particular way of combining life and thought. In the face of this conquering and colonial logic, whose aim is to subdue, the logic women weave in their discourse seeks justice. They are trying to find new ways for men and women to relate, new forms of solidarity with the earth. They want to create new ways of being the church and living together in society. The solidarity logic that accompanies women in their reflection does not just propose a vague sort of humanism, such as has existed up till now. It seeks a humanism capable of integrating freely and creatively the aspects denied by the conquerors' logic, aspects concerning the right to integrity, goodness, and beauty of triply oppressed women.

A fourth characteristic of traditional theology is its _one-sided viewpoint._ From this stance it defines the world, persons, and things, and does not acknowledge the validity of other viewpoints. Every meaning and explanation given to what exists is circumscribed within the limits and boundaries of this single, one-dimensional view of life. This creates a closed system, which offers security because it explains and justifies an order within what is always already known. It closes off imagination, re-creation, life's multi-sided dynamism, and dimensions of existence not previously contemplated. It shuts off the challenging voice of the Spirit. Traditional theology is one-sided because it was originally male theology and therefore believes that the way things have been is the way they should be because it is *natural* they should be so.[33] The traditional *machista* destiny society has assigned to men and women acquires an obvious and evident character. Because the way things are is self-evident, this continues to legitimate unequal relationships that oppress women. Now women have begun to suggest that the evident is not so obvious and the obvious not natural, that what is obvious from an androcentric viewpoint is not so for women. Women point out that reality includes that which has not yet been tried and that it is possible and necessary to open up this closed system in order to enrich theology with other aspects of life. One of the spheres offered to theology to overcome its one-sidedness is the sphere of daily life. Here it can find new meanings and values in the differences between women and men, which do not necessarily involve unequal relationships.

In close connection with the above-mentioned characteristics, traditional theology is also *one-voiced*. Even though it imposed itself on the world, and Latin America in particular, as a generic universal discourse, in reality it was not. It was the voice of androcentric European thought.[34] It is one-voiced in its choice of themes, which are not always appropriate to the vital needs of the Latin American situation, and even less to those of women. This single-voiced, male, European character leads traditional theology to select certain aspects and marginalize others. It believes that its language expresses the popular vision of the cosmos, but this is far from the case. For this theology humanity is restricted to *man* and effectively expresses only a male view. It gives primacy to speculation and marginalizes the experience of ancestral cultures. It degrades the popular, everyday, and simple culture present in the symbols, activities, and language of the poor. For this theology the tenderness, affection, humor, celebration, and optimism that belong to the Latin American identity are not experiences where divine revelation occurs. Because it ignores the symbolic systems of Latin American cultures—with its oppressive elements but also with its traditions of protest, resistance, and subversion—this theology creates a huge gap between its one-voiced theoretical structures and what is deepest in the Latin American spirit.

A sixth characteristic of traditional theology, which has already been pointed out in many works, is its *dualistic character*, both in its own configuration and in the anthropology that supports it. This legacy of a theology that took over the paradigms and models of Platonist and neo-Platonist philosophy has enormous consequences, which are not only harmful to women but also hinder an adequate understanding of the biblical message. When this theology dominated ethics, metaphysics, and Hellenistic-Roman politics, it transmitted, along with this method, the contents of this particular way of understanding existence. It thus forced a reading of the gospel message that damaged the emancipatory essence of Christianity. Accordingly, humanity was not a living couple, man and woman in the image of God, but a male, who was a mirror of the Creator and mediator of woman. A human being—man or woman—was no longer a single body through the union of flesh and spirit. There was, instead, a permanent conflict between body and soul—and women corresponded primarily to the body. It was no longer humanity's vocation jointly to transform history but rather its task became to divide up the material and spiritual tasks to be done. The assembly of believers was no longer an egalitarian community of disciples, but an organization in which there existed superiors and inferiors. This split vision of faith and the world invaded all spheres of life, and in all of them women came off the worse.

Another aspect of this dualistic character is the tendency to construct a world of spiritualizing abstractions. Thus the experience of God in everyday life is separated from its explanation in theological discourse. Inner and outer are separated. Rationality is opposed to emotion and feeling, which are not allowed to nourish the understanding of faith. This dualistic character has led traditional theology into a way of thinking that has been damaging to women,[35] men, theology itself, and the church's own life. A theological perspective that is aware of these limits has greater possibilities to transcend them, because it no longer thinks of doing theology as simply doing more of the same. It puts critical reflection on faith— together with its objects and those doing the reflecting—into a new context. Here concepts can be reformulated, questions given priority, themes stressed, positions confronted, and particular viewpoints propounded. In this case liberation theology from the perspective of Latin American women is based on the historical and spiritual experiences of struggles against oppression by women. It seeks God's revelation in them and describes this theologically in its own words. This not only transcends the limits of traditional theology, but it also re-creates the method, presuppositions, and contents of liberation theology in general. In short, this is a believing process, which formally incorporates into its work the re-creative dynamism of the Spirit in the past and present lives of women. It also embraces what is not yet realized in humanity and in the experience of faith as promises to be fulfilled.

PART 2

WOMEN AS DOERS OF THEOLOGY

5

Methodological Premises for Theology from the Perspective of Women

As doers of theology Latin American women must lay down certain premises for their reflection. These premises are theoretical structures that allow a coherent understanding of faith to be formulated in terms of certain consciously adopted interests, values and objectives. They are concerned with anthropological, philosophical, and political options appropriate for the construction of genuinely equal and liberating projects. Making its premises explicit is a feature of feminist liberation theology. On the other hand, Elisabeth Schüssler Fiorenza notes, "theologians in the academy refuse to discuss publicly their political allegiance and preconceived bias and function."[1] This means they manage to conceal even from themselves the ideologies and interests upon which their work is based. One of humanity's current discoveries, backed by the sociology of knowledge, is how thinking and the historico-social reality of the thinker are related. All thought has a social context and is articulated in particular social practices, which decisively influence the process and also the content of this thought.[2] There is no thinking or thought that is neutral or without preconditioning. As Georges Casalis said in his time: "Good ideas do not fall from heaven."[3] So it is necessary that all reflection should be aware of its premises and objectives. As both thinking activity and socially situated work, theology does not escape this principle, even when its own internal logic is recognized to be a discipline regulated by faith. Nevertheless, it is still human thinking about the experience of faith in the Christian community in the light of revealed data.[4]

As Juan José Tamayo-Acosta notes,

However much theology tries to flee from historical reality and shut itself off in interreligious discourse, it always ends up having

81

a historical function and relating to the surrounding culture. Sometimes this is by resisting new cultural categories and legitimating an established order against those who are struggling for a new order. At other times it welcomes the new cultural climate, reformulating the faith in sympathy with it; it offers criticism in terms of the gospel and supports changes in the direction of greater justice.[5]

Theology claiming to be above history, or theology that is not conscious of its premises, ends up identifying with the dominant power in the church and society. This is to its own detriment and humanity's, because such a theology ignores the questions and deepest desires of the majority of human beings: the poor and oppressed of the earth. It becomes deaf to the urgent cries by victims of injustice claiming their right to life—in this case, women.

As we have already seen, in Latin American liberation theology, although women share the hermeneutical locus of the poor, some theologians do not accept women's special needs and demands; their work is androcentric. As for traditional theology, following Schüssler Fiorenza "it has identified humanness with maleness and understood women only as a peripheral category in the human interpretation of reality, the new field of women's studies not only attempts to make women's agency a key interpretative category but also seeks to transform androcentric scholarship and knowledge into truly human scholarship and knowledge."[6] The work done by women tries to end their exclusion from theological knowledge. This work is based on a conscious commitment to the liberation of the poor, the subjugated races, and women who are triply oppressed.

An Egalitarian Anthropological Perspective

Women's theological work in Latin America is aware that not all theology bothers to make its anthropological presuppositions explicit.[7] It is very important to do this because theology in Latin America is trying to become relevant to the masses who "are poor, enjoy no adequate quality of life, and lack respect, bread, love, and *justice*."[8] So, if theology is about the meaning of our actions and our life and death, it must be about the meaning of human existence and humanity's destiny seen in God's supreme light. Hence the inseparable connection between theology and anthropology. In fact all theology is indebted to anthropology. As human word and understanding of faith, theology expresses a person's self-understanding in relation to God's mystery; it enunciates the ultimate foundation of human life and what it is called to be in terms of the Christian message. So theology implies an anthropology.[9] Word about God's mystery is always historical within the determinations of human reality. But as Ivone Gebara and María Clara Bingemer note,

> The human word becomes divine word when it touches on the heart, the core, what is deepest in the human. This deepest aspect in turn points to the personal and collective history of human beings. It refers to that which in fact allows the right to life and respect for all beings. Hence, the various religious texts called "revelations" of the divinity point to something that affects the deep fulfillment of every human being. It is as though beyond the differences that distinguish us, we were walking on a common ground that impelled us to recognize that we are equal, similar, complementary to one another.[10]

In this light we are seeking an anthropology that does not suffocate women but allows them total fulfillment.[11]

Today the recognition of women as active subjects and persons is not limited to the emancipation of some bits of their lives, because life is not a sum of isolated components but a single reality with many interrelated aspects. The heart of the question is the conception of humanity as a whole and the understanding of what constitutes a human being. Therefore the debates around women's subordinate positions in the church and society have to do with different anthropological ideas underlying the various theological and political positions.[12] For example, readings of the Bible are determined by a conscious or unconscious anthropological assumption. This gives rise to "the doubt to what point — at least in certain parts — it is dominated by an *androcentric image of the world*, which does not necessarily belong to the fundamental deposit of revelation."[13] This means an androcentric reading of the Bible has encouraged an unequal view of humanity and supported male superiority. Here an androcentric anthropology is dominant, when in reality the fundamental structure of revelation is dialogical — one of mutuality (the I-thou of God's self-communication to humanity: women and men and both to each other). This requires an equal view of humanity. Karl Lehmann points out that, women do not owe their dignity to men, but to God. . . . The dignity of the person requires an immediate relationship with God and an unassailable freedom. Only God guarantees this dignity, which must always be unconditionally respected. This equality of rank must be made possible today economically, socially, and legally. When the demand for *self-realization* is a search for personal dignity through women's equality, it deserves every support from Christians and the church.[14]

Therefore the anthropological — and consequently theological — emphasis must be on the affirmation of women's and men's rights to full humanity as equals, because each relates as a person to the same divine reality. This premise rejects out of hand any subordinationist anthropological positions. Saying that women are constitutive members of humanity means recognizing them as persons with full rights in all spheres of life. This applies even more strongly when we take into account the oppressive situation of women in Latin America and the Third World in general. Poor Latin American women in particular are "ranked third or fourth in the cruel categorization of the class system in which we live. Not all of them are saints; they are not pure, but they are people who beget and sustain life in the midst of the trash produced by what is supposed to be 'civilization.' "[15] Therefore the theological and anthropological perspective of women in Latin America pays special attention to women who are oppressed and at the bottom of the human ladder established by dominant androcentric thought. This emphasis does not ignore the cry for life and full humanity by the oppressed races in Latin America and the Caribbean. On the contrary, it commits itself to their cause and to working out an anthropology of equality in terms of the Christian faith.[16] This anthropology does not want to diminish the struggle but to *restore* to each his or her just right to be a person. Otherwise it is impossible for Christian revelation fully to come to pass. More fundamentally, if the human reality is not considered in its wholeness, this gravely damages the understanding of the Christian faith, as happened with the unfortunate legacy of Greek anthropology.[17]

A liberating anthropology means opting for a model that can do justice to the masses whose humanity has been denied and, in particular, women today. At the same time it means consciously opposing the long tradition of an anthropological perspective that is unequal, both in its view of humanity and of public and private relationships. Without any doubt one of the major tasks confronting women here is the overcoming of Augustinian and Thomist notions, whose anthropology derives from Platonist and Aristotelian philosophy.[18] Their influence continues to be considerable in both traditional theology and church structures. Even with the differences pointed out by feminist investigation, the anthropological views of Augustine and Thomas Aquinas share *dualism* and *androcentrism* as fundamental elements of their doctrine.[19] These characteristics were assimilated by classical theology; hence its marked androcentrism. As noted by Kary E. Børresen,

> The relationship between men and women is stated one-sidedly from the man's point of view, not from the viewpoint of the reciprocity of the two sexes. This means that the woman (*femina*) is referred to the man (*vir*), considered as the exemplary sex. This leads to the identification of man as the masculine sex and "man" as humanity (*homo*).[20]

The tendency to use the term *man* (understood as just the male sex) to denote *human being* is a typical feature of current anthropologies,[21] but the same thing happens in the field of theology in general, including liberation theology. This would mean that women should try to understand themselves as *man*, not as woman.

For Augustine and Thomas women's subordination is a given fact, which it is not necessary to prove or argue. Women's physical inferiority and imperfect intelligence is natural, because it is part of the order of creation.[22] For Augustine, the meaning and purpose of the sexual difference between women and men finds its ultimate justification in procreation. The existence of woman as *femina* is ordained solely for the purpose of procreation. In Thomas, the biological purpose of women's existence is explained by the good of the species.[23] Women are subordinate through their auxiliary—and therefore inferior—procreative function.[24] In both cases women's inevitable destiny is for purposes of procreation. These ideas are the basis for the unequal division of social roles between women and men in society and the church; they support the gender constructions that make the masculine superior. Women signify weak and inferior, and men strong and superior.

This theological view of women as subordinate combines with the vision of others who have enormously influenced androcentric Western thought. One good illustration is Darwin. In his theory of evolution women are clearly inferior, because they show greater powers of intuition, rapid perception and imitation, faculties "characteristic of inferior races, and therefore belonging to a former inferior state of civilization."[25] From any point of view in an androcentric anthropological system women are the losers. Women's biological condition has been used to make women inferior in all fields of life—the religious, political, social, public, and private. Women's biological characteristics also have been made the excuse to exile them to the domain of housework and childcare. So it is not surprising that from the perspective of women a reevaluation is required of these one-sided anthropological ideas underpinning current theological reflection. One of the premises of women's thinking is the recognition that humanity—men *and* women—has a profound unity created in the image and likeness of God. So when women demand recognition as individuals, they are not asking for a charitable concession by androcentric civil structures or the church hierarchy. They are demanding a natural right.[26] Anthropology and its foundations must be reformulated in a way that does justice to human life and restores the theological and spiritual weight of the human person. The broad outlines of a proposal for an egalitarian anthropology from the perspective of women in Latin America follows.[27]

A Human-centered Anthropology

Whereas traditional Christian theology was constructed on the basis of an anthropology centered on man as the masculine sex, thereby acquiring an androcentric character, an egalitarian anthropology stresses the human-centered view, which places humanity—men and women—at the center of history.[28] The first point arising from this displacement is that men are no longer the only bearers of God's presence, and they cannot appropriate God's relationship with humanity for themselves alone. On the contrary, it is the whole of humanity—women and men—who become bearers of the divinity and can reveal it fully. Through the incarnation all human flesh is assumed in God so that it becomes God's temple and dwelling place; humanity is a race of priests, where the Spirit of God dwells in every member.[29] There is no hierarchy that assigns to the male sex the private role of representing the divinity. Gebara and Bingemer note that from a human-centered viewpoint "The male expression of humanity is not privileged at the expense of the female; nor is there any effort to affirm the latter in order to downgrade the former. A human-centered anthropology seeks to grasp the revelation of the divine all throughout the human and accepts the historical and theological consequences of this stance."[30] Such a human-centered view rescues women's historical action for the reign of God, so that it ceases to be subordinate as it is in traditional anthropology. It also rejects theological views that do not express the real experience of women and men in their daily lives:

> The aim of such criticism is to restore the value of each human being through what is autonomous and original in each one. This is related to God's presence, to the presence of transcendence in man and woman ... the human-centered perspective is actually revelatory of divine and human transcendence because it does not diminish the human by dividing it into higher and lower beings, but rather does justice to God's absolute justice, which is above our hypotheses and theories about God.[31]

A Unitarian Anthropology

Traditional anthropology is characterized by the dualism of an opposition between spirit and matter. The aim of a unitarian anthropology is "to overcome this dualism by affirming the deep unity of the human being, who is born material and spiritual, inseparably material and spiritual, so much that we cannot conceive of the human being except on the basis of this reality which is proper to humans."[32] A unitarian anthropology also affirms the existence of a single history, as opposed to the traditional dualist idea of two histories, one sacred and one profane, one divine and one human, as if they were two parallel processes, where, in order to affirm the reality of the meta-historical, one has to disqualify the real reality of this world. According to Gebara and Bingemer, affirming the unitarian of history means that "our true history is neither ahead nor behind us, but is this history being built with sweat, blood, tears, in the unceasing advance of generations one after another."[33] Consequently, the unitarian perspective "not only restores the reality of human existence, which shows the imprint of different periods of history, but they also bring human existence to share deeply in the mystery of the incarnation."[34] It also allows women and men to share in the making of history as creators of what they become, agents of their own destiny, and not accessories to a pre-established ineluctable plan.

A Realist Anthropology

A realist view of anthropology assumes human reality as it is presented with all its contingencies, conflicts, contradictions, struggles, and hopes. It is a conscious rejection of idealist positions, which set the truth of humanity beyond history, hide the real presence of the poor and oppressed, paralyze people's transforming power, and, worst of all, establish in the name of an invisible order the domination of minorities who consider themselves to have been chosen by heaven to rule history.[35] Idealist anthropology does not allow making historical reality the starting point of theology. "It allows only a theology superimposed on reality, creating an unreal world in the attempt to make up for the crack opening in the human heart due to dissatisfaction, all kinds of dissatisfactions piling up one after another throughout history, and especially in the history of the wretched of the earth."[36]

Realist anthropology, on the other hand, enters deep into history and struggles to transform the realities that cause death. It assumes objectivity and subjectivity as fundamental dimensions of human reality, it accepts the laws that govern life in all its expressions, it is critically open to the world of science, it enters into dialogue with different cultures, it views human history in a less rigid, divided, dogmatic way, without preestablished models claiming to be valid for all cultures. Finally, as realist anthropology does not eternalize historical models, it accepts "the creative power of the Spirit of God who is ever renewing all things, who effects rebirth, who restores energies, who brings back to life what seemed to be dead."[37]

A Multi-dimensional Anthropology

This view is the opposite of a one-dimensional anthropology, which is merely an expression of essentialist idealism.[38] In one-dimensional anthropology,

> the starting point for its reflection is a closed definition of the human. It already knows what is human, natural, unnatural, true, false . . . . Therefore anything said that differs from what has already been said of God, and of men and women, is unacceptable. . . . [It] consecrates the male-centered vision as the one laid down and willed by God. . . . Hence, this anthropology cannot in any way ground efforts toward equality between men and

women. . . . [It] consecrates male images of God and situates man, the male being, as the first and most important in the order of creation.[39]

For a multi-dimensional anthropology, persons are not just an idea or definition, but historical faces marked by space and time. Human beings fulfil themselves in many dimensions. There is no need to suppress what is different; on the contrary a multidimensional anthropology accepts the challenge and mystery of our extraordinary diversity.[40]

An egalitarian anthropology that is human-centered, unitarian, realist, and multi-dimensional sees human reality as sacramental; it both evokes and reveals God; God gives human life its consistency and is its origin and destiny. Therefore

> it attributes to the human all its density and worth, and perceives there the divine breaking through, in humankind's seeking and accomplishments in history. The human is not hidden beneath the divine, as though the divine were choking, sometimes caressing, sometimes heeding, and sometimes rejecting the human. The divine takes place in the human, in its entire flesh, in its precarious wholeness.[41]

This statement points toward the full restoration of the human body, in particular women's humiliated bodies. Spiritual, cognitive, physical, and emotional experience never happens outside this bodily dimension. Women and men have no other way of being persons except in their bodily existence. This is how they relate, interact, communicate, and express their lives. It is part of the Christian faith that the body is not to be annihilated but wholly fulfilled through the life-giving action of the Holy Spirit in the resurrection. While it is being transformed into a strong and incorruptible body, it anticipates the longed for fulfillment through faith, whose guarantee is the same divine Spirit.[42] Liberating anthropology recognizes that the mystical and the spiritual, as well as the material, occur in the body. This is where the human person does both spiritual and material things and nowhere else. Indeed, "every human action, passion, or experience is both bodily and spiritual, psychophysical, psycho-organic . . . for example, knowing (which is the most spiritual of acts) only happens by the use of experience gained through the senses."[43]

This anthropology cannot be impartial, therefore, toward the historical and spiritual experiences in which women and men fulfil or fail to fulfil their bodily dimension. For the Latin American masses this bodily dimension, that is to say, their very lives, is permanently threatened by malnutrition, disease, unemployment, hunger, lack of secure food and lodging, repression, and untimely death. And women's bodies are threatened by the destruction of their sexuality through violence, rape and in their harsh struggle for the survival of themselves and their dependents. Within the church the reigning anthropology still gives the male body the exclusive right to represent the sacred, even though it cannot be denied that women's bodies are essentially creative of life; they are intrinsically co-creators with God. Thus an egalitarian anthropology insists on the integrity of life without any exclusion of certain aspects or persons. As Gebara and Bingemer assert, "Such an anthropology is not necessarily exclusive to women but it must be open enough to encompass the difference, multiplicity, non-homogeneity, and creativity of the human—man and woman."[44]

The Word as Affirmation of Full Humanity

Another presupposition of women's theology is the affirmation of their full humanity through the use of the word as an instrument to enable them to express their understanding of their own special identity as active subjects in their own right. Living in a context where they have been denied full humanity, women are concerned with their own identity.[45] They want to know who they are in a world that until recently has not offered answers that meet their concerns or start from their historical circumstances, but merely reproduce the common mode of being, that is, the androcentric way of understanding life. Women no longer agree with these answers, because even the way the questions are posed continues to deny their full humanity. Women want to name themselves and identify themselves in a context they also want to appropriate for themselves.[46] Women want to contribute to the creation of new meanings that will help people understand human differences, whether sexual or racial, in a fuller and more liberating way. This is because they have become aware that until now these differences have been explained by dominant Western thought, using categories of inequality to justify the subjugation of those considered inferior, especially oppressed races, peoples, and women. This vast majority of humanity simply has not reached full human stature according to the colonists. Therefore poor women from the oppressed peoples want to look at themselves and clarify their own identity.

Finding Their Own Identity

For Ana María Tepedino, women's discovery that an identity has been imposed upon them does not lead them to weep and lament but to stand up and walk on their own two feet. "The human person was not made for suffering, or to be kept down. People were made to stand on their two own feet and walk, to make their own way, participate in society, and initiate their own historical protagonism."[47] A fundamental part of this process is the appropriation of the word "in a conscious and coherent way, with delicacy and firmness, with determination and persuasion."[48] Lack of recognition that they are persons with full rights impels women to describe their own humanity in their theological work.[49] Elsa Tamez says that becoming actors on the historical stage is a gift given by the grace of God to human beings. It is an inalienable divine right, which must be unstintingly acknowledged, especially in the Latin American context, where capitalist patriarchal imperialism condemns the impoverished masses to death and women to non-personhood.[50] This condemnation to subhumanity and actual death perpetrated by the colonists of yesterday and today is a flagrant violation of these people's divine right. The question of the quality of women's humanity today is in no way a peripheral one. The question arises out of the reality of their measureless suffering and also from women's new awareness of their own power and original way of being. Carmen Lora observes that

> women are considered second-class human beings lacking certain fundamentally human capacities. This is a familiar daily experience for women in various spheres of life. There are two aspects in which this denial of women's humanity is flagrant: creative intellectual capacity, and sexuality in its aspects of pleasure, communication, and affection. ... The questioning of the humanity of the oppressed is perhaps the most characteristic feature of a relationship of oppression.[51]

When woman's full humanity is not respected, neither is what she says; at best, her words are regarded as mere babble. In our theological, social and ecclesial history no one asked what women had to say about themselves.[52] In theology, the creators of answers simply did theology believing that they were expressing the meaning of human life as a whole and the entire significance of the faith. It did not even occur to them that there could be other ways of understanding; no doubt even arose. It was regarded as a matter of fact that women were incapable of understanding the "great" definitions, which had to be well argued, well understood, and well said. Otherwise their essence was tainted. Furthermore, it was believed that the answers had already been given and the truths described, when in fact all theologians were doing was justifying their domination of those whom they claimed had a diminished humanity and whom they forbade the use of their own word. They imposed their own word as the only valid one. This was humanity seen from the point of view of the possessors of the word, the answer-givers. This was a Western androcentric paradigm of humanity. It is a model designed from an unequal position of economic, social, ecclesial, and sexual superiority, which has denied oppressed women and impoverished peoples the right to utter their own word. Its excluding logic denies the construction of a full life for humanity in solidarity. Hence the use of the word is primary in women's liberation process. As Lora indicates, it permits women

> to verify for themselves that they are human beings. This verification has a most important form in the word they discover they can speak. . . . For these women speaking means participating in their assemblies, expressing their opinions, criticisms, and views: speaking means telling their problems, learning to be outspoken about things, speaking means learning to have the right to think; it means learning to converse with husbands and children, learning to defend rights. For many women speaking means regaining their native language, lost because they are afraid of contempt. For all women it is a re-encounter with their culture, expressing it in dance, songs, craftwork, and food. These women's language has color, savor, sexuality through its content and form, which are not only verbal but include physical actions.[53]

In Latin America the right to the word is connected with the question about the essence of humanity, with the search for one's own identity. In the eyes of the colonists — and Western theology in many cases — this question may appear superfluous and anachronistic. But for the colonized it is not, because our true human quality continues to be judged in terms of a Western human archetype, from Europe first and then from North America.[54] Humanity's tally is not yet complete.[55] The growing number of exploited peoples, subjugated races, and oppressed women is witness to the fact that the debate that was first broached in the confrontation between Las Casas and Sepulvéda is still very much alive.[56]

One fact that cannot be ignored in the construction of Latin American thinking — and therefore in its theology — is that we belong to a continent that has been and still is a colony under global powers. This fact has meant that Latin Americans have been regarded and treated as sub-human and non-persons.[57] When we inquire what it means in Latin America to be a woman as a person with full rights, we have to take this reality into account. So how do we see ourselves, we who are the vast majority of mestiza, indigenous, and black women on this continent? How can we name our own identity unless we begin from our own historical circumstances? How can we assume the difference and idiosyncrasy of each person without denying his or her full human quality? How can we strengthen the power of the people as makers of their own history without dissolving or subsuming sexual differences? We cannot avoid these questions.[58] The view of humanity put forward by women when they do theology is fundamental because through it they continue their progress toward their own identity.

Renaming Humanity

Women challenge the Western *machista* tradition simply by claiming their right to use the word. They question models that disallow the human quality of women and oppressed people as well as their right to seek their own identity. The colonists never question their own model of humanity and will never cease to consider it as the supreme human paradigm, to which every other people and human person must conform. They begin by presupposing the superiority of their culture and the truth of their word. This is why they find it very difficult to meet the deepest values of those they consider inferior. Latin American women do not accept the Western view that there exist men and sub-humans. Neither do they accept the distinction between the universal abstract *man* as model for the human and sub-human women, who must imitate and copy the generic androcentric model. On the contrary, they stress the originality and idiosyncrasy of each person.

Women and men are different, but this difference is no reason to obliterate what is peculiar to each person; it merely fleshes it out. Because we are different and each person is special, we can claim equality. We are equals, with equal human quality, equal intellectual power, and equal creative powers, each in our own way. Thus we form humanity.

When we speak of humanity we must integrate individual differences into our structure of knowledge. Humanity expresses itself in intrinsically different ways; men and women, though different, are two actual ways of being human. This difference does not in any way imply that one is greater or lesser. It simply indicates a single equal quality in two different modes. Although the modes are different, they posses one same original quality. A notion that makes the differences between women and men antagonistic creates competition and not mutual solidarity, because it tends to impose its own world of values as absolute and universal.

Here I must note how some Latin American male theologians are reticent about the equality claimed by women.[59] They believe that what is being claimed is in terms of biological equality or equality of physical powers and a denial of any psychological differences. This means they have not understood the problem. What women seek is a different way of valuing what is different. They emphasize the capacity of women and men to be alike and also to accept what is different, without trying to subsume this difference. To deny difference annihilates the other's individual humanity. Men and women are alike in being different individuals, and this should draw us together rather than separate us. Equality does not depend on one person being a copy of another, but on the individuality of each: that is, men and women, white, black, Indians and mestizos in various cultures are alike in being different, distinct, diverse. Diversity is what makes us alike and should not be allowed to become a reason for diminishing the humanity of others. Every human person is like others through possessing an identity, an individuality, a personality, and a unique language and word.[60] Each individual person is called to fulfil his or her own humanity.

The creation of women's and men's original identity must go hand in hand with the elimination of the profound differences among social classes. From the point of view of the poor and oppressed, it is not possible to speak of full human integrity when the vast mass of humanity is engaged in an inhuman struggle merely to survive. Thus women's appropriation of the word enables them to recover the human quality that has been denied them and to build equality in difference. This involves even more far-reaching solutions to the changes sought in Latin America alone: the full liberation of the impoverished masses from economic and political dependence, the end of cultural and ideological colonialism, and the emancipation of women from every form of patriarchal oppression that condemns them to inferiority.[61]

The End of Gender Rivalry

Why are Latin American women concerned with their own right to speak?[62] Because we are looking for a theology that recognizes us as persons, we are seeking the word—*logos*—which makes us women full persons in our own right and with full humanity. We want to overcome the view that condemns us as "babbling barbarians." We must start by looking at theological work whose starting point is the Latin American reality. Liberation theology from the perspective of women stresses not only the doer of theology but also the origin of this reflection and the particular problems of reality as women engage in a liberation process in a conquered and colonized continent. The word emerges from our dependence and the *machista* context from which we wish to escape. The authenticity and strength of a train of thought comes from its origin, from its capacity to assume the vital interests and goals corresponding to its own historical community. So the originality of this theology is that we women are starting from our own problems, from ourselves, and the problems we share with other men and women of the oppressed peoples.

This theology does not imitate or repeat problems and questions that are alien to its reality. It assumes its own reality in order to transform it. Therefore it has the freedom to have recourse to contributions from other theologies, particularly feminist liberation theology done in other countries. It does not reject these contributions but welcomes them and processes them in accordance with its own reality, knowing it must construct its own answers. The theology done by women in Latin America is original in its personality, its individuality, its perception that universality requires the fulfillment of all women and men who have been diminished in their humanity. It knows that in order to be recognized as an authentic theology it must not copy the model of Western androcentric theology. It knows that women's full humanity will not be achieved automatically, neither does it come about as an *a posteriori* gain from revolutionary changes eliminating the obstacles to their fulfillment. It understands that demanding women's integrity and full humanity from the first as an intrinsic factor for change is essential to its achievement. This is why we women need to speak for ourselves.

Latin American women ask about themselves and their faith from the starting point of their own situation. They also take on board the findings of anthropology, theology, and the Western Christian tradition. In spite of the achievements and the heights these areas have reached, they are unable by themselves to end the inhumanity suffered by the oppressed peoples. In the case of women, they have not even tried. Traditional theology appears unable to promote the full human quality of women and the oppressed, the non-persons. Caught up in pure rationality and involved in a schema for humanity propounded as valid for all times and ages— and thus imposed on the colonized—this theology never considered that others could lay claim to their own humanity and right to speak.[63] This observation does not deny the value of classical theology, but it recognizes the spirit in which it approached the problems and questions of its own historical circumstances. Although the answers it found to the questions about its own reality, using the tools available at the time (Platonist and neo-Platonist philosophies), cannot provide solutions to our problems, what remains is the spirit belonging to all Christian theology; that is, the permanent effort to give an answer to questions about present reality in the light of revelation and the best contributions of Christian tradition. What remains is the spirit, the attitude with which it confronted its own history. This does not mean that its solutions are valid for all times, all ages, and all peoples.[64] If its model of humanity does not include women as full persons in their own right, then this theology does not fulfill the aspirations toward full humanity for women and men. It does not respond to women's expectations. This theology, and others that deny women's word and human quality, shows its cynicism in continuing to speak in the name of all humanity when in reality it subordinates a majority.

Women try to establish a perspective that does not deny the expectations of their comrades but that does oppose a view that denies them full humanity or condemns oppressed peoples to keep haggling for their rights. Women doing theology are creating a word that cancels the sub-humanity to which they have been condemned; they are adopting a logic that cancels the inhumanity to which oppressed peoples have been relegated; they are creating a way of thinking that has grown up from the needs and liberating goals of the Latin American reality. So this theology has the previously unexplored possibilities of new thinking that cancels subordination and *machista* prejudices in the interests of real human liberation.[65] In this process it rewrites history, without plagiarizing but striving to produce a true chronicle of human life always open to God's profound mystery.

Sexuality as a Source of Liberation

When we women do theology, we have to speak about sexuality. Sexuality is an aspect of ourselves that we exercise in the very act of doing theology. Doing theology involves mind and body, reason and feeling, intelligence and pleasure, tenderness and firmness. It also involves sexuality. Depending on the meaning given to it, sexuality can be experienced as a source of liberation or of unhappiness, as it appears to have been much of the time for women.

Sexuality Is Part of Human Life

There is no other field in which Christian morality, *machista* culture, and society in general have been so disturbing and guilt-ridden for women. Denial of the goodness of sex, contempt for the body, and the exclusion of pleasure have been constant throughout history in societies governed by the influence of Western Christian androcentric thinking.[66] Here women's sexual identity becomes the object of repression, guilt, and sacrifice rather than a source of human fulfillment. Even when the church has tried to combat dualist deforming schemas of sexuality, it cannot be said even today that it has succeeded in confronting this aspect in a satisfactory way for women. According to the well-known study of the Catholic Theological Society of America, the suppression of sexuality obeys various factors:

The church's tradition is marked by an historical development extending some three thousand years. It has been subject to a plurality of religious, cultural, and philosophical influences. Although rooted in the Bible, which itself witnesses to a moral evolution and comprises a variety of theologies, Catholic teaching comes down to us from the Church Fathers and medieval schoolmen, bearing the limitations of their pre-scientific historical condition. Inadequate knowledge of biology, as well as religious taboos, *the tradition of subhuman treatment of women*, and a dualistic philosophy of human nature have all left a distinct imprint upon Catholic thinking. In addition to the complexity of the subject itself, there is the complexity of Christian anthropology. At the very core of being human, sexuality can be viewed properly only within *the context of the whole person and the whole of human life*.[67]

In this perspective sexuality is understood in its broader sense as an inherent aspect of human existence and not as something external to the body and spirit of men and women. Rather than being reduced to the sexual act alone or to mere genitality, sexuality is seen to have a dynamism that invades, influences, and affects people's activities in every aspect of their life. Sexuality is to be found at the core of life; it includes the biological, psychological, and spiritual. As an inherent aspect of human existence it is always in relation to their nature as social, communal, and relational beings. Sexuality should bring humans fulfillment both as social beings and as individuals. Because of its relational character, it should lead to a mutual loving relationship of solidarity between the couple and of the couple with the community.[68] From the theological viewpoint, as Lisa Sowle Cahill points out,

> Sexual differentiation as male and female is good, is part of humanity as created (human *nature*), and is not incompatible with the inclusion of both male and female in what is meant by *image of God*. . . . Sexuality and sexual difference are fully personal, not reductionistically or dualistically limited to the reproductive organs. The fact that humanity is characterized by freedom makes impossible any narrow confinement of the expression of the masculine and the feminine to propagative and species-survival functions. A human being has as such dignity that transcends the species and the value of its maintenance, and has freedom in regard to the fulfillment of that dignity.[69]

Sexuality configures individuals as men or women, forms part of their being-in-their-body in the world, whether this is admitted or suppressed. Therefore, even though there are different ways of living with sexuality, it must be incorporated as an aspect of people's whole liberation and fulfillment. This dimension must be incorporated into every emancipatory project, since economic and political liberation cannot take place at the expense of sexual oppression, suffered in particular by women. The particular forms in which human sexuality is experienced and understood are historico-social products.[70] They can contribute to personal fulfillment or act as a profoundly oppressive factor. Every human society has created a specific meaning for sexuality and established personal and social norms. The problem from the perspective of women is that these meanings and norms have always been constructed in the interests of men and resulted in a *machista* culture. The androcentric viewpoint has displayed great capacity to accommodate itself in the various social conformations that have arisen.

> The meaning of sexuality does not come to us given by nature once and for all, with a permanent unchanging value. Sexuality has a meaning, but this can be investigated; it is never exhausted and it is open to new insights by different cultures. This meaning is the legacy of culture rather than of nature. This explains why in the real world we find all kinds of different attitudes and customs. ... Likewise these cultures are susceptible to study, analysis, and confrontation.[71]

In Latin America women are evincing deep dissatisfaction with the social, political, cultural, and religious forms that have confined their sexual lives, both in the biological and the emotional sphere and in their gender identity. Consequently, it is imperative not to approach these questions in a fragmentary way but with an articulated vision of a full-scale project of liberation and participation.[72]

The Importance of Sexuality in the Construction of Identity

As I indicated in previous chapters, women have come to realize the importance of sexuality in their search for new forms of relationship with men and other women. In the popular social movements women take part not as asexual members of the movement but as women who are triply oppressed. Maybe these claims have not yet been systematically stated. But no one can deny that women in these movements have always been threatened by an economic system that excludes them and by *machista* violence. This explains why sexuality and the construction of a new gender identity were matters articulated very early in political struggles. Likewise, the political character of women's subordination was also discovered quite early. Nonetheless, a phenomenon that has come to light only recently is the sexual violence faced by women in the couple relationship. Women are physically and psychologically ill-treated because it is taken for granted that the husband or partner has the *right* to use their woman's body. It is not easy to disclose this violence publicly, either through fear of increasing it or because it is considered a private matter.[73] Yet, it appears certain that most men beat women to resolve family conflicts, and both parents often beat their children. In Nicaragua and Mexico it is a widespread practice. In Peru 70 percent of all crimes reported by the police are women beaten by their partners; in Quito (Ecuador) 80 percent of women have been beaten by their partner; in São Paulo (Brazil) alone eighteen thousand cases of battered women were reported between 1986 and 1987.[74]

As well as this physical violence, women unfortunately have to deal with guilt feelings resulting from the church's attitude to sexual relations as sinful. Women today are discovering that their sexuality is a fundamental part of human life and should not make them suffer violence and repression. They are resisting. Sexuality has to do with what is deepest in humanity; therefore it has to do with life and liberation of the human person and of peoples. It has to do with men and women living together in solidarity. Thus women insist on the need to incorporate women's experience of sexual oppression and liberation into their analysis of the Latin American reality.

Nevertheless, Carmen Lora notes, "the male view of reality will tend to underrate the influence of the sexual dimension, because men do not feel that it really defines their lives." She goes on to say that this view is not only held by men but is "the reigning one in a society where men have been predominant in all areas of social life and therefore it also affects that society's actual schemes of knowledge."[75] Whereas men's incorporation into social life does not immediately confront them with their sexual identity—because the public sphere has traditionally belonged to them—for women the opposite is the case. Entering the public arena immediately brings a woman up against "her husband's disapproval, the difficulty of combining this with the care of her children and domestic work. This experience makes women incorporate aspects related to their gender identity into their thinking and their demands."[76] Thus all women's activities are marked by their sexuality, and this needs to be taken into account if liberation processes are to advance. The sexual dimension is related to all the other dimensions of human existence. It is not separate or autonomous. That is why women see that, however difficult and challenging, it is necessary to begin creating a new kind of relationship between men and women and between peoples. This requires profound changes to take place in daily life, in family relationships, in relationships between couples, friendship, the equal division of tasks, common production and social reproduction, in the expression of warmth, gestures strengthening solidarity, and every experience that makes life human. For life without emotional and sexual experience simply is not life.

Lastly, if sexuality is to become a source of liberation, this means restoring its political dimension to daily life. Collective solutions must be sought for problems which up till recently have been seen as solely personal and private.[77] For women, both private and public life need to change. Changing the unequal relations between men and women is vital to any liberation project.[78] When women say they want sexuality to recover its liberating character, they are restoring the savor of life to knowledge and experience. Sexuality

serves the development of human persons by calling them to constant creativity, to opening themselves up, fulfilling all the potential of their personality, the constant expression and discovery of a more authentic self. Procreation is an aspect of this call to creativity, but it certainly cannot be said that it is the only reason for sexual activity. Sexuality also serves authentic personal development by making people recognize more clearly their relational nature, their absolute need to go beyond themselves to embrace others and reach personal fulfillment. Sexuality is the ingenious means used by the Creator to draw individuals out of themselves toward others.[79]

The Logic of Life in Women's Strength

In their theology Latin American women are searching for new concepts that truly express women's experience and commitments in their daily struggle for life. In the field of theological epistemology this effort means exploring new hermeneutic categories, which not only do justice to women's active participation but also express women's special contribution to the liberation process, both their particular struggle and the liberation struggle as a whole. In the quite recent past theoretical formulations ascribed certain categories to women—weakness, darkness, rest, passion, the irrational, and so on. Today these do not seem to correspond to what women find in their own personal and collective experience. Women's *properties* created by androcentric thinking and raised to the category of being, have been interiorized by both men and women. New thinking, which tries to take account of the liberation struggles by women of the oppressed peoples, requires serious effort to overcome these internalized stereotypes.

Women's daily lives must be looked at, interpreted, and described from a new perspective in order to restore women's strength, authority, leadership, and wisdom. These aspects are incorporated into the biblical and theological reflection of Latin American women and act as theoretical structures serving to name women's contributions to the transformation of oppressive realities. These new formulations from the perspective of women are bound to conflict with the myths, theories, categories, and horizons of androcentric thinking.

Before I go any further I should note the following point. The aspects I stress here as presuppositions for women doing theology in Latin America have not as yet been developed systematically in terms of knowledge as intrinsic to theological epistemology, but as characteristics of women's new initiatives in politics and the church. Nevertheless, as they contribute to the theological collection of women's experience and knowledge, they become hermeneutical categories and the source of new and fertile ideas, which allow aspects silenced by androcentric thinking to attain the level of critical reflection. They also make possible self-criticism as well as the articulation into the liberation process of Latin America and the women's struggles for their right to life. The presuppositions I present here can be found in all theological reflection where the starting point is the situation of women in Latin America. All these aspects revolve round the same nucleus: Against the unjust irreversible logic[80] of the present system, which produces so many deaths, women adhere stubbornly to the logic of life.

On the other hand, although I am not trying to create interpretative criteria *exclusively* for women, I do wish to emphasize the particular contribution women make out of their own experience, both collective and personal. What I describe here is not a finished product. I merely wish to point out those new elements we are discovering as appropriate for understanding our own lives.

According to Ivone Gebara a key note characterizes the women's liberation movement today.

> This is women's *collective power*, a power which is beginning to be recognized and used in various popular organizations in a special way by women themselves. This is a sign of our times! What is this power? It takes many historical forms and no doubt there is both positive and negative mixed in it. That is human life. Any action, expression or feeling is always a mixture of positive and negative. All human striving contains these two forms of energy, which is indispensable to the evolution of nature and history.[81]

So, while not forgetting the possible ambiguity inherent in human experience, I describe the positive aspects of this collective strength, which is permeated by the constant search for life.

The Originality of Latin American Women

Although I have already alluded to certain ideas in this area, I now want to look at the originality of Latin American women in our present context. Latin American women have not *assimilated* the imposition of values, tasks, models, or socio-religious projects involving the loss of their human quality or the denial of their rights to be actors in history. With particular power today, but also in the past, women have struggled to fulfill their own calling. Fortunately they were never *molded* by their oppressive conditions, even when there was no talk of becoming aware of their situation. Rebellion was always present. This lack of compliance with alien subordinationist projects crystalized into a collective will to create and re-create justice and life. Women wanted to define their own features, hear the sound of their own voices, and feel the texture of their own skin. Finally, through hearing their own songs of joy and sorrow, they have found the "coin" they had lost. They have recognized themselves as they are—Indian, black, mestizo, and white women involved in struggles, resistance, and hope. Latin American women have never renounced their ancestral cultures, their compassion, their right to life. If they sometimes thought they had lost their identity, today they realize that instead they are weaving it anew.

Resistance

One of the clearest expressions of women's collective strength is their response to the various forms of imperial domination. Ivone Gebara notes that

For the last twenty years in Latin America women's resistance has taken the form of defending life and refusing to submit to social and political forces organized for death. Women have broken out of the purely domestic sphere and engaged in demonstrations against dictatorial regimes, all kinds of authoritarianism, all kinds of sexual and racial discrimination, raising of food prices, and for other social struggles. They have realized that the struggle for their own and the children's lives also takes place outside the four walls of home. Women shout and march in the streets demanding freedom for political prisoners, respect, and justice. Some call it collective hysteria, others call it lack of judgment. But those who have understood what it means to fight for life with all their strength call if a gift of the Spirit.[82]

Women's resistance is manifested in the many forms they invent to oppose the inhumanity and the condemnation to death of themselves, their children, and their comrades, a death decreed by the present *machista* and patriarchal socio-economic system. Struggles for survival, for collective work, for the self-direction of popular projects, for food increases, for a better quality of life become an expression of their huge resistance and their clear insistence that the present order can never belong to Latin American women or peoples.

Creativity

For Gebara, creativity is another manifestation of women's collective strength. She particularly dwells on the changes in human relations produced in recent years by women's conscious irruption into our societies.

By the conversion to themselves, to others, and to history, women have been able:
— by their new way of behaving to help change patriarchal atti-

tudes in force among us. They are still there but consciousness of change is becoming stronger and stronger;
—to change the status of "destiny" accorded to the hierarchically organized family with the man at the top;
—to begin living more equally with men and even change certain aspects of the masculine role. They have become aware of the value of housework, never previously recognized as work, and have fought for it to be given proper recognition and status.

This creativity is a way of re-creating the world at various levels, to the extent that we can now talk about a "before" and "after" the awakening of the historical consciousness of Latin American women.[83]

But women's creativity is not less active in other fields. It can be seen, for example, in the extraordinary personal and collective contribution they have made to intellectual renewal,[84] the arts, craftwork, poetry, popular song, painting, liturgy, theology, and even military service. All these contributions creatively reconstruct what for centuries has been denied them.

Heartfelt Solidarity

In the face of the dominant logic reigning in the power centers and their local allies and in the face of the spirit of imposition in the patriarchal institutions, women of the oppressed peoples understand that such systems cannot have any part in their aims or horizon. They do not accept them because they exclude the mass of humanity, they exploit and oppress poor countries, races, and women. Women have a different vision of the relationships among peoples, between men and women, and of both with the earth. They refuse to give up this vision that they have inherited from their past. It is a legacy they are welcoming today as the source of their deep identity. I am referring here to women's sense of *heartfelt solidarity*.[85] This is not just an urge to alleviate others' want, pain, and suffering. It is a genuine compassion for those whose lives are threatened. This logic of solidarity was not planted in the hearts of Latin Americans by the conquistadors. It comes from those Raúl Vidales calls the "deep peoples," our legendary and ever present peoples.[86] Everyone feels the human warmth, tenderness, tact, and affection that characterize the Latin American cultural ethos, especially its women. Although this may seem a trivial matter in this study, acknowledgment of the warmth of Latin American women is a point worth making. To be *affectionate* is not a defect or weakness; it is a central value of the original humanism of the Latin American people. It shows their capacity to form communities that do not exclude people and at the same time it expresses the spiritual strength that unites the women and peoples. Their relations are imbued with solidarity.[87] The central characteristics of our people are not the selfishness and greed of the colonists, but rather a constant spirit seeking justice, peace, freedom, and human fulfillment in harmony with the earth. Solidarity lies at the heart of Latin American women's identity, and it is a presupposition we find throughout their reflection on the faith.

Freedom

Ivone Gebara states that freedom is another expression of women's collective strength. Freedom, she says, is

> a breath of fresh air blowing through our whole being enabling us to live differently. . . . Talking about women's freedom, especially poor women in Latin America, means talking about God differently. It goes beyond the mere concept, although this is often a useful tool. By a significant number of women God is no longer seen in the image of a man, father, husband, or son, but as Spirit, breath of life, energy refusing to be locked in a box. The women's liberation movement is a movement of theological creativity and freedom, that is, a search for God, for the fulfillment of divine signs, recognition of a miraculous presence in women's lives.[88]

From their own experience women stand up, impelled by the Spirit of God, who re-creates them and transforms their weakness into strength so that life prevails over death and spirit over letter and law. Gebara continues,

> The power called freedom for many women is like being pregnant with the Spirit. Their vision of God derived from their own lives goes way beyond the one imposed by our macho culture. God is, [God] is in us, and we live with [God] in all the originality of our female being, our history, questions, and limits. [God] is the power, the energy driving us towards ourselves and towards

others to seek for something new, something greater than ourselves, but which will come upon this finite earth.[89]

Freedom is an original feature in women's lives, and it is becoming more relevant now that they are setting out to explore new ways. It is a matter of fulfilling their untried potential. It is through their contributions that history, the church, the whole of creation can become different. Women's deep conviction that they are called to life shows them the way to refuse to continue treading the paths that lead to enslavement.

Hope

For women and oppressed peoples hope is crucial. It is a force that gives the liberation struggles energy and has at its heart the certainty that God is on the side of the oppressed, that their cause is just, and that what is at stake is not only the historical destiny of the poor and oppressed but also that of the whole of humanity. From those without power, from the strength of those considered to be insignificant, women from oppressed peoples know that although the sacrifice is immense, life must triumph over death, truth over lies, good over evil, love over hate, justice over injustice, solidarity over selfishness, grace over sin. Hope is not a far-off ideal or a palliative. It is a deep spiritual force—because it comes from the Spirit—that encourages the poor in their daily struggles. It is an objective reality, an anticipation of God's justice and love as experienced in the life, death, and resurrection of Jesus.

We have experienced this anticipation anew in the liberating passover of the poor and oppressed, whom Jesus said he was with. Latin America cannot give up a future of justice and love. Nevertheless, as Ivone Gebara observes:

If we look at the whole history of the poor in Latin America, particularly over recent years, we may well ask, why speak of a new future, when for most countries the number of poor people has increased, the distressed and needy have multiplied, injustice of every sort is eaten and drunk by the poor with their daily bread and water. How can we sing of our hope for justice, our longing for love in exile from our self and our country? We have more reason to weep than to laugh for joy! Nevertheless, we hope for a new future and this hope is the breath of life to us. It gives our lives direction, meaning and weight.[90]

Hope is a dimension that mobilizes all women's strength. It becomes a duty, a task, a passion for justice, combined with love for our comrades, for other women, our people, and the earth. Hope is also a weapon against those who create pessimism, sadness, and nightmares. Although hope includes pain and suffering, it also brings joy because we know that by giving life we are reconquering it for the whole of humanity. For a new earth, a new humanity, for the fullness of physical and spiritual life, it is worth spending energy in our daily lives; it is the only way to anticipate utopia. All in all, as Gebara stresses, hope

> is not something that exists in advance ready-made. It has to be sought, nourished, shared, supported, made actual through signs in order to remain true and strong.
>
> Women are the nightwatchers of hope, waiting for the day. They are certain that when night is over the bright sun will shine and that even in the middle of the night there are often twinkling stars.[91]

Hope is realized in actions, attitudes, in everyday language, even in the midst of great hardship and suffering. Neither women nor the poor of the earth can give it up. It is part of the horizon that gives them their identity, it is a constitutive part of Latin American theological knowledge, and a necessary condition for women doing theology.

6

Women's Contribution to Theology in Latin America

The Theological Method

It is clear that liberation theology from the perspective of women in Latin America must be set in the broad context of Latin American liberation theology, although feminist theology has particular features because of the social and epistemological locations from which it is articulated.[1] Theology done by women shares in the liberation process of the poor, but pays special attention to the liberation of women who are triply oppressed.

Broadening the field to include women's vision and speech is a way of criticizing and correcting the androcentric position of liberation theology, which would be hard to perceive without this contribution from women. Their contribution profoundly modifies the expression and content of liberation theology to date, including even the very concept of *liberation*. In principle, this term bore the meaning of *liberation of the whole of man and all men . . . without excluding any man*. The perspective of women reviews the total meaning of liberation, with two results. On the one hand, it criticizes patriarchal structures, androcentric vision, and *machista* attitudes in the whole social context of oppression. On the other hand, it includes women in the production of knowledge, the making of theology, and the creation of a new liberating reality. This is not just a change of language, but also a change in liberation theology's *epistemological horizon*.

As María Clara Bingemer points out, today it is recognized that women's entry into the field of theological reflection "brings with it a new way, a new method of thinking and expressing theology."[2]

What does this new way, this new method consist of? What are its characteristics? As a first response I note a few observations made by Elsa Tamez, who begins by explaining this theology's methodological links with liberation theology and then goes on to point out the advance it represents with respect to theology in general: "Liberation theology," says Tamez,

> does not remove the experience of oppression from the experience of God, or the life of faith; it has demonstrated another methodology in making its point of departure the practice of liberation within this context. Women involved in the theological arena welcome this way of doing theology; dealing with concrete experience means dealing with things of daily significance, and that means also dealing with relationships between men and women.[3]

Indeed, daily life becomes its *point of departure*, whereas in a large part of traditional theology there is a tendency to avoid or spiritualize Christians' daily lives. The perspective of women emphasizes a change of attitude toward daily life without neglecting the transformation of power structures.

The Primacy of Desire

In the past, theology has generally given primacy to rationality. Theology done by women starts from actual experience and therefore, as María Clara Bingemer stresses, "is closely and indissolubly linked to desire."[4] This is trying to give back to theology its full power to express life, which is also made up of sensitivity, generosity, affection, and silence.[5] It must recognize women and men's spiritual experiences, as they try to love and seek justice in their daily lives. Hence women doing theology feel that the primacy of rationality must be replaced by the primacy of desire. The cold and cerebral character of the purely scientific

> must give way to a new system which springs from the desire that lies deep within human beings and which includes and mixes sensitivity and rationality, generosity and efficiency, experience and reflection, desire and rigor. *God is love*, says scripture (1 Jn 4:8). If this is so, God must be first and foremost an object of desire—not of necessity, not of rationality. Theology—which is

reflection and discourse about God and God's Word—must therefore be driven and warmed by the flame of desire.[6]

This means that reason, science, and systematic rigor must not suffocate the Greater Desire, or domesticate the divine *Pathos*, or extinguish the flame of the Spirit.[7]

In doing theology women incorporate the primacy of desire, because purely rational concepts do not take sufficient account of experience. This methodology is inherent in the way women work and think. María Clara Bingemer points out that,

> it is unthinkable for women to divide themselves into compartments and consider their theological work as a purely rational activity. Impelled by desire, a totalizing force that penetrates their whole being, women's theological work is done with the body, heart, and hands, as well as with the head. The mature fruit that is beginning to emerge from their fertile wombs is a result of slow and patient meditation on deep and intense experiences of life, confronted with the traditions of the past, the pilgrimage of the people of Israel and of the church. Here the Spirit, who is the divine desire poured out upon history and humanity, finds fertile soil. As well as constantly and faithfully referring to Jesus of Nazareth as the ultimate and definitive norm, it opens the future with infinite possibilities for invention and new ways of expressing the Christian mystery.[8]

Therefore the language of poetry, play, and symbol becomes an appropriate way of expressing the understanding and wisdom of the faith, because it is the means of expressing the human person's deepest and most genuine aspirations and desires.[9]

If we think of desire as fundamental to life or as the primary vital impulse, then clearly Latin America is a continent where desire is systematically threatened and denied fulfillment. Hence, Bingemer observes,

> the liberation process begins to occur when the poor become aware of the desires repressed inside them and allow them to emerge. They are let out like a cry and felt as a motive force impelling them to struggle. It is in this liberation of desire that theology is called upon to speak and in our particular case, theology done by women.[10]

In a context where life itself is threatened, attacked, and violated, where the masses are struggling to assert their right to act, liberation theology from the perspective of women is called upon to take up women's words and deepest desire, for life and hope in the midst of pain and struggle. For Bingemer,

> being a woman means knowing how to combine experience and practice, how to fight oppression, how to glimpse amid many misfortunes the superabundance of grace. In the midst of great contradictions women have the power to integrate and perceive contrasts and differences in a unifying and enriching way. They can contemplate and discern in the pain of the cross the breath of hope and the weight of glory that is now beginning to shine. They do not lose the thread of desire, which from the depths of disfigured reality groans with unutterable groans announcing the delivery of a New Creation that is now appearing.[11]

Desire activates women's capacity to be integrated, integrating, and full of hope. It gives them immeasurable strength, perceived as a gift to be shared generously for the benefit of the oppressed, theology, and the church, for the sake of their common liberation. Thus Latin American women understand that theology is merely a response of faith to God's merciful manifestation in the present-day reality of the immense suffering masses of humanity. Driven by desire, it is an attempt to eradicate their own suffering and that of others, and to restore the deepest desire of the poor and oppressed. By stressing the primacy of desire, this theological viewpoint

> inaugurates new ways of listening to Revelation, of speaking about the experience of faith, of reading and interpreting God's word, thinking and working on the great themes of theology. All this is done through being possessed by desire that inflames and summons, that keeps the flame of love burning without being consumed, against everything that threatens to extinguish it. It leads all creation, wounded by sin back to the Great Desire from which it came.[12]

The Option for Women in the Option for the Poor

Liberation theology from women's perspective is indissolubly linked to the option for the poor. Its origin and basis is the Latin

American reality, the urgent reality of the martyrdom, and the hope of the poor. It is directed toward promoting life and overcoming oppression. Nevertheless, the women's perspective gives a special place to one aspect of the option for the poor: it wants to reach the questions, historical and spiritual experiences, knowledge, memory, desires, and expectations of women, not only as part of this suffering world, but primarily *as women*. It is important to stress this aspect because on occasion, even when the option for the poor is recognized as fundamental to liberation theology, women are often neglected. Liberation theology fails to see them as a collective group that experiences in multiple forms the profound inequalities in society and theology.[13] So, for a theology that makes women's vision and interests explicit, the option for the poor becomes in particular an option for poor women.[14]

This option also becomes its principal hermeneutic perspective. Thus this theology is enabled to develop a fruitful dialectic — between the social location from which we learn about the problem to be examined and the epistemological location from which we put this knowledge to use — in order to deal adequately with our problems in a way that furthers the process of women's liberation.[15] In Latin America, says Ivone Gebara,

> the poor have many faces: workers, peasants, beggars, abandoned children, lost young people and others. They are men and women, but now we need to single out the women. The poor woman today is poorest of the poor. She is the other: bleeding and burdened, housewife, mother, daughter, wife. She is both subject and object of our option for the poor.[16]

The option for poor women must obviously look inward. We must look into ourselves. We must also look outward: to commitment, social struggle, militant action. Both these aspects are very necessary because the risk of lacking inner unity becomes ever greater as historical urgency increases. So the option for poor women assumes a *woman's option for herself*.[17] The option for the poor and for herself is not something outside a woman's self and work. Gebara notes that women's participation in popular social movements is often described without touching upon the nucleus of this commitment: the necessary first step toward themselves, the call to accept themselves and welcome themselves as women first and foremost.[18] This is a journey into self that restores a woman's inner unity. She is reborn as a woman, discovers the creative source of her being, and comes back into contact with her own roots. This inner journey is necessary in order to open herself to others:

> "To love others like oneself" is a key phrase for Christians and also for others. It tries to show how love of others is not distinct from love of self or love of self from love of others. They are two poles of the same loving movement and one cannot develop fully without the other. . . . The option for ourself is a personal act but not a solitary one. It also means being open and welcoming to others.[19]

Hence the option for the other springs from the same source. Both flow into a conscious option for a new future of justice and love.[20]

The Practice of Tenderness

As I have emphasized, the starting point for this theology is daily life. It makes a clear option for poor and oppressed women and stresses the primacy of desire over rationality in order to take account of experience. But there are other crucial elements. Ana María Tepedino adds that this theology "also starts from our experiences of faith, lived from the underside of power and authority. From these two starting points we reread revelation and reality with a view not only to individual liberation, but to liberation of an entire people."[21] This theology understands that it must contribute to the transformation of situations and structures that cause misery and dehumanization. Therefore it cannot ignore the culture of patriarchal and *machista* systems, which worsen women's economic and social oppression. As this theology is concerned with daily life it must necessarily incorporate the relations between men and women. "Consequently," Tepedino continues,

> the starting point for feminist theology goes beyond the experience of oppression, the experience of God, and the struggle for justice; it must also be the "practice of tenderness," that is, seeking to create brotherly and sisterly relationships, which should not exist simply between men and women, but also among the elderly, adolescent, and children—and indeed among all people.[22]

This aspect is incorporated into theology because it is part of real life. It is not something outside human experience and reflection on the faith. Warmth and desire lose their fragmentary character as they become integrated as part of the cognitive process. This warmth is the opposite of the historical coldness of a purely conceptual approach. In fact, women's warmth and commitment have not been seen in the language of faith as a deep spiritual experience giving light and content to formal theological discourse. In this respect Ivone Gebara observes that

> The persistence of women in the struggle for life and the restoration of justice have been linked together and lived out as expressions of faith, as the presence of God in the struggles of history. Many women see in these developments the expression of their desire to struggle for a more human world, in which certain values presently dormant may be aroused, where people can accept affection, where life may triumph over the powers of death.[23]

The practice of tenderness humanizes theological discourse and restores its meaning for the daily life of the oppressed, and it also integrates women's experience into theology.

Feminist Analytical Tools

In this theology — as in all liberation theology — the social sciences become vitally important for knowing and transforming the situation, especially that of poor and oppressed women.[24] I have already indicated some fundamental elements in the use of socio-analytic methods from the perspective of women (Chapter 1). It should also be noted that theology from the perspective of women critically adopts the scientific method used by liberation theology. However, inasmuch as certain disciplines do not help it analyze and change the real situation of Latin American women, this theology finds it necessary to resort to others that do move toward women's liberation. Some of the analysis done by Latin American theologians has not contributed to the understanding of women's oppression and has even clearly shown an androcentric point of view. Hence the importance of interdisciplinary feminist investigation stressed by women in their theology. Ivone Gebara notes:

> We cannot fail to recall the inestimable contribution of the social sciences — anthropology, psychology, and different theories about

language—as elements that have been changing, directly or indirectly, women's understanding of themselves. These same elements have contributed to the emanicipation of women's power in the social dimension of human relations and in the way these relations are organized.[25]

Nevertheless, we cannot say that to date liberation theology from the perspective of Latin American women has developed an analytic method capable of encompassing women's problems. This points to an inner methodological weakness and is also a big challenge for feminist theology in our context.

María José Rosado Nuñez's remarks are important here: "In Latin America, when we tried to understand our societies and the way they function to produce a situation of structural injustice that is unacceptable from the Christian point of view, we turned to the social sciences. We looked to European writers, including non-religious ones, for the explanation we lacked to support our theological thinking."[26] If we want to understand and transform oppressive situations unacceptable to women as part of humanity and the church, we must resort to the sciences that help us understand women's particular situation, that is to say, *feminist theory*,[27] and not just that relating to theology but also to other areas, including anthropology and philosophy, from the Latin American viewpoint. The important task is to understand "fully what happens in the unequal and unjust relationships existing between women and men in society and the church."[28] Feminist work is trying to find new answers, new ideas, new paradigms, new ways of understanding that are more whole and that do not exclude people. Whereas men's analyses tend to conceal women's real oppression, feminist analysis makes explicit the oppressive structures working against women, men, and those depending on them. Hence Rosado Nuñez suggest that:

> we must overcome certain prejudices in relation to first-world feminist theory, seek from it what can help us understand things that are happening in our own countries. . . . We should approach these theories critically, making use of what is helpful, and adding what is peculiar to us in Latin America. We can correct these theories when what they say does not seem valid from our perspective of commitment to the cause of liberation for the poor and the transformation of society.[29]

On the other hand, Latin American feminist theory is already quite well developed — as I have shown in this book — and it can act as our reference point. Although this field is of particular interest to women, it should also interest male theologians, because, as I have repeatedly said, women's liberation is not just a matter for women. In liberation theology it is a matter of equal liberation for all.

Tasks and Methods of Feminist Theology

This theological work by women is interested in gathering the historical and spiritual experiences of oppressed women, looking at them, and interpreting them in the light of faith in order to contribute to their own liberation and the liberation of all humanity. Therefore everything that has to do with the creation, re-creation, and defense of life for the poor and for women's work of solidarity has theological significance for their particular way of understanding the faith. Women's activities to secure their own survival and that of those who depend on them intrinsically bear the seal of compassion, solidarity, justice, love, freedom, and passion for God's cause in the cause of the poor, together with large doses of strength, daring, and courage. In these personal and collective activities women discover the signs of God's presence.[30] They are therefore related to the contents of the faith and are where, above all, scripture is read and critically interpreted, along with the church's living tradition, the systematic formulations of theology, and the teachings of the church. For women the key to this reading is *life*,[31] and their hermeneutic starting point is the option for poor and oppressed women along with the option for the poor. Hence we arrive at theology's second stage. For this, a contextual and particularized method is proposed, which Ana María Tepedino summarizes as follows:

Feminist theology in the Latin American context arises out of the realities of daily life. This theology (a) seeks to know life through personal experience as well as through human and social science; (b) seeks to interpret in the light of the Bible (with the understanding that God's revelation was given to human beings and articulated in human language, thus depending on a culture in time and in space — and accordingly, it can both oppress and liberate); we have to discover the sense that the Spirit reveals to us today through the ancient text of the Bible, and (c) tries to retrieve and give name to the experience of women in a patriarchal society in order to redeem the past, transform the present, and prepare for tomorrow.[32]

This summary gives a general idea of the process followed by liberation theology from the perspective of women. However, before describing some characteristics of its method I want to list the tasks it faces. This is a provisional list:

1. To discover and interpret the saving historical value of reality in the light of new theological criteria, such as the New Creation, full humanity, God's *basileia*, God's reign, the new earth, equal discipleship, salvation, grace, sin, compassion, justice, power of the Spirit in the whole community, and others. It is a matter of giving positive value to projects and tendencies that give salvation a historical setting and anticipate God's liberation plan. Likewise, this theology denounces and rejects situations generating inequality, injustice, and exclusion of some people. It condemns the androcentric and *machista*, because they are at odds with the Christian vision. This criticism is not only of the reality today but also of the androcentric dynamics of scripture, tradition, Christian theology, and social and ecclesial structures promoting sexism, racism, and classism, and ecclesial and social colonialism.[33]

2. To unmask and dismantle theological formulations that support and perpetuate the interpretation of humanity and its history in terms of the androcentric patriarchal vision, which marginalizes the experience, knowledge, and contributions of women. On the one hand, such a theology consciously seeks to bring women's contributions to light, and on the other, to restore to theological language the power to touch the vital heart of human life.[34]

3. To recognize and describe women's history, showing their presence when many would like them to be invisible. If revelation and divinity are presented with a male character and serve to legitimate women's powerlessness and subordination, feminist theology must denounce these tendencies and show forth God's presence and revelation in women, who are also mediators of grace and God's presence in mind and body. In their bodies they prove the mystery of real life and therefore experience God in a special way.[35]

4. To show up the rigid positions, supported by androcentric and patriarchal dogma, which not only imprison the *real truth* of human life with its hopes and miseries and conceal the sin committed

against the poor and oppressed, but also block the life-giving power of the Spirit. As well as systematically opposing divine grace, these rigid positions show their ignorance of the hermeneutic structure of all knowledge, which is not pure, sterilized, totally objective, and disinterested. Thus Christian theologies, primitive writings, and doctrine are not definitive and do not wholly explain the meaning of human life inasmuch as they set aside and conceal women. Those who stubbornly exclude women are opposing divine revelation itself. On the other hand, women's perspective proposes a point of view able

> to view life as the locus of the simultaneous experience of oppression and liberation, of grace and lack of grace. Such perception encompasses what is plural, what is different, what is other . . . to grasp in a more unified way the oppositions and contradictions, the contrasts and differences as inherent to human life. . . . Such behavior enables them [the women] to avoid taking dogmatic and exclusive stances, and to perceive or intuit the real complexity of what is human.[36]

5. To recover and reconstruct the words, gestures, memory, symbols, experiences, desires, and struggles of the women who preceded us and who have left us a legacy of resistance, leadership, and commitment to the defense of life. This task is particularly urgent in our case, given the aggressive nature of the conservative neo-colonialist projects intent on reconquering Latin America for their own interests. These interests are obviously not those of Latin American women and the impoverished masses. In this task women have a fundamental role.[37] This work of reconstruction has three complementary strands. We must reconstruct: (a) our own history of Latin America; (b) biblical, theological, and ecclesial history in solidarity with women in other contexts; and (c) humanity's harmony with the earth, stressing women's ancestral closeness to it.[38]

6. To affirm and rescue what is theological in every authentically liberating process, regardless of its theological definition. The theological criterion of authenticity does not lie in words, but in the work of real liberation. Liberation theology done by women affirms the presence or absence of God according to whether or not both women and men are incorporated as actors with full rights in historical situations.[39]

Liberation theology done by women stresses certain key qualities.

These qualities help to distinguish this theology from liberation theology in general. We remember that from its beginning this theology has been a specific form of women's struggle for their right to life.[40] The Final Statement of the Latin American Conference entitled "Theology from the Perspective of Women," identifies the key characteristics of its methodology. This theology sees itself as:

—Unifying, bringing together different human dimensions: strength and tenderness, happiness and tears, intuition and reason.

—Communitarian and relational, bringing together a vast number of experiences that express something lived and felt, in such a way that people recognize themselves in this reflection and feel challenged by it.

—Contextual and concrete, with its starting point being the geographical, social, cultural, and ecclesial reality of Latin America, which detects the community's vital issue. This theological activity bears the mark of the everydayness of life as a site where God is made manifest.

—Militant, in the sense of taking part in the totality of our peoples' struggles for liberation at local and global levels.

—Marked by a sense of humor, joy, and celebration, virtues that safeguard the certainty of faith in the God who is with us.

—Filled with a spirituality of hope whose starting point is our situation as women, and which expresses strength, suffering, and thanksgiving.

—Free, with the freedom of those who have nothing to lose; and open, capable of accepting different challenges and contributions.

—Oriented toward refashioning women's history, both in the biblical texts and in those figures of women, who, acting out of their own situation, are symbols of struggle and resistance, wisdom and leadership, solidarity and fidelity, justice and peace.[41]

These features, together with those I have noted in previous chapters, give feminist theology a special character with respect to liberation theology in general. Feminist theology stresses the wholeness of human experience and attempts to reconstruct women's history. It stresses that its exercise of theological understanding is animated by the Spirit and aims to build something new:

We have discovered these characteristics, fully aware that it is the Holy Spirit who arouses us and moves us. The same Spirit draws us women out of our own lack of self-esteem and out of the oppression we experience because of our gender, toward an effort to break out of old frameworks, and to build a new person (woman/man) and a new society.[42]

Finally, we should emphasize the inclusive nature of this theology done by women. Women are not trying to replace men with women but are working to overcome the evils that cause death and inhumanity for women and men. Through their theology women want to contribute to a change that will cease to make the difference between men and women the cause of their inequality.[43]

The Hermeneutics of Suspicion and Daring

Investigations into the field of biblical hermeneutics from the perspective of Latin American women are beginning to look promising. There is great interest in studying the Bible because of the importance it has in women's lives, especially in the base communities. As in other areas, the rereading of the Bible in a way that supports women's human integrity and their liberation struggle is more likely to happen in the daily life of the Christian communities than at the level of systematic study. All over Latin America and the Caribbean there is a growing desire to *name* a new vital force that has entered women's lives: a reencounter between liberative biblical revelation and women's liberation process. In various countries meetings, workshops, seminars, and study days are being devoted to rereading the Bible from the perspective of women; a few works also have been published.[44] These concerns center around three key areas. First, there is the certainty that, although the Bible was long withheld from the people by the clergy, it belongs to the people of God, the poor and oppressed, and therefore also to women. Second, there is a growing awareness that forms of *machismo* are also to be found in the Bible; it contains negative remarks about women and is couched in androcentric language. These texts and traditions cannot be divinely inspired, especially when through Jesus' life and ministry we discover that God does not condone any discrimination against women. Third, stress is laid on the importance of reading the biblical texts in the context in which they were written and also in terms of the everyday experiences of the reader,[45] with readers being aware of their own situation.

Two important points are made about interpreting the Bible. The first is that God's saving will—carried out fully in Jesus Christ and accepted by the men and women who were with him—is not just localized in the biblical text. This is not simply a factual account of historical events that occurred, but includes interpretations assigning theological value to these events. Therefore the biblical text is conditioned by its socio-historical context and is the product of an androcentric and patriarchal socio-religious order. Often the text is patriarchal, and the writer has a patriarchal point of view. Therefore it contains values and traditions, some oppressive and others liberating. So it is necessary to adopt a critical position that notes the texts, traditions, and values—with their subsequent interpretations—that support the subordination of women, and also those that strengthen women's position as persons with full rights. As Gebara and Bingemer note,

> The written text should always generate within us the suspicion, or better, questions about what has not been written, what has been lost, or what has been omitted by choice. A written text is always selective. The author or authors choose some events they believe important, and they interpret them, while leaving aside others which from another perspective might be regarded as the most important.[46]

We must, they continue, bear in mind that if the good news of the reign of God is for humanity as a whole,

> this must of necessity involve the participation of men and women, even if the texts written by men and from a patriarchal viewpoint leave out the active participation of women. . . . That is the reason why we must take up a critical stance that can open space for us to reconstruct and recover the history of the past and thereby grasp the revelation of the God of life in the lives of women as well.[47]

The latter point recognizes that divine revelation is not exhausted in the biblical writings. It continues to operate in the historical processes of human liberation, in the signs of life present in the people's advance, in personal and collective activities that humanize life and generate relationships of greater solidarity, participation, and justice.[48]

God's revelation is also present in women's liberation struggles, and those of all the oppressed under the auspices of divine grace and the power generated by the constant activity of the Holy Spirit. Women's work in interpreting the Bible takes these aspects into account. This means that present experience of women's oppression and liberation is a criterion for discerning where and how God acts in the Bible and in life.[49] So, as Gebara and Bingemer point out, women interpreting the Bible turn to it not only in order to understand the texts of the past and the stories it tells as illustrations, but primarily to "understand and reactivate the past for the sake of today's liberation struggles."[50]

The Importance of the Bible in Women's Lives

It is striking what an important role the Bible plays in women's lives in Latin America. In the base communities it is called "the light of our lives," "source of energy, spirituality, and commitment," "word of life that strengthens my faith," "liberating word that illuminates the value of the whole human person." For these communities the Bible is the word of God, the power, and good news that nourishes them.[51] Starting from experience, likenesses are sought in the biblical story, which is reread to relate Bible and life in a simple and creative way, giving priority to faithfulness to life rather than abstract reflection.

Everyday experience is understood in the light of liberating biblical events anticipated by the women and men who participated in the decisive events of revelation. Thus biblical study is not done purely for its own sake. As Tereza Cavalcanti notes "In women's hands the Bible is transformed in the base communities into a dynamic force for the transformation of society and the church. Reading and interpreting it give members a new awareness of liberation, which they express with joy and humor."[52] In readings that link Bible and life there is critical stress on what does and does not correspond. Some examples include the certainty that we cannot infer or justify male superiority from the Bible by referring to Genesis; women's struggle for survival and to defend life finds references in Exodus; women's leadership, wisdom, strength, authority and solidarity is encountered in countless women in the Bible; women's new awareness of their value, their full rights to humanity, can be inferred from Jesus' liberating behavior in his relations with women; women's committed, believing, critical, and innovative participation is to be found in Mary, the mother of Jesus; the equality sought in the church relates to the women in the primitive Christian movement; women's suffering can be linked to the experiences of many people in the Bible as well as to their hopes and songs of joy and victory.[53] It is clear that in Latin America the process of women's liberation has gained energy from the Bible and new meanings are found in the Bible arising out of present experience.

We may note the special way in which women in the base communities establish this dialogue between Bible and life. Ivone Gebara notes the fact that many women

> are especially gifted with a deep intuition about human life and able to counsel, to intuit problems, to express them, to give support, to propose solutions, and to confirm the faith of many people. They explain biblical passages on the basis of their experience and respond to doctrinal questions by simplifying them and setting them on the level of existential reality. Some of these women are illiterate.[54]

Indeed they are, but this is not an obstacle. Tereza Cavalcanti observes that many "memorize words and stories from the scriptures, applying them to different circumstances. . . . Adopting the biblical language as their own they read events in the light of faith."[55] This is not a single reading. The dialogue to which I refer takes place in a critical spirit: "the critical consciousness awakened by reading God's word in contact with real life leads them to discover certain forms of machismo both in present-day society and in the Bible itself and the church. Then there are denunciations and protests against sexual discrimination, which is not always recognized by society or even by the members of the base communities themselves."[56] In many cases their way of reading the Bible places women in situations of real conflict within their families, in their own communities, or with the religious or civil authorities. Supported by the good news of the gospel and the power of the Spirit, they dare to claim their rights and the rights of their people.[57] Many of these matters arising from the experience of oppresson and liberation have deepened research into biblical hermeneutics, as we shall see.

Feminist Suspicion as a Theoretical Category
in Biblical Interpretation

One of the primary insights women bring to their study of the Bible is the option for the poor. They point out that "any reading of the word of the Lord must be a reading from the viewpoint of the poor. When Jesus explains the scriptures, he rereads them (Lk 4:16ff) in the light of his own situation as a poor person and in terms of his struggle for justice. Rereading the Bible means trying to understand its central message in order to live by it in the daily struggle."[58]

The perception that Bible reading in Latin America should be done from the viewpoint of the poor is of crucial importance for exegesis and biblical hermeneutics. This change leads to a rediscovery of the Bible. People have begun to see it as subversive, because it supports the struggle of the poor for liberation. Many men and women in various Latin American countries have suffered persecution simply because they had a Bible. As Elsa Tamez says: "This rereading of the Word from the point of view of the poor has been consolidated and has become so evident that Holy Scripture is regarded as a threatening or dangerous book by some sectors of society that do not share a preferential option for the poor. ... Some religious circles have even decided to avoid biblical discussions. Do they fear the Bible?"[59] This shows the dominant view—that the Bible is neutral—fails to recognize its own underlying position and that underlying the biblical text, thereby depriving it of its spiritual power and also weakening its historical efficacy. In spite of this "the ancient book of Christianity has indeed become new and defiant when it is read from the perspective of the poor."[60]

Nevertheless, gradually the *suspicion* arose that we cannot take for granted that reading the Bible from the viewpoint of the poor and reading it from women's point of view automatically correspond. This means it is necessary to make poor and oppressed women's interests explicit in order to avoid generalizations that overlook them. According to Tamez, the core of the problem appears to be that the poor "find that the Word reaffirms in a clear and direct way that God is with them in their fight for life. Women who live in poverty, however, even when they are aware that the strength of the Holy Spirit is on their side, do not know how to confront the texts that openly segregate them. These texts sound strange and surprising to someone who is not familiar with the culture of the biblical world and believes in a just and liberating God."[61]

Latin American exegesis and hermeneutics have long emphasized the great biblical liberating processes, which are clearly about the liberation of the oppressed—Exodus, the prophets, the gospel. This is a necessary task in our context, but it has failed to consider the biblical texts and traditions referring to women's oppression and liberation. They have been ignored or regarded as secondary "because the main criterion has been to experience God as a God of life who has a preferential option for the oppressed, including women."[62] Thus women's exclusion was regarded as something not fundamental, an afterthought. This attitude in hermeneutics is consistent with the way in which women's problems have been postponed or considered secondary in other fields.

Part of the problem lies in the encounter and mutual reinforcement between two deeply *machista* and patriarchal cultures: our present society and the culture of the biblical world.[63] Attempts to overcome this have not been adequate. The first thing necessary for reaching a nonsexist (and also non-classist and non-racist) understanding of the Bible is *to take the problem seriously*. Reading the Bible solely from the point of view of the poor may overlook the relations between the sexes, as well as concealing the biblical traditions that have contributed to the consolidation of the sex-gender system with men on top, which was and continues to be the determining factor in the subordination of women today.

In Tamez's opinion it is important to consider three key points. First, it is necessary to be critically aware of the conditioning that goes with every reading of the Bible. Often anti-feminist readings are determined by a long tradition that imposes on the text an ideological slant deriving from a patriarchal and androcentric society. These readings may be even more negative for women than the text itself. One example is the reading of Genesis, chapter 3, which has become the basis for "creating a mythical framework that legitimizes women's inferiority and their submission to men."[64] Such a reading of this text raises the reader's androcentric views of women to the category of a divine ordinance. The same thing happens with other texts, and the result is "a legitimation and legislation, as if it were holy, of an order unfavorable to women. Women are called, therefore, to deny the authority of those readings that harm them."[65]

Second, says Tamez, even when women succeed in rescuing certain texts and reading them in a liberating sense, they cannot always find their meaning *for women* because these texts merely reflect the inferiority accorded to women. In this case "its exegesis will show only the patriarchal ideology of the author, the commentator, the culture, and the historic moment in which the text was elaborated."[66] Women can merely make explicit and denounce these traditions and texts that oppress them. Nevertheless, the existence of texts that are clearly *machista* does not destroy the Bible's central message, which is intrinsically liberating. Therefore, Tamez says,

> From my point of view, it is precisely the Gospel's spirit of justice and freedom that neutralizes antifemale texts. A reading of the Bible that attempts to be faithful to the Word of the Lord will achieve that goal best when it is done in a way that reflects the liberating meaning of the Gospel, even when sometimes fidelity to the Gospel forces the reader to distance herself or himself from the text.[67]

In this case it is important to recognize that texts and traditions promoting women's inferiority and legitimating their subordination "are not normative; neither are those texts that legitimize slavery normative."[68]

Third, she says, it is necessary to reevaluate the principle of biblical authority. There is a contradiction in Latin American women's experience of reading the Bible. They regard it as the word of God, therefore having the authority of revelation, but they do not agree with patriarchal and *machista* texts and do not put them into practice. But those occupying positions of power in the church resort to these same texts to call women to obedience when their activities become a threat. So, can we say that these misogynist texts and patriarchal traditions that oppress women belong to revelation? Should we allow them the theological authority of Christian revelation? Tamez claims that this means we must "reformulate the principle of biblical authority, from the point of departure of our Latin American reality."[69] This must be done not only in order to criticize the patriarchal texts but also to reread the entire Bible from a point of view that does not exclude women.

New Guidelines for Reading the Bible

The formulation of theological criteria for the critical evaluation of biblical texts and traditions has always been recognized as a necessary task by the church. Throughout history various hermeneutic models have been followed. These have been competently analyzed by Elisabeth Schüssler Fiorenza.[70] Despite the variety of models, biblical research from the perspective of women requires its own particular criteria in order to bring out women's experience of struggle against oppression, which is normally overlooked by androcentric hermeneutics. It is becoming ever more necessary to formulate new guidelines with sufficiently inclusive and liberating criteria so that the Bible ceases to be used as an instrument of women's oppression. Women must be enabled to link their struggle for liberation with biblical revelation, which is life, fulfillment, and justice.

Tamez proposes three indispensable guidelines for rereading the Bible in terms of Latin American women. These are an initial approach to the large task that remains to be undertaken in the future. The questions Latin American women are asking about the Bible have given rise to what we call "hermeneutical audacity."[71]

First, Tamez indicates that for a Latin American rereading of the Bible it is necessary to adopt a dialectical process of *distancing and approaching*. We need to distance ourselves from traditional interpretations that we have assimilated over the centuries. We must really challenge the underlying presuppositions, interpretative models, and traditions, which have been consciously or unconsciously internalized over the years in a one-sided reading of the Bible. This means being *suspicious* of our own conditioning and that of the text. If we are not aware of these presuppositions or "prereadings," they will continue to act as keys to interpretation, blocking out other more liberating ones. So this distancing means "take up the Bible as a new book, a book that has never been heard or read before."[72] We also need to approach the text with the questions that arise from our daily lives, questions about our pain, joy, hope, hunger, repression, celebration, and struggle.[73] The dialectical relationship between these two processes will enable us to arrive at the meaning of revelation for women in their struggle today and also to reformulate the principle of biblical authority.[74]

In the second place, although the task of interpreting the Bible from women's point of view emphasizes women's specific interests, it must still keep the hermeneutic perspective of *the poor*. For Latin American women, the Bible must be read from the standpoint of the values, sufferings, and expectations of the Latin American masses, for whom the present system offers nothing but death or an inhuman life.[75] In Latin America any reading claiming to be liberating must start from the poor and oppressed. As Tamez reiterates:

They are in a privileged place, hermeneutically speaking, because we conceive of the God of life as One who has a preferential option for the poor. Besides, the mystery of God's reign is with them because it has been revealed to them (Mt 11:25). Therefore, a reading from a woman's perspective has to go through this world of the poor. This will be a guarantee that it has a core theme of liberation, and it will shed light on the other faces of the poor, such as blacks and native peoples. This kind of reading will also give us methods to develop specific approaches to salvation in each of their situations.[76]

This key will enable us to abolish the use of texts and traditions and their *machista* interpretations to oppress women.

Third, a reading of the Bible that aims to eliminate women's oppression requires a *clear feminist consciousness*. Without it we may not recognize the oppressive dimensions present in the biblical texts and traditions. This means, Tamez continues, that

> To read the Bible from a woman's perspective, we must read it with women's eyes, that is to say, conscious of the existence of individuals who are cast aside because of their sex . . . and a conscious effort is needed to discover new women-liberating aspects, or even elements in the text that other perspectives would not bring to light.[77]

It is not only texts referring to women that need to be read critically, but the whole Bible. This new awareness should not be exclusive to women but shared with men, so that they too may be enabled to read the Bible in a nonsexist way. Feminist awareness in biblical interpretation contributes to broadening the field of research, because women bring their own experience of struggle against oppression.

> They can pose new "ideological suspicions" not only to the culture that reads the text but also to the heart of the text itself by reason of being a product of patriarchal culture. Furthermore, their "ideological suspicions" are also applied to biblical tools, such as dictionaries, commentaries, and concordances, tools that are regarded as objective because they are scientific, but that are undoubtedly susceptible to being biased by sexism.[78]

Finally I should point out—with Elsa Tamez—the need to advance the field of Latin American biblical hermeneutics from the perspective of women and starting from our own historical circumstances. We need to take into account the contributions of other biblical scholars, who are developing new criteria and new hermeneutic models consistent with women's liberation and the liberation of the oppressed in general. This is the case with Elisabeth Schüssler Fiorenza with her major work *In Memory of Her*.[79] The methodology she proposes supports the common feminist task.

The God of Life and the *Rachamim* of the Trinity

Paradoxical though it may seem, systematic reflection on God is one of the least developed areas of theological work done by Latin American women. Nevertheless, speaking about God is mentioned in most of these works. God's mystery, as experienced and expressed by women, lies at the center of all theological reflection. Often it is not explicitly dealt with as a topic but appears in relation to the daily experience of faith. In fact, "any search for theological expression geared toward finding new ways," says María Clara Bingemer, "must be centered on the main mystery, the source, on the basis of the Christian faith and theology: God."[80] New ways are being sought to formulate God's image, an image that is beginning to look different through women's faith. Women's faith in God is the foundation of any subsequent systematic formulation.

As we shall see, women's experience of God is the deep root from which sprouts a new way of understanding themselves in Latin American history. And vice versa, women's participation in the Christian base communities and the popular liberation movements helps shape their understanding and experience of God. In this the rereading of the Bible from the perspective of women has played an important part. From women's perspective the difficulty in speaking about God is whether present language—even liberation theology speaks in a androcentric way—is capable of interpreting and expressing women's attempts to describe their own experience of God.[81] For the moment I will outline certain points that women stress in their understanding of God. The question of God is not asked in a context threatened by unbelief but by the attack on life itself.[82] Latin American women Christians live in a context of daily struggle for their own lives and that of their people. The answers they seek must meet the challenge of this reality. As I mentioned, for Latin American women faith in God is not something external. It is fundamental to who they are. So they feel it to be a challenging vocation and an opportunity for hope rather than a burden. Here the central questions are not about God's existence, but about how to discover God in a reality of suffering and inhumanity. How can we uncover God's true face in a context where women are reduced to insignificance? Is there any room for women in the mystery of the Trinity, the center of the Christian faith? What does it mean to speak about the God of life to people whose daily experience is being despised because they are poor women of oppressed races? In some Christian communities women deliberately sharpen the questions: If God is merciful and omnipotent, why do we have to suffer so? What role can we have in this dominated and oppressed society where life has so few possibilities?[83] These are ancient questions. Today they are asked with reference to the oppression of women.

Reencountering the God of Life

For some time there has been a notable change in the way in which women conceive and experience God. The traditional image of God as a judge, a warrior, a patriarchal lord, an abstract and timeless ruler, is being replaced by that of a God whose essence is love, a God who freely conceives and creates, whose peculiar mode of being is compassion and mercy. Of course this change is connected with the change in the way women see themselves, that is, with their new awareness of *causality*, as I noted in Chapter 2. This awareness of causality has contributed substantially to the effort to seek new meanings for history and women's role in it. Consequently, women's view has been affected. Once women realized that their ancient oppression could be lifted, and moreover that God is on their side, this realization challenged the traditional view of God ruling in the male interest. Gradually it questioned the view of God as a patriarchal judge and ruler justifying women's subordination. Awareness of causality is leading to a reorganization of the way in which women understand their lives, including their idea of God. We can also see how the perspective of women broadens and deepens liberation theology.

Women's active participation in the liberation processes in society and the church has given rise to a change in the expression of their faith. Ivone Gebara observes that

Entering the labor force has changed the expression of women's faith. From their previous horizon of home and family, women have opened out to a broader reality. God is no longer one who addresses a world limited to the activities of home and family; God becomes the one who addresses socioeconomic and political challenges in the new militancy of Latin American women. The image of God is no longer that of the father to whom one owes submission; rather, God is basically the image of what is most human in woman and man, seeking expression and liberation.[84]

First, Latin American women have rediscovered the God of life. The starting point for this new experience of faith is the general context of suffering and oppression of the Latin American masses. In the light of faith this situation is *unnatural*, and God is not indifferent to it. On the contrary, realizing that this immense suffering is against God's plan for fullness of life for humanity has led to the discovery of God in the suffering faces of the oppressed. And it has also led to the recognition that faith in God means a commitment to transform this situation, which is not accidental but has perceivable causes. Moreover, the biblical revelation presents God as always acting in favor of life. God generates and guarantees life; God is fullness of life, become tangible in the life of Jesus. This encounter with God in the faces of the poor, of women, and all the oppressed has given faith a new meaning. As Luz Beatríz Arellano notes,

We have gone from an experience of oppression, marginalization, and suffering to a realm of hope that is impelling us toward change, toward transformation. . . . We were also discovering that God was different from what we had been taught. We were discovering God as the God of life, closer to us, as one who journeys with us through history.[85]

From this experience God emerges as the one who truly protects and defends those who have the least life.[86] There is a kind of resonance between the God of life and women's own experience, or at least life has fuller meaning by analogy with God's activity. For Arellano, "being essentially bearers and sustainers of life, women find a new meaning in the discovery of God as God of life, and they themselves become stronger and more conscious as defenders and bearers of life, not only in the biological sense but in all its dimensions. . . . "[87]

Aurora Lapiedra points out that women have a special link with everything to do with physical life, and also its psychic and spiritual dimensions: "Through their closeness to life women have a great interest and sensitivity in studying the Bible. I think they have a special talent for being in tune with the God of the Bible who is the God of life."[88] Ana María Tepedino suggests that women's experience of the God of life is also connected with their capacity to carry children in their womb during the nine months of gestation.[89] Women's union with the God of life is supported by their experience of faith as a single whole embracing all life and relationships. On the other hand, precisely because life is preeminent for women, they feel called by God—like the biblical prophets—to denounce every threat to it.

Tereza Cavalcanti has some interesting reflections on the prophetic tradition. From questions arising out of current experiences of the communities, she rereads the biblical texts that refer explicitly or implicitly to women's prophetic ministry in the light of women's activity today. Cavalcanti sets out various prophetic elements derived from women's activity in the Hebrew Scriptures that she considers to be highly relevant to the Latin American context.[90] These include women claiming their rights; acting with authority, leadership, and wisdom; women as symbols of popular resistance; solidarity with the people in the option for life; faith in God who sides with the oppressed and makes a covenant with his people; cries and lamentation to provoke a response from God; canticles and hymns that preserve memories, urge people to struggle for freedom, and express the hope of the poor; the freedom and faithfulness of those who know that God is on their side.

When Cavalcanti establishes the link between women's prophecy in the biblical tradition and today, she is also bringing us to the same affirmation of the God of life. The certainty that God sides with the oppressed is ultimately based on God's self-revelation as a God of life, in opposition to anyone or any systems and institutions—the idols who do not hear or see—who threaten it. Cavalcanti concludes:

The women prophets of the Hebrew Bible are of the same prophetic line as Jesus (José Comblin). Theirs is a prophetic ministry dedicated to life and the reconstruction of life—in spite of threats and danger. . . . Where there was death and sterility, they demonstrated the strength and value of living. We believe that this same attitude is reborn today in a surprising way in the struggle of the Latin American people and their many women leaders. It is a tireless struggle; it is rooted in faith.[91]

This new understanding sees a God who is near, who generates hopes, shares in daily struggles, and at the same time is still to be discovered in the mystery of human life. The presence of this God is felt in the anticipation of the New Creation.

The Divine Rachamim, Speaking of God in the Feminine

Systematic reflection on God has advanced more consistently in the identification of God's feminine and maternal aspects. This is not apart from the growing perception of the God of life but the identification of other characteristics that belong to the divine being. The suspicion that the patriarchal image of God that exists in Judaism and Christianity is rooted in the unequal relationship between men and women at the expense of true love and solidarity has shown the need to seek new ways of thinking and speaking about God. God must not be identified with male power, but must be able to integrate women in a way that neither suppresses their difference from men nor endorses their inequality. María Clara Bingemer has addressed herself to this task.[92] Her aim is to "trace the clues leading to the revelation of the feminine in God. By the end of our search, we should be able to believe in and call on God using feminine appellation without having strayed from the Church or the Good News of Jesus Christ."[93]

There are various key points underlying this view: God's image identified with the masculine is incompatible with Christian revelation and its preaching of universal love. The archetypal models in which God has been conceived have been polarized toward the masculine, to the detriment of the feminine. Cultural, anthropological, and theological dualism has strengthened the androcentric nature of God's image. It is necessary to overcome these limits in order to reach a fuller, more communal, and relational understanding of God, in which the masculine and the feminine can be equally expressed. The Christian God is not a self-sufficient patriarch but a community of love among persons (Father, Son, and Holy Spirit). This does not suppress the differences or give priority to the masculine; rather, it includes the feminine dimensions in its inner life.

María Clara Bingemer explores the semantic nuclei and biblical images that enable us to reach a greater understanding of the feminine in God's trinitarian mystery. In the first place, this theological reflection tries to recover the biblical roots of the experience of God contained in various terms such as *rachamim* (mother's womb), *ruach* (wind, spirit, breath of life) and *hochmah* (wisdom or in Greek, *sophia*). The point has been stressed that *rachamim* is used to refer to God. Bingemer writes:

> One of the biblical terms often used in referring to God is *rachamim*. It describes God's mercy. The root of the word is *rechem*, which means mother's breast, or womb; *rachamim*, then, refers to that safe place in a woman's body where a child is conceived, nourished, protected, where it grows and later is given birth. *Rachamim* is used to compare God's love to that of a mother.[94]

In the Hebrew Scriptures there are many texts referring to God directly as a mother or in terms of the womb (Is 49:15; Jer 31:20; Is 42:14; Is 14:1; Ps 77:10). The divine *rachamim* is even invoked as personifying God (Ps 79:8). Generally speaking, androcentric theology emphasizes God's power and dominion and leaves out his loving, tender, and compassionate side. The same might be said of the the divine *ruach* as a presence that creates the world and the breath of the creative birth (later identified with the Holy Spirit); likewise the *hochmah* as a feminine presence and mother of wisdom. As for the New Testament, Bingemer suggests that the term *agape*, taken from the theology of John, is the one that expresses God's love best. *Agape* indicates the divine activity that lovingly envelops the world, and God is love (1 Jn 4:8-16). "God's love for humankind, as it flows out of the trinitarian economy, is the image and form of God's deepest reality. The love of this mysterious reality is inclusive; the poor and the 'lesser' people have high positions; women and men live in harmony."[95]

The divine *rachamim* can also clearly be found in the New Testament, referring in particular to Jesus, the incarnate son, and the Holy Spirit. On the one hand, says Bingemer, Jesus speaks of God and God's merciful love for the sinner as like a woman who loses a coin and lights her lamp, shuts up the house, and carefully searches until she finds it. When she finds it she calls her friends and neighbors to celebrate (Lk 15:8-10).[96] Here Jesus shows God as like a woman. In the gospel there are also various passages showing Jesus acting in a motherly way or expressing feminine traits. For example, he weeps over Jerusalem, which murders the prophets, and compares himself to a mother (Lk 13:34); he is tender toward weak and defenseless children (Mk 9:36); he expresses joy and gives thanks for God's self-revelation to the humble and ignorant (Mt 11:25-7); he weeps for the death of his friend Lazarus (Jn 11:35).[97] We can say that the feminine is definitely assumed by the Word, the second person of the Trinity.[98]

Likewise, New Testament theology identifies the Holy Spirit (the creative life-giving *ruach*) with a mother who does motherly things. For example,

> The Spirit will not abandon us as orphans (Jn 14:18); the Spirit consoles, exhorts, and comforts us as loving mother (14:26). Paul talks about the Spirit as doing things usually done by a mother: teaching us to stammer the names of the Abba-Father (Rom 8:15) and Jesus Christ (1 Cor 12:3); teaching us how to pray in a way that is acceptable and pleasing to God (Rom 8:26).[99]

This activity of the Holy Spirit according to Bingemer, shows that the feminine is inherent in God's being. Therefore the emphasis on the masculine that androcentric theology places in its image of God merely reduces it and debases it.

This focus on the feminine and maternal dimension of the trinitarian God has gradually led the Christian communities to an understanding of God in which the masculine father ceases to dominate. God can be called a motherly father or a fatherly mother.[100] As Bingemer indicates, the biblical terms and images

> allow us to affirm that there exists a feminine principle in the divinity which makes it possible to believe, worship, and love God not only as the strong Father who creates us and liberates us with his powerful arm, but also as a Mother, full of tenderness, grace, beauty, and receptivity, who accepts the seed of life and feeds it in her womb, so it may become a full being in the light of day.[101]

God, understood as Father and Mother, who is merciful and whose essence is love, must allow for the forming of communities of women and men without domination or privilege. If the trinitarian mystery is primarily a community of love, a society and a church that exclude some are unlikely to manifest God's true face.

As I said at the beginning of this chapter, Latin American feminist theology is still in an early stage in its search for an appropriate language to speak about God. The image of the God of life offers no difficulty in the experience and reflection of women in different communities. It is in the communities that mystical, spiritual, and prophetic language is more fluently expressed, especially because it connects with the struggles and resistance of daily life. A great problem is presented by language about God connoting traditional gender concepts derived from cultural stereotypes and functions assigned to men and women in androcentric thought; that is, when God is presented in terms characteristic of the masculine or the feminine or traditional paternal or maternal functions assigned to men and women.

With respect to Bingemer's contribution, Tamez appears to distance herself from a reflection that maintains the archetypes of the masculine-feminine duality. From her point of view,

> In both Catholic and Protestant popular Christian communities it has occurred to no one to speak of Goddess, or to refer to the God of the Bible as mother. And generally speaking this is still alien to Latin American feminist Christian women, or at least we do not consider it an important issue—yet.[102]

In the light of what has been said here, I do not think the question of what to call God is a matter that can go on being set aside. Recent reflections by popular Christian women in different places in Latin America and the Caribbean do not allow us to avoid their challenge. In some communities, the biblical-theological tendency of the *rachamim*, as well as the God of life, is gaining ground.[103] So is talk of the fatherly mother and motherly father. For many, God is both Father and Mother.[104] Likewise in their search for a new language about God, other communities have created terms such as "Lifegiver," "Creative Force," "Befriender," "Friend," "Comrade," and many others.[105]

Women in the Christian communities are conscious of their right to their own word, to human integrity, and to full personhood. They are beginning to take on the task of seeking a new language about God that does not exclude their experience, knowledge, and expectations. I do not agree with Tamez that this is not a matter of concern in Latin America today. On the other hand, neither do I believe that a rethinking of God's figure and image must necessarily be in terms of the archetypical models of the masculine and feminine. Although it is an attempt to overcome the antagonistic character of sexual differences, this procedure risks consecrating the traditional functions ascribed to each sex, but now transported into the divine being. We must be careful about this risk. This is not really a way to change the androcentric view, since it is the source of these gender stereotypes. First, we must criticize these structures. Only then can we evaluate their appropriateness for expressing our current experience, as women, of the God of life. Useful efforts are being made toward a feminist theological construction of God's image—the mystery of the Trinity itself—by using other biblical images whose significance has not yet been explored. These include Water, Light, Way, Bread, Life, Word, Vine, Wisdom, and others,[106] including the Father and Mother images. We are not trying to create an exotic language, but rather to name this ineffable, challenging, and loving presence, which became tangible in the strength and vulnerability of Jesus Christ and now acts with life-giving power in the world of the poor and oppressed, in their suffering and their hope, in their weakness and their strength. By naming this presence we are naming ourselves.

Jesus Christ: Life and Liberation in a Discipleship of Equals

Saying who Jesus is for Latin American women today means taking up the question Jesus asked the men and women who shared his ministry: "Who do you say I am?" (Mk 8:27). The reply is in terms of the respondent's personal history and tries to express what Jesus means for her. Like many biblical characters, Latin American women Christians today feel *summoned* to share in a discipleship of equals in Jesus' ministry. An answer to Jesus' question is only possible in terms of a consciously adopted attitude about ourselves, that is, realizing that our own lives are deeply affected by the person of Jesus. The core of christological reflection from the perspective of women is that it is in Jesus—whose life, death, and resurrection was for the sake of the reign of God—that God's saving plan for humanity has been manifested. Through the power of the Spirit women feel called to share in the new world that has begun with Jesus.

Peter and Martha's Replies

New Testament hermeneutics usually takes for granted—erroneously, as feminist exegesis shows—that the central question put by Jesus to those who were disciples in his movement is addressed only to *twelve male* disciples, thus excluding women and other men.[107] This view is reinforced by the emphasis given, following the synoptic tradition, to Peter's answer: "You are the Christ" (Mk 8:29). This shows the patriarchal prejudice of androcentric hermeneutics, which disregards the messianic profession of faith that John's theology places in the mouth of a woman, Martha of Bethany, who proclaims: "Yes, Lord, I believe that you are the Christ, the Son of God, the one who was to come into this world" (Jn 11:27). As Ana María Tepedino points out, by this proclamation Martha "crystallizes the messianic faith of the community, being its spokesperson in her capacity as the 'beloved disciple' of Jesus."[108] Neither of these replies excludes the other and should not do so; they share the same space of equal discipleship. The problem is that preeminence has been given to the one that expresses only the androcentric interest, with the object of legitimating religious power in the hands of men. But both replies taken together enable us to understand more fully not only the person of Jesus but also the nature of the inclusive discipleship he offered and his own experience of God in a sharing community.

As Nelly Ritchie points out, Latin America women take up the question and answer it in terms of their own interest in taking part in social and religious liberation movements and the protagonistic role they are now trying to play in history. For them,

> the statement: that Jesus is Christ! covers new dimensions. It does not have to do with an applied doctrine but with a truth to discover, with a response which, translated into words and deeds, takes on historical truthfulness and liberating force. ... This attempt to give answers happens within our context as Latin American women.[109]

Latin American women's christology is based on our own experience of a historical reality, and this means our christology is *contextual*. To do this christology implies a commitment to the transformation of our own suffering, and that of others, to joy, liberation, and justice. Women's discourse about Jesus Christ is nourished by liberating activities in the church base communities and the various social movements of struggle and resistance.

So, knowledge and understanding of Jesus Christ has to do with the historical experience of the struggle against oppression and for liberation. This knowledge consciously distances itself from the theoretical and tries to become *sentient knowledge*. Both the woman seeking knowledge and Jesus Christ are significant in this process; they relate in such a way that if either is left out the very identity of the other is radically affected and will have to be reformulated.

Christian women in Latin America experience faith in Jesus Christ as a vocation and a call to participate. As Nelly Ritchie writes:

> Our reality means that we are women, we belong to Latin America, and we are members of the body of Christ. We are setting out on an adventure which will bring together all our humble contributions. We do so with the confidence that together we will enrich each other's lives, we will inspire one another, and share the work involved in liberating our continent. . . . What we hope to do is to provoke new questions and to open ourselves up to the marvelous revelations of God who, in Jesus, is shown to be the Liberator.[110]

Women's christological reflections express their vision and expectation of a new earth to which they are called in the power of the Spirit.

Some Presuppositions of Feminist Christology

Christology from the perspective of women welcomes the findings and aims of Latin American christology in general.[111] But it has different emphases and stresses aspects ignored by androcentric reflection. Among others, we may mention women's active participation in Jesus' movement; their full membership in the community summoned together by him; women's equal discipleship with men; Jesus' humanizing attitude toward women; Jesus' criticism of patriarchal social and religious institutions; and the prophetic wisdom traditions in Jesus. Up till now these aspects have been peripheral in the christology done by male theologians. This christology has failed to give the relationship between Jesus and oppressed women the importance it should have in liberation hermeneutics and which is present in the gospel itself. This means that systematic work on christology today is not automatically inclusive; it is necessary that the person doing it consciously choose that it should be so.

Those who believe that the new era of the reign of God initiated by Jesus implies the end of women's oppression must deliberately include this objective in their theology and make plain that the good news also announces the end of women's current subordination.[112] In order to find personal and social meaning in the gospel's liberating message for women, it is essential to participate in the historical struggles for change without reductionism or postponement of women's issues. Likewise, in approaching Jesus as an object of our theological reflection, we must clearly pay attention to the historical Jesus; at the same time we must make a conscious effort not to add more androcentric weight to that already present in the biblical accounts. This critical position will give us a broader access to the life and ministry of the historical Jesus. Our christological vision must not overlook fundamental aspects of Jesus' life and activity, one of which is his relation to women. He clearly viewed women not just as belonging to the impoverished masses, but simply as women; not just as receivers of the good things brought by the messiah, but also as actors contributing to the spread of the good news; not as appendices to do the housework, but as full members of the equal community he founded.[113]

Although Latin American christology may be lacking in these respects, the work done by women lays equal emphasis on Jesus Christ as liberator. It stresses Jesus' liberating mission in its historical, structural, personal, and eschatological dimensions. From the perspective of women, historical liberation is not a closed circle but points to a future still to be revealed. The present is only an anticipation of the fulfillment to come in an abundance of life for the whole earth.[114]

There are certain classical questions for modern exegesis about the liberation brought by Jesus. For example, the definitive gift of God's reign, freely offered as a blessing for the poor and oppressed, requires *responsible human action* for the transformation of the reality that produces inhumanity and oppression. As this liberation embraces all human relationships, it must change the unequal relationship between men and women in daily life.[115] This is because Jesus' liberation does not support a split between the personal and the social, private and public, the transcendent and the historical, men and women, above and below. Once again the criterion is the one I mentioned earlier: women's special way of seeing life as a single whole. Now I point out certain aspects of the christology elaborated by Latin American women.

From Patriarchal Christology to Jesus' Egalitarian Practice

One of the first things women's christology does is to examine the patriarchalization of christology, notorious in the New Testament texts and in later elaborations of Christian theology. Rosemary Radford Ruether has made a significant contribution here to the development of Latin American women's christology, as is noted in Bingemer's work.[116] For Bingemer the patriarchal roots of christology go back to the Old Testament messianic expectations, in which the monarchical Davidic messianism prevails over the Isaiah tradition of the Servant. Likewise in New Testament times, the Greek *logos* prevails over the *hochmah* (wisdom), culminating in the fourth century with the establishment of Christianity as the official religion of the Roman Empire. The convergence of these two processes in christology will have dramatic consequences for women in the fields of anthropology as well as christology and soteriology.[117] With the final stage in the patriarchalization of christology in the fourth century, Jesus became the image of the emperor—the *Pantocrator*, Judge, and Lord—like a temporal ruler. He thus becomes "the consolidation of the lordship of a masculine God, who can only have male representatives."[118]

The ensuing christology, together with Greek androcentric patriarchal anthropology, not only placed women in a subordinate position but also damaged understanding of the God of Jesus Christ. Bingemer points out two particular problems that this christology has passed on to the church today and that need to be solved. On the one hand, the exclusion of women from the ordained ministry appeals to the argument that women do not act *in persona Christi*. On the other hand, this christology

> makes women second-class citizens in the order of creation and salvation. As well as being christological, the problem is soteriological. Many women (especially now that women's liberation is growing fast) find it difficult to see this man, "the one whom men killed, God made Lord and Christ" (Acts 2:23-24), as God's salvation offered to humanity."[119]

Women are seeking ways to solve these problems and create an alternative christology that is also liberating for them. They are trying to reencounter the Jesus of the gospels in order to return to his relation with women and women's active participation in his movement.

A second feature in women's christological reflection is concerned with the primary link between Jesus and the poor and oppressed from the very beginning in the incarnation of God's eternal word. This link relates the person of Jesus with women, both as women and as oppressed. The undeniable fact, without which theology would cease to be Christian and without which Jesus Christ would lose his power as the savior and liberator of humanity, is that God's Word becomes flesh (sarx) (Jn 1:14) and chooses as its human dwelling place women and men, not primarily men. But the fact that really causes scandal is that God's Word does not just become human but becomes flesh in the humanity of the poor and oppressed, identifying with them in their life, destiny, and hope (Mk 9:37; Mt 8:20; 25:40, 45). Hence the acknowledgment made in the final document of the Latin American meeting on Women, Church, and Theology:

> It seems important to recognize that the incarnation of the Son of God takes place in the humanity of the poor, and his resurrection is the victory of the new humanity over death. Jesus' special concern for women lies within the scope of this fact: God becomes poor before becoming man or woman and God conquers death to become new humanity, cancelling the divisions of class, race, and sex.[120]

Without this fundamental recognition we cannot understand Jesus' action for women as people in their own right or the scandal that his behavior provoked. At the same time this perspective enables us to understand that Jesus' good news to the poor and oppressed is not given to women in addition to men, but because God has made taken on flesh and their cause.

The third important aspect is women's incorporation into Jesus' liberating plan, centered around God's reign. Unlike other Jewish groups and movements in the first century of our era,[121] Jesus' movement admitted women because of his special way of understanding of the reign of God and his experience of God. According to the gospel accounts, Jesus initiated an itinerant charismatic movement, whose central vision continues to be that God's reign has broken into history in Jesus' own person and ministry. This is a new reality that benefits the poor, sinners, and outcasts, for whom society offers no salvation. It is to this collection of needy men and women that God's reign belongs. It comes to them as a blessing and tells them that now is the time of salvation. It is the good news of liberation. The power of God's reign is already at work and will change the face of the earth. The triumph over the evils that deprive the poor and oppressed of life has already begun and can be seen in Jesus' activity, the signs of liberation created by him.

Characteristically, Jesus likes to express God's reign as restoring power in a common meal, shared by the most disconcerting groups of people: the poor, sinners, prostitutes, the impure, women. In short, he eats with those who are considered to be religiously and socially deficient by those occupying positions of religious power. For Jesus, God's reign means joy, superabundance of life and well-being, human relationships based on justice, solidarity, and constant human renewal. So God's reign proclaimed by Jesus and experienced by those who followed him is understood in terms of the fulfillment to which history, humanity, and the whole creation is destined.[122]

"Jesus embodied God's will to form a more human community by treating women as persons worthy to share in it together with men."[123] From the beginning of Jesus' ministry women form part of the community that follows him. Indeed, says Bingemer,

> It is common to the four gospels that women form part of the assembly of the reign of God summoned by Jesus. They are not merely accidental components, but active participants (Lk 10:38-42) and special recipients of his miracles (cf. Lk 8:2; Mk 1:29-31; Mk 5:25-34; 7:24-30). So women are an integral and principal part of the vision and messianic mission of Jesus. They are the most oppressed of the oppressed. They are the lowest rung of the social ladder.[124]

Jesus offers a different future, and women belong to his movement in a radical way.

> As they are at the bottom of the heap in the society of their time, bearing the weight of its contradictions, women are the ones who have the most reason to want to fight for the non-perpetuation of the status quo that oppresses and enslaves them.[125]

These women show the way in which Jesus turned society upside down.

*The Recovery of Women's Bodies as Belonging
to the Reign of God*

Another fruitful line of reflection for Latin American women is the rediscovery of Jesus' relation with women and women's activities within the new community. Women are not only recipients of messianic benefits, but of the power of God's reign, begun by the person of Jesus and his ministry, which is at work in them. There is no doubt about the active participation of women in Jesus' movement. They did not go along simply in their traditional role of suppliers of domestic needs, as the account in Luke appears to suggest (Lk 8:1-3). Just because Luke speaks about women does not mean he is speaking for them. In fact, Luke's own community kept up the traditional sexual division of labor.[126] Luke presents as a *public sinner* (Lk 7:37) a woman who was not a rich prostitute or a prostitute of any kind. Moreover, he appears to take a great interest in rich women.[127]

For Bingemer, Jesus' relation with women must be placed in the framework of the liberating project of the reign of God. And here it is important to describe Jesus' relation with women's bodies, given that it is precisely women's biological condition that causes their exclusion. According to patriarchal socio-religious laws women are permanently in a state of impurity and do not belong to the *holy people* because they are not circumcised.[128] Ana María Tepedino points out that an inherent part of Jesus' project is the humanization of the person; therefore women's bodies are restored as the primary place for divine activity. This cancels the inhuman logic leading to women's oppression. Jesus restores the dignity of women's bodies and proposes equal relations with women and all the poor and oppressed, thereby showing what it means to bring abundant life (Jn 10:10).[129]

At this point we may look at certain situations given in the gospel showing the relation between Jesus and women.[130]

• Peter's mother-in-law is healed by Jesus (Mk 1:29-31). He comes up to her, takes her hands, and raises her up, restoring her to health and life. She recovers her full human powers and "served them." We should note that this serving by the women is analogous to Jesus' serving. He came "to serve, and to give his life as a ransom for many" (Mk 10:45).

• The woman who is bleeding and therefore impure (Mk 5:25-34) not only suffered economic want but also exclusion from the community. She touches Jesus and is cured, restored. She is also called to live fully and share in the community.

• The dead girl, Jairus' daughter (Mk 5:21-24; 35-43) feels the transforming power of God's reign in Jesus and herself. Death changes to life, and the child walks on her own feet. According to the purity codex (Num 19:11-13) Jesus would become impure by touching the dead girl. But through his action Jesus promotes the logic of fullness of life, which is the driving force of God's reign.

• The Syro-Phoenician woman and the wholeness of life restored to her daughter (Mk 7:24-30) demonstrate a supremely important attitude to women. Their condition as women, even foreigners, poor and impure, is no reason to justify their exclusion from the community initiated by Jesus. The Syro-Phoenician claims her right and her daughter's with firm determination, replying to Jesus' negative by making him see that the abundance of the reign of God was not just for male Jews. Jesus recognizes this argument and cures this foreign woman's daughter. The woman's behavior shows two important things: she represents a special moment in Jesus' self-understanding in relation to the humanizing project of the reign of God; that is, it must be open to all and not just to the house of Israel. Moreover, it is she as a women who has opened the way to integrity, freedom and fullness for her daughter, for women and for all races. "The Syrophoenician woman whose adroit argument opened up a future of freedom and wholeness for her daughter has also become the historically-still-visible advocate of such a future for gentiles. She has become the apostolic "foremother" of all gentile Christians."[131]

• In an argument about marriage (Mk 10:2-12) Jesus defends women's humanity and integrity and criticizes the patriarchal structure of marriage. Jesus points out that a man must leave his patriarchal household for the man and woman to be joined as an equal couple united by love. The coupling by God "from the beginning of creation" (v. 6) of two equal persons is a relationship that no human being can break.

• The poor widow woman, who, Jesus told his disciples, put into the treasury everything she possessed, everything she had to live on (Mk 12:41-44), represents the poverty among Jesus' people. On the other hand, there are the rich who put in only from what they do not need. In Jesus' time widowhood was considered to be a state of absolute privation. But for Jesus this woman is the typical example of what it means to be *poor* and therefore one to whom the beatitudes of God's reign are addressed.

• The anonymous woman who anoints Jesus on the head with a very expensive perfume (Mk 14:3-9), as the kings of Israel were anointed by the prophets, is the one who through her symbolic action explicitly recognizes Jesus as the awaited messiah. Of this woman Jesus says, "wherever throughout all the world the gospel is proclaimed, what she has done will be told as well, in remembrance of her" (v. 9).

• The experience of human fullness and spiritual betrothal experienced by women sharing the discipleship of equals promoted by Jesus did not disappear even after the arrest and crucifixion of Jesus (Mk 15:40-41). In contrast to the fear and paralysis manifested by the male disciples, the women resisted strongly to the end. They shared in Jesus' ministry from Galilee to Jerusalem, they resisted persecution, at the cross and sepulchre. Therefore it is not surprising that they were the first to receive the good news of the resurrection (Mk 16:1-6). Women are called to extend the humanizing process they have experienced with Jesus beyond Jerusalem and Galilee. For them it is certain that God has raised Jesus and that God is on their side.

After this general consideration of how Latin American women perceive Jesus' relation to women, and in particular to women's bodies, I shall now point out the most significant features of a christology from the perspective of women.[132]

Features of Jesus in a Christology from the Perspective of Women

The principal feature in a christology from the perspective of women is Jesus' compassion and solidarity with those who have least. This solidarity becomes action to restore what is lost (see Lk 7:11-15). This restoration anticipates the fulfilment to which the whole of creation is called. At the same time it condemns those who grasp power over the lives of others. Hence the decisive feature of this Jesus is as the Christ of life. Jesus' whole life speaks of a God who is not indifferent to the unjust misfortunes of the poor and oppressed. He is not a magic deity trapped in ritual without any relationship to real life. Jesus proclaims the good news of a God who embraces in love and mercy those who according to the dominant religious system are out of favor with the divinity. In the new community men and women who suffer injustice can experience that God is on their side and defends their cause. Jesus shows a God who has inaugurated a new order, in which grace and freedom offer the beginnings of a new life (Lk 7:36-50, 4:18-19). He gives women abundant self-esteem so that they can choose a different life for themselves and become part of the current of life-giving power of the Spirit. Thus they discover Christ to be the Christ of grace.

Jesus challenges institutionalized religion, which claims to honor God without this involving any commitment to justice. Jesus attacks the false gods whose legal prescriptions damage people's lives. He sets the God of life within reach of those who hope to be freed from these imposed burdens (Lk 13:10-17). Many women laden with burdens that even the religious leaders cannot bear experience the true God's compassion and liberation. Jesus enables them to assume their proper human condition and become persons with full rights. Jesus' activity, person, and ministry free them and all the oppressed from the destructive power of sin and evil that enslaves them. In this way they discover Jesus to be the liberating Christ.

All these features presuppose a clear option for life to the full for those who suffer poverty and dehumanization, so that no one remains outside the blessedness promised by God. This is indeed choosing the better part, which will not be taken away (Lk 10:38-42). Following Jesus means commitment, and discipleship also involves sorrow, struggle, hard work, sacrifice, and renunciation. But with it all goes the conviction that this cause is the cause of God. The vision that goes with this commitment is of a total renewal of the present order. It is an option to make God's reign present through daily struggle to restore women and men to lives that are fully human. In this commitment Jesus is discovered to be the Christ of God's reign.

Finally, christology done by women in Latin America stresses Jesus' resurrection as the starting point for the experience of faith, just as it was for the early Christians. Women are the first witnesses of the resurrection and the first to meet the risen Christ (Mk 16:6-9; Lk 24:5-8; Jn 20:11-17), the first who are sent to proclaim the good news (Mk 16:10-11; Lk 24:9-10; Jn 20:17-18), and the first to proclaim the new life God is offering humanity. In spite of the androcentric character of the biblical accounts, the paschal witness shows the presence of women at Pentecost (Acts 1:14; 2:1, 17-18). They also played a crucial part at the birth of the church. Women belong to the sphere of the New Creation anticipated by Jesus. "From Jesus' resurrection," writes Bingemer, the Spirit is poured out on all flesh, creating a new humanity, which is the body of Christ. And this body of Christ, the collective new creation, which the Spirit continues to form and give birth to "in labor" (Rom 8:22-23) continues to make God's original creation present in the world—male and female (Gen 1:27). This is Christ the firstborn of every creature.[133]

So women's christology stresses that both men and women constitute the new humanity and the body of Christ. Consequently, the writer continues, "in this christology women are not only spokeswomen for the risen Christ but also identified with the same Christ. They too speak, live and act *in persona Christi*. They too are *alter Christus*."[134] Jesus' resurrection has finally cancelled any form of inequality between persons, so that it cannot be said that only one part of humanity is destined to represent Christ in the world.[135] Otherwise the resurrection, and with it the whole foundation of the Christian faith, loses its power.

God's plan for fullness of life for humanity and especially those who lack it—as anticipated in the life, death, and resurrection of Jesus—must involve women as well as men. It is not possible to conceive of God's fullness when the great majority of women continue to occupy a subordinate position in the church and society. Accepting Jesus' liberation and proclaiming God's plan require us to commit ourselves to wiping out every form of suffering, sin, and death afflicting these women. Taking on their cause and that of the great oppressed masses anticipates the glory of the resurrection in constant hope of the day of total fulfillment. Thus, for Latin American women christology becomes working to establish their own identity and develop spiritually as women and as members of the people struggling for life and liberation in the following of Jesus.

Spirituality: A New Way of Acting in the Power of the Spirit

From the viewpoint of Latin American women, spirituality is a new personal and collective experience marked by the power of the Spirit. It is "an ongoing movement of women to live and incarnate their faith in a way that is consistent with what we are experiencing."[136] It is speaking about the living experience of God through the personal, social, and ecclesial transformation processes innumerable Christian communities are undergoing in Latin America. "Spirituality," says Consuelo del Prado, "is a way of living; it is also a way of following Jesus."[137] As Tereza Cavalcanti says: "It relies on the power that comes from the Spirit who gives encouragement on the way. The Spirit generates love and energy in us, permeating everything to the point where we are prepared to give our lives. This is where following Jesus day by day may lead."[138] Spirituality is a *whole* style of living the faith within history through the power of the Spirit.

When I speak of a special way of living and expressing the faith from the perspective of women, I am referring to the women's unique way of looking at life, starting from the most basic daily level. Consequently, spirituality is not seen as something concerned with cultivating the *soul*, or as a separation between the religious and the profane, the spiritual and material, body and spirit, mysticism and practice. On the contrary, it is a way of experiencing ourselves in the power of the Spirit. It embraces every dimension of life. This characteristic, essential to women's way of knowing, stresses certain theological features harder to see from a different epistemological position. Women and men have equally been endowed with the Spirit through their baptismal calling to a discipleship of equals, and this points to a need to change the church and society. When we speak of spirituality from the perspective of women, observes del Prado, "we are referring to an accent, not proposing a polarization. Nevertheless, that accent must be strong enough to emphasize the just claims of the silent or neglected aspects of ordinary speech."[139] The usual way of speaking is, even in matters of spirituality, that which sees men as the supreme expression of human life, the paradigm to which women must conform. This leads to an androcentric and *machista* spirituality. Del Prado quotes the literary expression that José María Arguedas places in the mouth of Matilde, with whom Christian women identify: "I sense God in another way." Del Prado goes on to say, "This phrase demands the right to sense, and thus also to express our distinct experience of God differently.[140] Women *as women* have their own self-understanding, commitment, and spiritual way.

In the Latin American context women's spirituality is marked by suffering. Women's spiritual journey requires them to integrate conflict, because it forms part of the structure of our societies. According to Cavalcanti, our historical circumstances, which may lead women into rivalries, disputes about leadership, intolerance, resentment, tensions, and discouragement, are also opportunities to rethink, reevaluate, and acquire a more critical vision of the mechanisms operating. Then we can redirect our behavior and not fall into despair.[141] So spiritual experience induces us not to give up. The actual situation changes into an environment where we can listen to God's word and respond to it in faith. In the presence of immense suffering, we can change the environment into one of joy and liberation.

> Knowing how to listen to God in the midst of conflict, in the midst of contradictions and the ambiguities of everyday life is an apprenticeship that women are undergoing, especially those who are on the opposite side to that of wealth and power. Listening to God and listening to the poor are two faces of the same coin. This spirituality is a dialogue, because knowing how to listen means also knowing how to speak, how to utter our women's words.[142]

From the perspective of women it is a spirituality that springs from conflict and connects formally reflected practice, mysticism, and our behavior in daily life.

In a special way this connection enables women to see that their suffering is not wanted by God and does not come from God. It is caused by the excluding character of patriarchal imperialistic capitalism, which condemns women to subordination and inhumanity. Elisabeth Schüssler Fiorenza says that feminist Christian spirituality gives rise to another kind of ecclesial community; it raises women's consciousness and leads to the rejection of all forms of oppression and slavery, including the alienation of sexism.

> [This spirituality] rejects the idolatrous worship of maleness and articulates the divine image in female human existence and language. It sets us free from the internalization of false altruism and self-sacrifice that is concerned with the welfare and work of men first to the detriment of our own and other women's welfare and calling.[143]

It is undeniable that in men's spiritual journeys, according to Christian tradition, there seldom has been any special concern for women's work and well-being in accordance with women's interests. Men merely designated functions for women in reproductive and domestic tasks for the benefit of men.

Women's awareness that the Spirit gives life and makes all things new is creating a spiritual revolution in them. Women's lives are changing radically. They are undergoing the paschal experience of passing from slavery to freedom, the freedom for which Christ liberated us. Luz Beatríz Arellano notes that women's strong presence in the processes of social change is full of this vital experience of the Spirit.[144] Women are questioning the *machista* models traditionally assigned to them. In the patriarchal model, a woman

> was idealized as the reverse side of the exploitation she suffered as victim: besides her sexual image, her idealized image was one of motherhood, which gave her back, or tried to give her back, as a mother, what had been taken from her as a human person and as woman: her dignity, her participation, and the chance to be not just one who reproduces human life but also one who creates new life and transforms her own society and her own culture.[145]

In our time women are attracted by the freedom that the Spirit gives women and men; they feel called to solidarity and common responsibility in the building of structures different from those operating at present. They know that fulfilling their own vocation, supported by the power of the Spirit, means struggling to create a space in the Christian community where women and men can share fully in the charismatic and ministerial outpouring of the Spirit upon God's people.

This new way of seeing and experiencing the action of the Spirit in women's lives is closely connected with the biblical tradition of the divine *ruach*: God's living presence and creative breath. Nevertheless, as I noted earlier, the divine *ruach*, which behaves like a woman in labor, was progressively subjected to the patriarchalization of the biblical literature and Christian theology from the first centuries onward. *Ruach* is a female term in Hebrew. It became the neuter Greek *pneuma* and ended up as the Latin masculine *spiritus*. Finally it became the *Father* (of the poor) in the Western Christian liturgy.[146] Nevertheless, today we are recovering the prophetic wisdom tradition present in early Christianity. According to this tradition, says Schüssler Fiorenza, "the theology of the Christian missionary movement identifies the resurrected Lord not only with the Spirit of God but also with the Sophia of God. (This was possible because in Hebrew and Aramaic both terms are grammatically feminine and can also be interchanged with the Shekinah, the presence of God)."[147] In the new community women and men share in the new age of the Spirit; both share a capacity for prophetic preaching (Acts 2:17ff) and perform certain tasks for the benefit of the community (1 Cor 12:4). Through baptism women and men belong to the new order of the Risen Lord, in liberating Wisdom (2 Cor 5:17). They are "brought into glorious freedom as the children of God" (Rom 8:21).[148] In the new age of the Spirit it is this divine presence that gives wisdom and eloquence at the hour of persecution for the sake of Jesus and the gospel (Mk 13:11). Jesus himself is identified with the Spirit of God: "Where the Spirit of the Lord is, there is freedom" (2 Cor 3:17). Through him we "are being transformed into the image"—ever more glorious—of Jesus Christ, God's wisdom and power (2 Cor 3:18). Through baptism the new community begins the New Creation (2 Cor 5:17) and has a new life, reconciled in justice. The Spirit makes women and men spokespersons for Christ (2 Cor 5:20), and both act in the same power of the Spirit.[149]

Latin American women recognize the presence of this Spirit of God at the dawn of our history, but their spiritual journey is also a dialectic between death and life, crucifixion and resurrection, fear and hope. Amid conflict and opposing interests, women recognize that life is already present in death; the resurrection in the crucifixion; and fear need not paralyze but can be transformed into boldness through the Spirit.[150] The New Creation is anticipated through the conscious and committed action of the poor and oppressed, but this cannot avoid the period of painful birth. The divine presence is felt within this tension between death and life, oppression and liberation. Luz Beatríz Arellano observes:

Instead of allowing themselves to be trapped by fear, however, [women] live this situation in a dialectic of boldness, rashness, and weakness that becomes strength. Their weakness comes not from being women, but from being human beings who know that the life of their people is continually threatened and under attack. Thus women are not arrogant in their boldness. Their boldness leads them to move forward, transcend themselves, take on new things they have never undertaken before, but they are weak in the face of death-dealing attacks. Nevertheless, they do not become paralyzed, but march forward and believe with hope in a world that is new, just, and human: the promise of the spirit emerging, like wheat in the midst of weeds.[151]

Because of where they direct their energy, we can say that the popular social movements today, where many women are found, can be described as those that historically welcome the action of the Spirit of God. Consequently, they are currently the most favorable place for Christian spiritual experience. As Leonardo Boff and Clodovis Boff write, "the history of the struggles of the oppressed for their liberation is the history of the call of the Holy Spirit to the heart of a divided world."[152]

The Spirit of God enables women and men to act. Amid conflict it gives them strength in suffering. It transforms them to enter the New Creation, because women and men are called to form the new humanity in Jesus Christ. Thus men and women walking in the Spirit must take account of their differences without this leading to antagonism. This means that this spiritual journey must favor the integrity of women as women and men as men, without diluting their special characteristics. There must be human relations between them as they try to build the New Earth and the New Creation. So Latin American liberation spirituality cannot propose any current version that suggests that women should change into *men*, in the way that patristic androcentric spirituality proposed. It can no longer tell women to become liberated men as a route to spiritual fulfillment. Women will not fulfil themselves by becoming *free men*.

These androcentric proposals, usually made by clergy who are celibate, must be radically modified through fruitful dialogue with women.[153] As I have repeated, it is not just a matter of changing the grammatical gender, but of adopting a *non-excluding epistemological position* in theology, and in particular, in the relations between men and women. This position must be adopted in the same way we approach questions of class and race. It is not the poor who exclude the rich, it is not the black and indigenous races who exclude the white, and it is not women who exclude men. The contrary is the case. Theological reflection must eliminate this hierarchical view of humanity. Here I note the observation of Rosemary Radford Ruether on the sexism of the dominant consciousness reflected in androcentric language: "Language is the prime reflection of the power of the ruling group to define reality in its own terms and demote oppressed groups into invisibility. Women, more than any other group, are overwhelmed by a linguistic form that excludes them from visible existence."[154] Truly liberating spirituality should call into being what does not exist so that it may be.

Nevertheless, the special features of Latin American women's spirituality are still in the process of maturing. Luz Beatríz Arellano recognizes that "One thing is clear: it is impossible to come to a definitive conclusion about the new women's spirituality."[155] Still, we can distinguish certain elements. Tereza Cavalcanti points out three stages through which women seeking liberation, including control of their own lives and spirituality, pass. The first stage is bitterness and indignation as they become aware of the centuries of personal and social oppression. In the second stage they start to value themselves and recover their self-esteem and they take part in the various liberation struggles of the popular social movements. In the third stage they recognize the commitments, claims, and rights of women as women in defending and creating life, in the creation of mutuality, and the rebuilding of a humanism that accepts human differences.[156]

This process takes place in the spiritual journey of many women. So it needs to be seen in collective terms. Consuelo del Prado stresses women's commitment to themselves and the whole community in the development of a spirituality that expresses their own special characteristics. As well as strengthening women, this task enriches the spiritual life of our peoples.

Christian spirituality is deeply enriched when we develop the gifts received from the Lord. We have received and been enriched by a wealth of spirituality which is born in our poor believing community and is nourished by the testimony of disciples such as those born each day on this continent through the experience of following Christ.

We have something of ourselves to give to the Christian community. . . . We would do well to make use of our own spirituality and theology, that which flows from those whom we have called the "masters of spirituality," much in the same way the book of Proverbs advises: "Drink the water from your own cistern, fresh water from your own well."[157]

So, rather than defining Latin American women's new spirituality, we can point out certain features of a shared spiritual journey.

The Cry for Life

From the perspective of Latin American women, we cannot speak of a spirituality of suffering. But we can speak of the meaning suffering acquires within a particular spiritual experience. Del Prado writes that "women of the poorer sectors suffer and weep much over their situation. They live in an estranged world."[158] Suffering is not wanted by God. It is caused partly by the selfishness of our own human condition, but above all by the internal logic of the present structures that produce death and inhumanity. Del Prado continues:

There are many women in the poor sectors who . . . go from their own experience of poverty and need to serve the community, often through their commitment to organizations set up to help others. Living this way gives them a new sense of the God of Life because it demands that they give up their individualism for the good of the community where they feel they are worth something and their lives and experiences are appreciated. This is what is meant by the living God's call to life in abundance.[159]

The Spirit's presence and activity—which makes all things new, re-creates life, and calls us to life—is strongly in evidence in women's spiritual experience.

Comfort and Joy

When we say there is joy in women's spiritual experience, this does not always mean well-being and lack of worries. As Arellano says, "Joy accompanies the people's journey; we can always celebrate it when life overcomes death, when justice overcomes injustice, when women find their place in society as men have."[160] Joy is there when suffering is shared, in the mutual support of the poor and oppressed, and in bearing sorrows together to transform them into happiness and hope.

As del Prado points out, "The joy that conquers suffering, that does not buckle under pain, persecution, hunger, death, and martyrdom, lives on in a resurrection spirituality that comforts the sad and makes the happy reflect."[161] This is an evangelical joy that celebrates the *cause* of our joy even in the midst of death and oppression.

Courage and Love of Mercy

Strength is a typical feature of the vital breath of the Spirit. This is not a male force but a characteristic of women. I mean the action that passes from fear to strength and boldness. This is what gives women their enormous capacity for resistance. "In solidarity and service, Latin American women are forging a courage that will allow them to keep going, in spite of poverty and suffering, in their struggle for life and love."[162]

The love of mercy is also a fruit of the Spirit, and love casts out fear. Indeed, the greatest love is to give your own life so that others may have life more abundantly (Jn 15:13). This evangelical quality is a deep part of women's lives. It is a love that takes up the desires of the poor and oppressed; it commits itself to the transformation of human misery. It makes women break with fear and self-disparagement. They break with their history of personal humiliation to set out on the path of liberty, their own spiritual journey in solidarity with other women and fellow pilgrims.[163]

Solidarity, Hope, and Generosity

The Spirit generates communion and sustains the community inside and outside the church. Communion and solidarity are salient points in women's spiritual experience. "Opening ourselves up to communion," says del Prado, "is a great calling, our highest aspiration; at the same time it is a challenge. . . . Only in community can we overcome the fear that clings to our life. Only in communion will we be able to live out the solidarity to which the poor and Christ call us."[164] Nevertheless, solidarity requires a special emphasis in the relations between women themselves. It must strengthen women's struggles as women and not just in view of the poor masses as a whole.

In a context where the reality is often a source of discouragement, hope and generosity become very important. The presence of women makes people see that a new order is possible in justice and solidarity. Hope is not an evasion of a commitment to the reality of massive suffering but an anticipation of the victory of life. "Hope in the resurrection in no way means escape from present reality but, rather, it means a deeper involvement in the struggle against death,"[165] because God's plan is to bring history to its fulfillment. While this is happening, women are called to a commitment that is both effective and generous. Full liberation is a gift of the God of goodness and mercy, but for it to happen requires the active participation of women and all the oppressed.

Indignation and the Body Restored

Perhaps it is surprising that indignation and rage form part of feminist spirituality, but it should not be. Feminist spirituality is a radical opposition to evil and sin; it rejects machismo and sexism because they oppose the justice and compassion of God. Women's ancestral oppression in the church and society should unite both men and women in indignation at this injustice so that it becomes effective solidarity. An understanding of Christian love "does not need to deny our hurt and anger or to cover up the injustice and violence done to women in the name of God and Christ."[166] The androcentric perspective regards this rage with suspicion, but there is nothing suspicious about it in women's spiritual experience as those who suffer the violence. Here we must emphasize the importance of *bodily integrity* in women's spiritual experience. As Tereza Cavalcanti says, it is not just a question of whether women have more freedom of bodily expression for their feelings, affections, sorrow, and pain.[167] Something more fundamental is at stake: women's bodies, their inner and outer life, their flesh and spirit, their guts and their mind, that is to say, their integrity as sacraments of God's mystery. Women's bodily integrity mediates God's mystery, and women's bodies are not alien to the church's spirituality as the body of Christ.[168]

Martyrdom and Ecumenism

Latin American women's spirituality is a spirituality of martyrdom. Because of their commitment to justice, peace, and the life of the poor and oppressed, countless women suffer persecution, rape, mutilation, and torture. In the power of the Spirit many women have borne witness with their lives to God's tangible presence, urging history toward liberation and justice. Women's martyrdom is twofold: they give their own lives, and they suffer anguish at the torture, disappearance, and murder of their children, lovers, comrades, and friends.[169]

Women's spirituality is one of solidarity and community. So they try to overcome social and sexual divisions and also divisions arising from the patriarchal church. Schüssler Fiorenza points out that,

Such a movement of women as the people of God is truly ecumenical insofar not only as it has in common the experience of patriarchal ecclesiastical sexism but also as it has as its central integrative image the biblical image of God's people that is common to Jewish as well as Christian religion.[170]

Even beyond the church there is an ecumenical spiritual experience in which women claim their rights and dignity, even though this may not be put in religious terms. The Spirit is present in their work to eradicate their own suffering and that of the poor masses, and they are inspired by the vision of a new earth with abundant life and sufficient goods for the whole of humanity.

Finally, I must stress the enormous importance of Mary the mother of Jesus for Latin American women. Mary is the paradigm of faith, prayer, and solidarity with all the oppressed and all women on earth. As Arellano notes, "We contemplate her as the new woman, the liberated woman, prophetess of the God of the poor, who surrendered her womb and her whole life to the realization of God's liberating plan in history."[171] Mary is important to women's faith because "this strong women is an example of so many others who, weighed down with children and pain, also bear the cross of the poor."[172] Poor women identify with her because they share the same hope and the same language as women. "A woman of the people, a believer and mother," says del Prado,

> Mary becomes for us a companion on the road in following her Son. So it is that we are taught the piety of Mary which is so deeply rooted in our continent. We can reclaim her name for our spirituality; in the best sense of the word, our spirituality is Marian.[173]

Latin American women's spirituality is difficult to pin down in theoretical categories. We are at the limits of human language and sometimes what we mean can only be expressed through gestures and symbols. It is a deep experience of freedom, which women are only now beginning to put into words. After centuries of demeaning colonial experience we recognize with del Prado that

> the quality of our spirituality may increase with the depth of our experience of freedom. . . . These are women who are joyful in spite of the suffering which cannot dry their fountain of joy. These are humble women who are open to community from their own experience of solitude, and who enrich it with the gifts they

have been given freely and who learn to give freely what they have received. These are women who are responsible in their roles in history and have discovered the value and the efficacy of the unconditional. Women who are warm, welcoming, and creative in the way they come to the Lord and to their brothers and sisters.[174]

Women's spiritual experience generates new attitudes, frees them from inner constraints, activates great potential, and makes them free to choose a different way.

The Church—Baptismal Community of Equal Discipleship

Ecclesiology is one of the most difficult areas from the perspective of women. In the tradition of the Roman Catholic church women automatically belong to the laity. But unlike laymen, who can rise to the ministry or the governing bodies of the church, women are excluded because they are women, in spite of the fact that they do a great deal of the church's practical work.[175] In response to this sexism women are trying to work out how they belong to the church in their own right, in what way they too are builders of the church, and what a church would be like that embraced all in participatory communion in accordance with the equality practiced by Jesus and the early Christian movement.

Obviously the church's organization is selective, with men in its ministry and government. This is supported by equally selective androcentric-patriarchal hermeneutic principles that exclude women.[176] Women want to supersede these models in order to contribute to a new way of being and understanding the church as a community of faith that shares the vision of Jesus Christ, the power of the Spirit, and the call to God's fullness beyond the sexual or racial characteristics inherent in human life. Women's contributions are critical and call for creativity and commitment. They are critical because they point out the contradictions and problems in the Latin American church. They are a call to creativity because, although women see themselves as following in the liberating line of Vatican II, Medellín, and Puebla, they recognize that this continuity is different because it distances itself from androcentric ecclesiological views and invites those who share the faith to experience the novelty of a liberating and equal community. Women's contributions challenge the whole church to explore new ways for the poor and oppressed, women and men, to find their place as genuine members of the church, like the early Christians. Women's contributions are a commitment because they know that the fate of the church in Latin America is closely linked to what becomes of the poor masses. Consequently, women see the necessary changes in the church in relation to the socio-political transformations needed to create a new society. The situation of women in the church must contribute to their advance in society; vice versa, women's gains in society must affect their position in the church. Women want to make the church become what it should be: an all-embracing community formed by the Holy Spirit, sacrament of the whole Christ, God's priestly people, the sign and anticipation of the fullness of God's reign in history.[177]

As I said in Chapter 3, women's thinking about the church arises out of their personal and collective experience of doing church work and in particular from their work in the base communities. Here women find room to understand themselves as church members with full rights. Because of their communal structure and way of understanding the ministry—as vested in the whole community and not just a select few—the base communities give women the opportunity to affirm themselves as active members of the church *as women*. Nelly Ritchie points out that "the data of our reality are telling us that a new ecclesiology is underway."[178] However, at the moment the contribution of women to the debate on women in the church is not to offer solutions but to point to new approaches. Women want to be part of the process of a new *ecclesiogenesis* taking place in Latin America, which will also involve them in the liberation process for themselves and all the poor. This is not to underrate women's theoretical contribution. But what is most important about women's reflection on the church is that for the first time in Latin American history, women have formulated what they themselves consider to be the church's mission and their own role in it.

This is a reflection which is an ongoing process. . . . We are not accustomed to thinking from our own standpoint and holding opinions in defense of our rights. . . .

However, new fields are opening up and it is therefore useful that the work we are doing should be an ongoing process, so that we may be ready to look squarely at our thoughts and have an in-depth dialogue—correcting each other in love and patience and, above all, being prepared to pursue humbly together, and with our comrades, a new course of action and reflection to which, with the acknowledgement of each other, we may contribute our efforts.[179]

In order to understand women's situation in the church today, María Clara Bingemer stresses the importance of Vatican II, both for its vision of the role of the laity—in which women are defined— and for its challenges to theology.

In the Council documents—especially in the dogmatic constitution *Lumen Gentium* — two ecclesiologies exist side by side: a legal ecclesiology and an ecclesiology of communion. Although the latter has been imposed on the former, through the central notion of the people of God to whom all Christians belong in equality and communion, the fact that the two ecclesiologies exist has an influence on other connected ecclesiological themes.[180]

Women as laity and as women is one of these themes.

The legalist view of ecclesiology derives from the church of Christendom. This is characterized by its institutional-hierarchical view of the church. "The legal-institutional dimension prevails over the dimension of mystery," says de Almeida.

Only the Catholic church possesses all the marks that Christ left his church. Only the Roman church can be identified with the mystical body of Christ; only the baptized not hindered by heresy, schism, or excommunication are members of the body of Christ. The church is centered on the pope and the curia. The bishops are the pope's vicars rather than independent pastors of local churches. The laity are passive objects of initiatives by the hierarchy rather than active sharers in the work of the church.[181]

In this model the actors in the church are the clergy, who are the church's proper leaders. This creates a pyramid with the laity at the bottom. The origin of this institutional-hierarchical model is usually seen in the birth of Christendom (around 313 C.E. when Constantine gave public recognition to Christianity, followed in 380 C.E. when Theodosius made it the official religion of the Roman Empire).

Nevertheless, as feminist research has shown, this view of the origin of Christendom does not take account of patriarchy, which did not arise with Christendom but culminated in it.[182] Consequently, women's exclusion goes back to the triumph of patriarchy over the early Christian tradition of equality, which took place in the late apostolic and patristic era.[183] It is true that both the process of hierarchicalization and patriarchalization reached their dogmatic peak in Vatican I with the definition of papal primacy and infallibility.[184] This resulted in the strengthening of the church hierarchy to the further detriment of women. Likewise, through this historical experience the church emphasized its condition as mother and teacher; the hierarchy possessed the hegemony of knowledge and thereby established the rigid distinction between the *teaching church* and the *learning church*. The laity, especially women, became religiously and legally dependent on the hierarchy. They became "pupils and apprentices needing the message passed on by pastors,"[185] as if they were incapable of exercising their own judgment and interpreting their own lives.

The church as a Christian institution sees itself in opposition to the world. The church is the perfect society (*extra ecclesiam nulla salus*), which brings salvation to the world; the world is the place of sin. The baptized belong in the sphere of salvation and grace through the habitual practice of the sacraments. This vision of the world and the church's role in it, says de Almeida, rests on the dualism between "nature and grace, natural and supernatural order, the baptized version of the polarity between sacred and profane, that exists in all religions."[186] This division leads to the separation of tasks. The clergy are in charge of the sacred sphere, and the laity of the profane. Men have authority, leadership, and church power; women are in charge of the private domestic sphere. Women are at the bottom of the ladder; they have the lowest theological, spiritual, human, and ecclesial significance.

This legalist ecclesiology endured in Vatican II in spite of its advances in other fields. Bingemer notes that

> in chapter 4 of *Lumen Gentium*, no. 31, the Holy Synod defines as laity "all Christians except members of the holy order and religious state established in the Church." That is, the laity are defined legally in a negative way: anyone who is not clergy or religious, anyone who has not been given a charism or vocation or special ministry in the church, and has only baptism.[187]

Nevertheless, as I pointed out, in Vatican II we also find an ecclesiology of *communion*, which gives priority to the notion of the people of God, the church as the universal sacrament of salvation and mystery of communion. Here women begin to rediscover their original vocation and place within the church.

The ecclesiology of communion tries to overcome the opposition between clergy and laity, religious and non-religious, teaching church and learning church, sacred and profane.

More and more today, particularly in certain recent theological tendencies, we see an attempt to overcome these oppositions. They are seen as possibly impoverishing or even reducing the breadth of spirit of the conciliar ecclesiology based on the all-embracing notion of the people of God.[188]

Latin American women's ecclesiological thinking is going in this direction. They are returning to the older biblical and ecclesial legacy where they find the basic outlines of what they believe the church community is called to be. Feminist theology often uses the same concepts as traditional theology but gives them new content. This is what constitutes the novelty of women's contribution. Although they use concepts belonging to the historical and theological legacy of the church, they rethink them from their own perspective and give them new meaning. Here are some of these concepts.

The Church as Mystery

The understanding of the church as mystery derives from its essential relationship with the mystery of Christ, its foundation. Women recover the original biblical notion of mystery to express God's eternal plan for humanity, the earth, and the cosmos, which was previously hidden but now is revealed in the life, ministry, death, and resurrection of Jesus Christ. This revealed mystery is what the visible church prolongs and manifests to all humanity. Instead of defining itself as the perfect society, the church sees itself as a saving and transcendent reality, visibly manifest in the traditions, services, organizations, rites, and symbols peculiar to different cultures. Thus, says Aracely de Rocchietti, "the Church has a function that it cannot abandon, as a sign and sacrament (a *particular* reality) and as an expression of the very mystery of Christ (the *universal* reality)."[189]

As a human and divine reality, the church orders itself according to God's plan for humanity; it is an anticipation and sign of the reign of God, which has already begun. At the same time it is God's instrument for imposing this reign upon history. The church anticipates the fullness of life desired by God for women and men, in particular for those who are deprived of life or whose lives are cut short. "The church is a mystery because it fulfils in a public and official way the plan of communion that God wants for all humanity. . . . It is where the call of the Spirit and the Gospel can be heard."[190] Salvation is offered by God to all humanity including those outside the church, because Christ's victory reaches the whole of history, impregnates it with grace, and leads it to its eschatological fulfillment. The church is the sacrament, that is, the sign and instrument of this salvation.

The Church, Community of Salvation

Christian faith states that God's restoring action in the world has been offered to women and men through the incarnation of God's eternal word. Jesus Christ did not offer this to individuals but to persons in a community, within which distinctions do not exist (Gal 3:28).[191] Discipleship of Jesus becomes mutual responsibility for women and men to show solidarity and do justice in a community of faith. Nelly Ritchie says that

Those who gather around the purpose of the God of life constitute, and actively take part in, a community. Those who respond to Jesus' invitation and follow him are the company of his associates. Those who with one mind and heart wait for the fulfillment of the promise that they will not be alone as they face the struggle are those who receive the power and dynamism of the Holy Spirit, and this makes them active participants in this new reality, this new way God has of being present in the world.[192]

The New Testament term expressing this experience is koinonia — communion, closeness, sharing in something held in common, solidarity. This word, continues Ritchie, "also translates an attitude: one does not enter into a relationship of dependence and passive acceptance, but one enters the sphere of creative communication, of common interests, purposes, and efforts."[193] Thus the community is the fundamental reality where we experience intimate union with the God of life, Jesus Christ, and the Holy Spirit, the divine wisdom-giver of all goods. In this vision of the church "word, sacrament, mission, and service to the world, especially the poorest, constitute the basic theological supports of the Christian community."[194]

The Church, the Body of Christ

Unlike the legal view of the church, the new ecclesiology does not identify the male body of clergy with the body of Christ. It emphasizes the communal character of the church and Christ's all-embracing wholeness. The whole community, women and men, embodies the crucified and risen body of Jesus Christ. Members share in it in different ways but with equal responsibility and possibilities. The cohesion and internal unity of all ministries and gifts are based on the common experience of the life-giving power of the Spirit throughout the community and through faith in Jesus Christ, whose practice of equality has been ratified by God through the resurrection. The Spirit is given to the whole community without regard to sex or class. Equality is based on the fact that no one is preferred because God's justice has been manifested through faith in Jesus Christ for those who believe; now there is no difference (Rom 3:21-2). As Ritchie observes, the image of the *body* used in the New Testament by the apostle Paul tries to show the interdependence of church members: all depending on Jesus Christ. This organization of the church's being and doing is for the sake of its mission.[195] Consequently, this image cannot be used as an argument to legitimate the subordination of the laity to the hierarchy, or the subordination of women to men, or the subordination of the poor to the powerful. Christ's whole mystery, as New Creation, draws all humanity and the whole cosmos toward itself.

The Church, the People of God

The biblical and theological term *people of God* has influenced Latin American thinking about the church as a whole and also about the contributions of women. It indicates the fundamental equality and common dignity of those who have received the gift of the Holy Spirit. If we look at the term *people of God* in the Hebrew Scriptures, Ritchie tells us,

the biblical texts point toward the formation of a particular people, God's own, a holy people who can make known its own acceptance by the true God in its options in history.

This purpose, which in the Old Testament seems to be restricted to one race, is in fact a universal purpose. God reminds Israel over and over that truly belonging to God's people goes beyond race. The universal nature of this calling becomes explicit in the incarnate God. In Jesus of Nazareth is revealed the Messiah who continues to create and recreate his own people from among all peoples.[196]

God makes a covenant with the whole people (Dt 29:9-17) and includes both men and women. Hence, sharing in the divine election is not confined to a single race or sex. The condition for membership in God's project is accepting Yahweh as the true God and a commitment to respond faithfully to this faithful God.[197] The *qahal Yahweh* is identified with the New Testament *ekklesia*. "It is the summoned and chosen people united round a common faith and historical-eschatological project."[198] In the New Testament we see clearly Jesus' refusal to form an exclusive community and his firm solidarity with the poor and oppressed. Jesus' practice of equality subverts the existing oppressive structures. He forms a community where there is room for all people, particularly those suffering dehumanization and misery at the hands of evil forces. This automatically includes the subversion of androcentric patriarchal structures.[199] So women can occupy a prominent place in this community in their own right.

Likewise, in the primitive Christian movement, stresses Ritchie: "We find that equality in Christ is a basic thesis: man/woman, slave/free, Jew/pagan — all are viewed as persons. There is an attempt to live out the new humanity that has been announced. Thus we find women fully involved in the total ministry of the church."[200] In the early Christian communities women and men were equally able to hold positions of power, authority, and leadership. According to Schüssler Fiorenza,

All members of the community were Spirit-gifted people of God who had received the power and endowment of the Holy Spirit for the building up of the community. Different members of the community may receive different gifts and exercise different leadership functions, but in principle all members of the community had access to spiritual power and communal leadership roles. God's gift and election were not dependent upon one's religious background, societal role, or gender and race.[201]

In the early Christian community there was no room for hierarchical stratification in the newborn church, or for division of roles by sex.

But in this new community, the new people of God, women became progressively excluded as the patriarchy took hold of the institution. This process was consolidated by the Fathers of the church.[202] The clericalization of the Christian ministry and its appropriation by men was reinforced by the patriarchal socio-political context and the philosophical-anthropological dualism of the Fathers. For them, men were the paradigm of humanity and virility the symbol of the divine.[203] Women must either progress toward the *perfect man*, become male, or have no chance of belonging to the sphere of the sacred because, unfortunately, they continue to be women. Toward the end of the third century the question of the resurrection of women was of serious concern to some. Will women rise again as men?[204] As Schüssler Fiorenza notes the change that occurred in the second century

> was not a shift from charismatic leadership to institutional consolidation, but from charismatic and communal authority to an authority vested in local officers, who—in time—absorb not only the teaching authority of the prophet and apostle but also the decision-making power of the community. This shift is, at the same time, a shift from alternative leadership accessible to all the baptized to patriarchal leadership restricted to male heads of households; it is a shift from house church to church as the "household of God."[205]

From then onward the notion of the people of God as a key concept in the Christian experience is gradually lost. This brief summary partly helps to explain the positive and dynamic impact of Vatican II's recovery of the term *people of God* for the church's life today.

Nevertheless, we have to recognize that although Vatican II restores the centrality of the people of God and affirms the equality of all church members, such equality is in fact not possible for women in the present church structure. The communal current in conciliar theology opens new lines of thought about the church more as a mystery of communion than an institution; more as a community with a multiplicity of gifts and ministries than as a body in which the hierarchy govern the laity; more as a sacrament of God's saving plan for humanity than as the single perfect society that mediates salvation. But as María Clara Bingemer points out, we cannot ignore the fact "even in the conciliar text the dualism remains between hierarchy and laity, religious and non-religious."[206] And with few exceptions the distinction has been maintained between *teaching* church and *learning* church, especially in discussion of women in the church. *Lumen Gentium* (especially 18; 21:2; 31-32) gives rise to very real questions that cannot be ignored. How can we speak of the fundamental equality of all persons or in the name of the *whole* people of God, when in fact the document confirms the exclusion of women from "the sacred ministries" by appealing to Christ's *will*? Does the body of Christ express its wholeness through the exclusive mediation of men? How can we proclaim equality among Christians when important structural divisions are preserved? Jesus' practice of equality and the inclusion of women and the behavior of the early Christians give no support to the church's current exclusiveness.[207]

This makes it all the more important to continue exploring the implications of the term *people of God* so that the church may create a truly equal community of men and women summoned by God to experience, celebrate, and communicate God's plan for humanity and the whole earth: to make all things new.[208] In this way the church can become a sacrament of universal salvation and an anticipation of eschatological fulfillment.

The Church, Baptismal Community in the Discipleship of Equals

From the viewpoint of Latin American women the most important happening for ecclesiology has been the rise of the base communities, so important today in the Latin American church. This is a new way of being the church, *the church itself on a popular basis,* whose key membership consists of the poor and oppressed, who are emerging as new actors in the church and in history. The crucial characteristic of this new way of being the church is that it sees itself as "an all-embracing baptismal community, within which gifts are received and ministries exercised as services for the sake of what the church should be and do."[209] This is a new experience in which the church becomes aware of itself "from underneath, from among the poor of this world, the exploited classes, despised ethnic groups, and marginalized cultures."[210] This is the *resurrection of the true church*[211] or an *ecclesiogenesis.*[212] This new church gives rise to a new kind of organization. Bishops, priests, religious and laity, women and men set out together to experience God's compassion, justice, and goodness. They share an equal discipleship in the daily following of Jesus Christ and in seeking God's will in the power of the Spirit for the common liberation struggle.[213]

Instead of a polarization in the relationship between the hierarchy and the laity, here is a new model based on the relationship between the community and its ministries and charisms.[214] As Bingemer says, this new church is recovering the vision of the early church and in accordance with the true spirit of Vatican II:

> It is taking to its limit the priority given to the ontology of grace over any other distinction with the church. The gifts of the Spirit are given first place in the church, and the Holy Spirit acts upon the whole community and arouses different charisms to build the body of Christ. The church's ministry belongs to the whole church and not just to certain sectors.[215]

In this view the most important thing is the common baptismal calling. "Through baptism all are introduced to a new way of life: Christian life. So baptism is first of all a commitment to live life in the presence of the mystery of God's revelation in Jesus Christ. The choice of one state of life or another, this or that ministry or service in the church comes later."[216] This view transcends the dualism inherent in the legalistic ecclesiology that is still present in the church's post-conciliar organization.

Then the *laity*, a term used to designate women and non-ordained men, loses its meaning as part of the structure of the church. The term *laity* is superseded by a threefold *laicity* of the whole church. According to de Almeida[217] laicity in the church refers to the value of the human in relationships within the church; *laicity of the church* refers to the responsibility of all the baptized (and not just the laity) founded on an anthropology of grace, in relation to the temporal order, each according to their charism or ministry and in their own socio-historical context; and finally *laicity of the world*, that is, the recognition on the part of the church of the autonomous value of earthly realities. This implies overcoming ecclesiocentrism and replaces it with an ecclesiology of dialogue and ministry, in which the church is at the service of all, but especially the poor and oppressed. The church recognizes that it is not the sole depositary of truth but is open to the dignity and freedom of each individual, each culture, each historical situation, each political proposal, to welcome its original values and offer the word of the gospel.

Women can find their place in this model of the church. Because it is based on charisms and ministries, women share in it as active members at all levels. Women are bearers of the gospel and equally responsible for the church's mission according to the charisms and ministries they receive from the Spirit. In this new experience, Bingemer says,

> the last word is not that of this leader or that, this boss or that, but the word of the Spirit itself, passionately sought in dialogue and discernment. Likewise, in such a church one part of the community should not be subordinate, passively carrying out the orders of others. All must be active and responsible in a single common project. All will be full participants in a community of service, in which different services and ministries are carried out for the benefit of all.[218]

This model of the church is beginning to exist amid the suffering and hope in Latin America. It recovers the central vision of the Christian movement initiated by Jesus Christ and makes the church a mystery, a community of salvation, body of Christ, and new people of God. On the road to its eschatological fulfillment it anticipates in history the New Creation in Jesus Christ.

Sharing in a common liberation process, in the struggles to build a new society and in a new sort of church gives rise to a new ecumenism among those who come from different traditions — Protestant evangelicals and Roman Catholics, Christians and non-Christians. This is an ecumenism from below. Christian women from different traditions know, as Nelly Ritchie points out, that

> We must uncover within ourselves all our potentialities and help one another in this task of giving birth to all the fruits of this painful childbirth, which has meant, and for many continues to mean, letting our voices be heard, not being seen as a "threat" but as a force bringing about new realities.[219]

Mary, Prophetic and Liberating Woman

We cannot trace Latin American women's spiritual experience or understanding of faith without referring to Mary, as a woman, mother of Jesus, and above all as "a 'worker' in the harvest of the Kingdom, an active member in the movement of the poor, as is Jesus of Nazareth."[220] In the base communities Mary is seen in terms of commitment to the restoration of justice and the affirmation of hope. She gives new meaning to the existence of the people of God, because in her own person she ratifies God's compassion and power to turn the suffering of the poor and oppressed into joy and abundance. Women's thinking has contributed new dimensions to Mary because of her participation in the movement promoted by Jesus.

The prophetic proclamation of the Magnificat, which the New Testament text places in Mary's mouth (Lk 1:46-55), has become a key source for the spiritual journey and practice of Latin American women. As Tereza Cavalcanti says, "in liberation theology Mary has become a symbol of hope, which nourishes the people on their way."[221] Liberation theology from the perspective of women is now beginning to examine the figure of Mary in accordance with its own theological criteria for women's liberation. Current work does make certain key feminist points about the option for the poor, but it still moves in the context of the classical androcentric division between *the feminine* and *the masculine* and affirms Mary to be the feminine dimension of God.[222] Nevertheless, in recent years there has been a conscious effort to overcome the androcentric norms of traditional mariology.

Criticism of Traditional Mariology

An ancient tradition in Latin America venerates Mary more in her role as Jesus' mother (mother of God), virgin, and mistress of heaven than in her own person as a woman. In fact, in the history of the Latin American church this tradition has been unable to eliminate the predominant *machismo* in our culture. There is a convergence between the great reverence for Mary and the *machista* tendency of Latin American culture, which the church itself has also helped to maintain. The theoretical and practical correspondence between these two phenomena is not accidental. On the contrary, Mary has been presented as the best representative of women's *nature*. As such she symbolizes what women's deepest aspirations should be. In this sense mariology, like other theological disciplines, can be a source of either oppression or liberation. María Clara Bingemer points out that Mary has been proposed to women as a model to be followed, but the image of Mary has been that of traditional mariology, which "often shows a figure of Mary that does not promote women's liberation, but confirms and continues their oppression."[223]

There are two principal features of the traditional mariological model. First, there is the image of Mary as obedient and passive, resigned and suffering, humbly dedicated to domestic tasks in accordance with the *role* that is naturally hers in the private sphere. This figure of weakness and submission, of all the "typically feminine" virtues, becomes a symbol of the subordinate position women should occupy in the church and society. Second, there is the exalted and idealized image of Mary as the supreme symbol of purity and virginity, which neutralizes her human integrity and her sexuality as a woman. This timeless image represents the values the patriarchal view ascribes to women.[224] Both these features are supported by an androcentric anthropology, whose basic proposition is women's subordination to men,[225] and both are prejudicial to women's human integrity.

According to Ivone Gebara and María Clara Bingemer,

> Traditional Mariology speaks of Mary in "feminine" terms, idealizing her on the basis of certain qualities said to be feminine, a determination which is made from a male viewpoint. Thus Mary is "retrieved" by this traditional anthropologico-theological vision and goes on to justify it insofar as she is a product of that vision. So Mary, mother of Jesus, mother of God, as presented by the androcentric and patriarchal world, far from provoking conflicts, actually strengthens the cultural foundations of that world to the extent that she also becomes its great Mother. So we can understand the problems the leading figures of the partriarchal religious sytem have with re-readings of the life of Mary.[226]

This traditional image of Mary has been questioned by women active in the base communities and the popular movements. Women's new awareness of themselves as active members in their own right has led to a different view of Mary in terms of women's liberation and the liberation of the poor.[227]

A mariology that stresses women's *feminine nature* in its primary role as virgin, wife, and mother dependent on men has gradually ceased to express women's experience of faith and spiritual pilgrimage. For women who have begun to take charge of their own lives and destiny, the traditional notion of Mary is more a source of perplexity than a motivation for the liberation struggle.[228] Thus criticism of classical mariology and the need to develop a new theological discourse about Mary were required by women's own experience of the liberation struggle.

Mary's Liberating Features in Women's Thinking

We should note two points. The first is the fact of the church base communities as an expression of the church of the poor. Their context is one of oppression, conflict, struggle, resistance, and hope, and this is the starting point for women's thinking about Mary of Nazareth. The Christian communities recognize themselves in Mary's experience, and she encourages them to be faithful to the God of life. As Gebara and Bingemer point out, the church base communities find that

> conflict was always latent throughout Mary's whole experience, as the Gospels narrate it. She went through a "different" and unique kind of gestation and gave birth in the midst of the strains created by the Roman occupation force, far from her own land and relatives, an exile and uprooted with her newborn son. She was a follower of this same son in his project of forging a Kingdom, and then her son fell out of favor with the religious and civil authorities of that period, and she became the mother of the one sentenced and crucified. Thus Mary represents the people faithful to God, bearing oppression and persecution so the Light may shine and liberation may become reality.[229]

Mary's attitude is repeated today in that of the poor Christians in the base communities. This attitude does not deny reality and is not blind to God's self-revelation in it, but takes it seriously and actively shares in faith in the God of life. This connection between Mary and the base communities is central to Latin American women's thinking about her. Mary is thought of not as an object of worship but as an active participant in liberation processes.

The second point is women's return to liberative scriptural sources and traditions. Latin American women's thinking about Mary is aware of the difficulty pointed out by Kary E. Børresen in the doctrine of Mary and its biblical basis. "The main problem with Catholic discourse about Mary is the disparity between the biblical data and the doctrinal interpretation put on it."[230] In Latin American popular devotion Mary is seen more in terms of the church's teaching about her than as the living figure in the New Testament text. Tereza Cavalcanti recognizes that "there is a gap between popular devotion and the New Testament biblical sources."[231] This gap is gradually being closed by new hermeneutic tools for reading the Bible. Cavalcanti observes that when the church rereads the Bible in dialogue with life a new figure of Mary emerges, one that is prophetic and liberating, committed to the struggle for justice, faithful to her God and her people.[232] Mary is identified with the interests of the poor and oppressed, and her own experience is of a God who is on their side.

Now the figure of Mary cancels the model of the passive woman submissive to man. Instead, there is a new vision of her as a person active and committed to change. The emphasis is on her historical responsibility, together with the other women who shared in Jesus' movement and the beginnings of the first communities. Gebara and Bingemer go into great detail about this.

> The elements highlighted in the New Testament's understanding of Mary are thus very different from those which have been put forth in traditional piety's view of Mary and which had led generations of Christians to venerate her as that humble and obedient woman, submissive to men and to the structures of her time. It is the former, the Mary of the Gospels, on whose lips is placed the Magnificat, God's program for the messianic era; it is that Mary who does not hesitate to leave her house or to contradict her son (see Mark 3:31-55), who remains at the foot of the cross to the end and in community with the emerging church; it is that Mary who is seen as a colleague, reference point, and symbol by women from around the world who are rediscovering that they have their own identity and a mission in society and church.[233]

In this view the stress is not on Mary's individual virtues but on her solidarity with the common project to create a new order. Mary constantly says yes to the God of life and no to an unequal socio-religious order that sacrifices human lives and condemns the majority to a subhuman existence.[234]

Women's thinking about Mary gives great importance to her relationship with the reign of God, seen as a collective happening. She is not seen exclusively in terms of her role as mother of Jesus but in relation to God's reign that is bursting into history through the creative power of the Spirit. For Gebara and Bingemer the concept of the reign of God is fundamental because "it includes God's deeds on behalf of men and women throughout the ages, deeds that are signs of the saving activity of this same God in the history of human-kind."[235] They point out that God's reign cannot be thought of solely in terms of christology, because this dilutes "what is specific to the female way of living and proclaiming the Kingdom."[236] The sense they give to the concept of God "goes beyond the person of Jesus. It extends to the whole of his movement in which both men and women were active participants."[237] This broadening of the concept, they say, makes possible a new and different mariology.

It can provide the basis for reading Mary's actions in the various images she assumes in scripture and tradition, as well as in particular traditions, as actions that bring signs of the reign of God to the fore, concrete actions that make the presence of salvation in human history manifest. . . . Mary announces the Kingdom, like Jesus and so many other men and women. Every action of Mary, of Jesus, of the prophets, apostles, disciples, male and female, converges toward the Kingdom, toward this way of being reborn in the midst of the old human race.[238]

These observations appear to indicate that these two writers want to make the nature of the reign of God less christocentric and more human-centered. This is in order to lessen its possible andro-centric patriarchal bias and also to offer a basis for women's experience of the divinity as represented in Mary and the activity of women in the early Christian community. Mary is the paradigm both as a woman and member of the people. Nevertheless, Marian theology should not lose its fundamental relationship to Jesus Christ, in whom the salvation of God's reign becomes a tangible reality. Otherwise mariology acquires an independence that is not in accord with the New Testament texts. We should also note the tendencies to give Mary a redemptive character, corresponding to that of the Christ. All this goes to show that it is necessary to do more work on the relation between mariology and christology in the Latin American context.

Another liberating feature that women in the Christian communities find in Mary is her motherhood. For poor women Mary is not a heavenly creature but shares their lives as a comrade and sister in struggle. Her solidarity and prophecy become a program for these women and the communities themselves.[239] Mary's experience of fertility through the work of the Spirit becomes a source of inspiration for many women as it enables them to rediscover their own dignity. Mary's motherhood from the perspective of women acquires a sense of profound solidarity, friendship, and sympathy strengthening the relationship of mothers with their children and each other. Margarida Luiza Brandao stresses that this friendship "opens the way to understanding what is new; it makes women feel solidarity in the struggle for justice and against all forms of violence and discrimination."[240] Because solidarity and friendship are also features present in the social movements and the communities in which the women take part, Mary's motherhood is seen in terms of close collaboration between God's saving work and the painful gestation of the New Humanity.[241]

Finally, I must mention how fruitful the religious experience of the Latin American people is in regard to Mary. She acquires countless faces and special features, which are linked to history and the symbolic cultural world of the ancestral peoples. Nevertheless, as Gebara and Bingemer point out, the multiplicity of names and characteristics "are all the face of Mary, simultaneously a 'projection' of the suffering face of the people and of a yearning for the restoration of life."[242] Although not all Marian devotions lead people toward their own historical responsibility and not every vision of Mary contributes to the human integrity of women, there is a rich tradition of Marian piety that needs to be explored, for example, Our Lady of Guadalupe and other important figures in the history of Latin American religious experience. Gebara and Bingemer's book, *Mary, Mother of God, Mother of the Poor*, makes an important contribution to this work. Just as we have begun the historical reconstruction of the origins of Christianity from the perspective of women, these two writers are proposing "a feminist reconstruction of popular Christian traditions, a work that must be undertaken courageously in Latin America."[243]

7

Other Themes in Latin American Feminist Theology

Now I would like to look at other areas into which women's theological thinking has ventured—areas deriving from the historical experience of Latin American women. I have chosen to group them under a general title, not because they are insignificant but because they have not yet been dealt with at any great length. This is the case with popular devotions; the theme of integrity, goodness, and beauty; and also Christian ethics from the perspective of women.

I am aware that there are other fundamental aspects that concern Latin American women, who want to reflect on them in the light of faith. For example, the themes of pleasure, the body, the eucharistic dimension of the female body,[1] the sacraments, and others all need more work. The absence of more systematic thinking on these important topics does not indicate weakness in recent Latin American feminist liberation theology. On the contrary, it only goes to show what promising fields are waiting to be explored. Here I will consider only the three areas noted above.

Women and the Theme of Popular Devotion

Popular devotion is one of the most challenging fields for theology from the perspective of women. The religious experience of poor Christian women moves in a world of symbols, which need to be examined. This is necessary in order to identify in their religious practice the crucial points of their experience of the faith, cultural identity, collective memory, desires for the future, and great capacity for resistance. We must also look at the tendencies in popular religiosity that are not helpful for solidarity, conscious organization, and the achievement of human integrity desired by oppressed women. Although popular devotions express liberating impulses that have helped the poor masses in their struggle to survive, especially when they are expressed in the language of resistance, it is also true that this same popular religiosity contains elements that legitimate submission to the oppressor. Because this environment has been basically patriarchal and *machista*, it is not surprising that women's religious expression also contains these elements.

The whole area is full of complexity and has not been much investigated by women.[2] But it has great potential because it not only contributes to a particular cultural identity but expresses in its symbolic language and behavior the course of women's resistance and struggles. What is needed is a collective reappropriation of Latin American women's religious experience with a view to rebuilding their human integrity. I want to indicate the basic features noted by women in their work on this theme.[3]

Women's religiosity is not separate from the rest of their lives. It is one of the dimensions that gives meaning to their whole life. It is a special way of experiencing the presence of the sacred in daily life. Popular religiosity embraces the whole of life and therefore is concerned with conception, birth, struggle, and survival.[4] Popular religiosity is not confined to matters directly relating to Christian doctrine as defined by Western theology; instead, it is a vision of the cosmos, a particular way of apprehending reality, of being in it, and intervening in it. It is a way of understanding life in terms of the ancestral cultures, Christian faith, and of a historical situation of oppression in which hope of liberation is also present. So it is closely bound up with the ways in which women live their daily lives, their particular way of looking at life and faith; it cannot be separated from their historical situation and cultural identity. Popular religiosity embraces all this in a single whole.[5]

As Aurora Lapiedra points out, it is important to see how all these things are related.[6] For example, a key point in the popular vision of the cosmos is the harmony it establishes among nature, people, and God. Nature is seen in terms of the earth and agriculture, and at the same time as the source of life, which governs the relations between men and women and of both with God. In this view the relations between the sexes have to do with nature, the human community, and the divinity.[7] In the context of popular religious experience women have a primordial role because their link with the earth constitutes the basis for understanding themselves, and it guarantees the principles of interdependence, defense of life, preservation of health, living in harmony with the earth, family and group cohesion—all of crucial importance to the people's cultural identity.

But when the reference point is not the land, as when people move to towns and urban areas, it is the women who seek new ways of reorganizing this experience. "Now it is not through the land itself, which they do not have," says Lapiedra, "but it is still in terms of symbols, which in their history derived from the land. This is what happens in the organization of festivals. Popular religiosity still has the function of creating harmonious relations."[8] Festivals, celebrations, and feasts, in which women have a crucial role, are of primary importance in keeping people together and maintaining the past, present, and future community. Looking at all the activities women engage in, let us note some features in their religious experience.[9]

1. Women's religious experience creates and maintains harmonious relations among nature, the earth, the human community, and God. In its content and ritual expression it displays poor and oppressed women's understanding of the Christian faith and the gospel in terms of their own historical circumstances, their own symbolic religious code, cultural identity, and expectations.

2. This religiosity is primarily relational. Women help maintain the principles of mutuality, living together in harmony and group solidarity.

3. Women's religious experience is rooted in daily life and covers both the public and private spheres, the personal and the social. Hence the predominant relationship between men and women in their own culture embraces both spheres. However, their religious experience also incorporates the dominant culture's modes of relationship.

4. Women's religious experience involves the whole of themselves. They speak with their hearts, bodies, and their whole being. In the popular world there is no split between understanding and feeling, as if they were two separate and opposite faculties. Both operate together in a peculiar kind of consciousness.

5. Women's religious universe is permeated by the fundamental values of fertility and abundance, which express the longing for a life as it should be. These values become a criticism of scarcity in daily life as it is.

6. Both in symbolic expression and in ethical rules life has deep significance in women's religious experience. Countless gestures of

solidarity and mutual support between women and the communities express their resistance to everything that threatens this life and the firm belief that life can and should be different.

7. Women are the main transmitters of religious, cultural, and social values accumulated by a people throughout its history. Women consolidate cultural identity and contribute to the safeguarding of the people's collective memory. There is an emphasis on the general values women transmit, but the memory of their own struggles and history as women is not always explicit.

8. Through their religious experience women have never lost the conviction that they will be restored to their full human integrity. In prayer, rituals, festivals, or their constant recourse to God, the Virgin, or the saints, women seek to affirm their own rights and dignity as women. This is part of their hope and expectation.

This is just a brief list of features in women's popular religion. Much more work remains to be done on the subject in Latin America. José Luis González makes the useful point that

> Respect for popular religiosity should not be an excuse for a naive idealization of it. It is riddled with contradictions. Not everything that appears to be associated with popular religious expression is functional for the popular culture; not everything in popular religiosity is helpful to cultural identity, solidarity, or the advance toward more human conditions of life.[10]

This is particularly true when we are speaking about women. Just as popular culture cannot remain untainted by the dominant culture, neither has it remained free from the patriarchal character present in our own ancestral cultures, colonial domination, and present-day *machista* capitalism. Future work on women and popular religiosity cannot evade this fact. There is a growing need for research, because there is a need to combat attempts to demolish the Latin American popular identity. We must eliminate all that contributes to weakening the transforming force of Christian faith. We must rebuild the cultural and religious elements that represent a genuine force for liberation and recover the religious currents that favor women's human integrity.

The Right to Integrity, Goodness, and Beauty

One of the most important aspects of the contribution of women to liberation theology is the principle that liberation is not total if it does not also emancipate women from their repressive attitude toward themselves. It is not enough to become aware of social repression and the struggle against it if this is not accompanied by the recovery of self-esteem and individual strength. From the perspective of women full liberation means the aspects I mentioned earlier, together with a recognition of themselves and their lives in all their integrity, goodness, and beauty.

Integrity means that a woman experiences and understands herself as a physical, psychological, and spiritual whole. It includes senses, organs, passions, emotions, aggression, rebellion, imagination, fantasies, and actions. Although I have already mentioned this aspect, I want to stress again that all these dimensions make up a woman's personality. This is her experience of herself and must be integrated. She need not feel guilt or shame if she reacts spontaneously, emotionally, sensitively, rebelliously, imaginatively, or even hysterically in a socio-cultural milieu that has established the male stereotype of a cold, calculating, rationalist, and conceptual harmony.[11] The task of building a self-image that consciously establishes new standards for valuing the many features of women's personalities has only just begun. It is a fascinating and painful process, first because it involves reappropriating ourselves and second because it requires a break with the norms of the dominant *machista* culture. The process is original and challenging.

When I speak of goodness or beauty I am not referring to two qualities possessed by some women or to certain cultural stereotypes. I mean something more fundamental: the intrinsic character of the self. A woman is good and beautiful in herself; she does not need to refer to androcentric archetypes of human perfection in order to legitimate herself. But are not these topics too trivial for liberation theology from women's point of view in Latin America? Isn't this pandering to feminist thought in Europe and North America? As María Teresa Porcile points out, they arouse "surprise and suspicion."[12] They are suspected of being a deviation from the main concerns of the Latin American oppressed women. Neither systematic theology nor any other theology has proposed that these questions should be addressed. Only feminist liberation theology has done so.

On the other hand, how can we say that women are good and worthwhile when they have a deep inner experience of being systematically marginalized? As Janet W. May observes, because of their marginalization women tend to despise themselves.[13] How can we say that a woman is beautiful in Latin America when Indian, black, and mestiza women do not fit the dominant stereotype of white beauty? Porcile goes on to say that "on a continent with so many faces of ugliness, injustice, poverty, and wretchedness, how dare we mention Beauty?"[14] In the Latin American context it is radical to speak of integrity, goodness, and beauty, especially when we are talking about oppressed women. Despite suspicions and uncertainty, the liberation theology done by women considers it necessary and urgent to affirm women's possession of goodness and beauty as their own.[15] Moreover, as we are speaking about a reality of oppression where there is no beauty but only misery and wasted bodies, we are also speaking about an inalienable right to an integrity women have been denied.

Further work with women has led us to see the growing necessity to emancipate their inner drives. This includes overcoming feelings of guilt, fear, repression, and bitterness, as well as the need to create networks for intimate communication, the development of confidence, mutual support, and reconciliation with our own feelings and our bodies. From the perspective of women, subjectivity is not at all superficial or a deviation from the struggle as a whole. On the contrary, it forms part of it. It is important because "women do not mobilize on the basis of a theoretical interpretation of their situation but because of very personal matters that affect their personal lives."[16] Women from different backgrounds in the liberation struggle all agree on this matter, even when they speak from different church, social, and political platforms.[17] They are affirming women's rights to personal integrity. This strengthens women's organizations and helps their self-recognition as women and as a social movement, which may obviously also flow into other social, ecclesial, and political movements, both close to home and further afield.

In the Latin American context when we say a woman is *good* or should be, the very expression is already supercharged with meaning. And this is not the significance women themselves have given it but one derived from the *machista* culture's views of women. Elisabeth Moltmann-Wendell's remark is illuminating here when she says, "In Christian experience and theological culture, being good no longer has a proper place. We are more familiar with the experience of being 'bad,' and of the theological language of being a sinner."[18] Generally speaking, women are only considered to be good when they conform to the image of mother, wife, and virgin. This stereotype has the disadvantage of not being realistic, because women are not good only insofar as they fulfill the tasks assigned to them by the patriarchal world. Yet because women internalize this model, when they do not fulfill these functions they feel guilty. They feel they have failed in life. As I said earlier, the goodness of women is not a moral quality but something more original and fundamental. This is what constitutes a woman's very self. This is good of itself because it is a creation by the love, compassion, and goodness of God.

Latin American women are reclaiming their right to be good. They know they are created by the divine wisdom. They are good in themselves and not by virtue of what they do in accordance with the reigning *machista* code. Because they are in the realm of divine mercy and goodness, they can produce fruits of life, justice, and goodness.

The experience of being good must be complemented with the experience of being beautiful. Here beauty does not mean the ideals of physical perfection created by men's imagination or the "beauty canons imposed by an inhuman consumer society."[19] According to María Teresa Porcile, beauty "has to do with the self; it is her self that makes a woman beautiful."[20] So in Latin America we speak of beauty as the "epiphany of the self," the display of what a person is in her own originality. This notion has profound biblical roots,[21] and is echoed in the taste and sense of beauty in the ancient Latin American cultures and current socio-religious experience.

The Latin American people are eminently sensitive to beauty. They perceive it in their cultures, even in their great suffering and hope, in the memory of their ancestral traditions, their songs, poetry, symbolic representations, words, and silences.[22] Beauty is deeply inscribed in the spirit of Latin American people. So, to contribute to their own epiphany they must explore it through liberating theological thought. This is of crucial importance to the theology done by women. It is important to speak of beauty precisely because women want to overcome the suppression of their self and end their condemnation to an inhuman life of injustice and subordination. That is why they want to transform the ugliness to which women and oppressed people have been condemned by those who create the norms of beauty and well-being at the expense of the misery and wasted bodies of the majority.

Liberation theology in Latin America must also recover the dimension of beauty for itself. As Porcile points out, "Theology must have an expression of desire, attraction, eros. This dimension will be combined with poetry and contemplation and also be prophetic and sapiential—a theology of play and free creation, capable of evoking God's mystery and human justice."[23] It will be a new theology, which will encourage us truly to reveal ourselves. Thus it will also be liberating. Part of this manifestation of the self is the vision of a new theology and a new reality where women "get the taste of justice" and men and women "weave the points of history," as we read in the poem below.

Prayer of Iztaccíhuatl

I have a silent skin
speechless eyes, love broken
My blood does not circulate
My spirit does not breathe
My heart does not dance

Sadness hurts
so does my hope
My eyelids weigh down
my soul
I am muzzled
    I am Iztaccíhuatl, the woman asleep

Popocatépetl!
Popacatépetl!
I want a hummingbird heart!

O gods, oppressors, murderers
you have ears to block out my pain
hands to bind me to the bed
a mouth to stop my protest
and feet to kick my children's home

    I will no longer bear it

Useless chiefs, charlatans
you have power and use it against me
call meetings to study my oppression
but devour me as the eagle does the serpent
and invoke the goodness of the murderous gods

You are my arrow's target

Mystery!
Mystery!
I want the spirit of fire
I want joy to run through my veins
And Popocatépetl swift with me
like a pair of running deer
my mouth to taste the savor of justice
and my body proclaim the pleasure of love
our hands weave the points of history
and the oppressor gods to go to hell

we are my people's hope
(Elsa Tamez, May 1979)[24]

Women's Liberation and Christian Ethics

Women's reflection in the field of Christian ethics begins as a theory preceded by commitments seeking to transform social and religious institutions that oppress them.[25] Their starting point is women's action for liberation opposing the present system as a *whole*. They have a "vision of a new world order, a new model of human life, not just for the Third World but for all humanity."[26] Christian ethics from the perspective of women does not try to reform the norms, virtues, values, and goals in force in present-day patriarchal imperialist capitalism. Thinking in terms of *reforming* or *improving* the existing order would mean keeping as our starting point the questions presented earlier: What has a woman to do in order to be *good*? How must she act in order to be considered morally acceptable? If an answer exists within the present situation, it will inevitably be given in terms of the moral coordinates operating within the system. Otherwise it would incur the sin of rebellion and pride.

On the contrary, one of the tasks facing women in the sphere of liberating Christian ethics is to criticize and dismantle the foundations of the present socio-religious order, which subordinates women. We must clear the way toward a new order whose primary ethical criterion is the affirmation of the fullness of life and the integrity of every human person. "The feminist struggle in theology," says Irma Janis Jordan, "is both a criticism of the myths and structures of society and the culture that oppresses women and of the theological myths and structures that join in this oppression."[27] So, in ethics women need to rethink all moral problems from the viewpoint of responsibility for others and themselves, and search for a historical alternative that enables them to leave the land of sorrow and set out for the promised land.[28] As Enrique Dussel observes, every system creates its reigning morality and sets up a collection of norms and behaviors describing the goodness or badness of actions in terms of its own system.

Any system of prevailing dominant practices (from Egypt or Babylon to Rome, the several Christendoms, or capitalist society) determines its established practices to be good. Its project (its end, its *telos*, its *beatitudo*, as the Latin theologians termed it) is confused with the "perfect human good" as such. Thus the norms that demand the execution of this project are "natural law." The prohibition, "Thou shalt not steal the private property of thy neighbor," for example, has been part of capitalism's "natural law" since the eighteenth century. The virtues of the project are now obligatory as the highest virtues of all.[29]

As in the case of property, the subordinate position of women and the legitimation of male superiority becomes natural law. So under this order, those who fulfill and adopt as central to their life the practices, norms, values, virtues, and laws of the system become worthy, meritorious, and just people praised by their peers. This explains why women are praised who diligently fulfill their functions as virgins, wives, and mothers and do the housework. Their acts are accounted *morally good* to the extent that they are in line with the established order.

In capitalist ethics the generator of life is capital and to it is owed respect and submission. Capital decides on the life and death of the immense masses of humanity. When capital becomes the supreme deciding factor in life, it becomes a fetish to which business and people must freely submit. But this takes from people their right to their own personality and their right to be protagonists in history. In this order the business sectors become the prototype of virtue and goodness, whereas the popular social movements struggling for an alternative order are merely the source of chaos, arrogance, and evil. Every effort to demand actual physical and spiritual life for the poor and oppressed is merely a perversion of the order through rebellion and pride; it is *unnatural*. This justifies repression, torture, massacre, murder, and condemnation to an inhuman life or even to death.[30]

The ethics of capitalism is wrong, and so are its theological and religious beliefs. For Ignacio Ellacuría,

> The intrinsic evil of capitalism is not seen until we see its effect outside the frontiers of rich countries who seek to export the evils of capitalism in many forms to the poor countries they exploit. It is not just the foreign debt or the exploitation of primary materials or the search for places for the developed countries to dump their waste, but also capitalism's profound dehumanization.[31]

The denial of vital necessities to the poor, the inhumanity to which whole countries are condemned, and the daily violence toward women and those who depend on them are the basis for our assertion that capitalism is a project of death. In feminist research Maruja González observes that "capital is interested in creating permanent conditions for its production and reproduction. This means it must guarantee the basic ruling power structures and will try to use women and make them function in its interests."[32] For example, capitalism is interested in maintaining the division of labor by sexes, in which domestic work is reduced to a merely biological category, when in fact it is an economic and social category. Many Latin American women think that because this function is theirs by nature they must make a bigger effort over and above the work done by men.[33] Present-day capitalism is interested in maximizing profits at the expense of women. Moreover, it is interested in reproducing and spreading the classic gender stereotypes in morality, custom, legislation, religions, and ecclesiastical structures. In the social, cultural, and religious orders it enthrones and maintains the hierarchical order of masculine and feminine models, racial division, and control over women's sexuality, reproductive powers, and work.[34] These, among others, are some of the characteristics that reaffirm the alignment of present-day capitalism with patriarchal structures.

Faced with the increasing deterioration of their lives, women have tried to create their own organizations. In these, women re-create their own values, struggle to overcome inequalities, and strive for social recognition. This struggle is a threat to capitalist patriarchal ethics. Often women run into opposition from leaders of traditionally male organizations. This is the case with the prohibition on trade unions among women workers in assembly plants and factories and the permanent hostility to women's unions.[35] In this case the *machismo* of the male trade unions converges with capitalist *machismo*. They distance themselves from women workers and weaken the strength of popular organizations. It is worth pointing out here that those who weaken the people's organizational strength are not the women but the actual *machismo* of the male trade union leaders.

These observations show us why women's thinking on Christian ethics is opposed to the present system as a whole and why women subscribe to a new ethic of fullness and wholeness of life. In Latin America the ethical demands of the gospel cannot be identified with patriarchal capitalist ethics, which nevertheless offer a parody of the gospel in the commercial world. But neither are the ethical demands of the gospel fully met in certain socialist societies that dehumanize women and maintain male superiority.

Beatríz Melano-Ccuch holds that the key reference point for a Latin American ethic is the reign of God.[36] Although her thinking is not explicitly directed toward the development of Latin American feminist theology, she does make a contribution to it. She says, "The good news of the reign of God is not a philosophical system, or a dogmatic economic strategy. Neither is it a dream. It is a human way of life that involves individual attitudes and behavior and the socio-political and cultural structures under which people live."[37] As a new proposal for action and liberating relationships, as a new lifestyle and an anticipation of fulfillment, the reign of God expresses theologically the longed-for new society. So the vision of the reign becomes the final ethical reference point of all Christian practice. It illuminates historical realities and is the way to read the signs that anticipate the New Earth and the New Creation. As an eschatological horizon, it is a criticism of every system that makes life impossible for the majority and all unequal relations that diminish human integrity.

The reign of God is the radical constituitive principle of Christian ethics and the root from which all ethical discourse must grow.[38] The reign of God is the fullness of life to which history, humanity, and the whole creation is destined. From the vision of God's reign, a new code of ethics emerges that articulates in terms of daily life its vision of physical, psychological, and spiritual wholeness for all humanity, both women and men. "The news of the reign of God," says Melano-Couch, "shows me that I am created by God to be free and also to be the author of my own destiny in his sight, not a slave to other human beings. . . . The news of God's reign tells me that I am destined for God, not for torture, or the death penalty, but for freedom, peace, joy, and fulfilment."[39]

Christian ethics is a basis for a new historical order where human life in all its dimensions is freely empowered.

The fundamental principle on which the new order is based is that all should have life and have it more abundantly (Jn 10:10). The historical experience of death, either through want and hunger or through repression, or through different kinds of violence, an experience that is so common in Latin America, shows the fundamental importance of material life as the first gift from which all else follows. This life must be filled out by inner growth and in relation to others, always in search of more life and a better life.[40]

Christian ethics from the perspective of women — in the context of the reality of death that presses upon women from all sides — sees itself as a commitment and responsibility for the defense and promotion of life. In Latin America today *life, liberation* and *human integrity* are the most fundamental and necessary principles emphasized by Christian ethics. They are required by the reality itself and are the only honest Christian response to it. To take life as the primary ethical criterion leads to many particular tasks devoted to the eradication of structures and realities that deny the poor and oppressed the means of life and exclude women from their right and duty to be active protagonists. God's reign, as a vision of the new world God wants for humanity, particularly the poor and oppressed, becomes the global horizon of all Christian behavior and the most fundamental principle of Christian ethics. The reign of God involves attitudes, behavior, and values both in private and in public life. The imaginative construction of new relationships between women and men and both with the earth; the creation of new meanings and equal values for gender identity; and the achievement of oppressed women's human and spiritual integrity are anticipations of the fullness of life promised by God for the whole creation.

Conclusions

My first aim has been to investigate and describe the principal characteristics of theological work done from the perspective of women in Latin America. I have tried to clarify what this work is doing, its aims and presuppositions, its method and content. Thus I have highlighted its internal methodological coherence, which until recently has been scantily explored. My reference point has been the formal contributions of the women themselves and other less systematic contributions.

Another aim of my work has been to describe the contributions made by women's theological work to the epistemology of Latin American liberation theology. I have indicated how this has to change when it incorporates women's experience and knowledge.

I have also noted that theology from the perspective of women is set within the field of liberation theology. This gave us our methodological tools (analysis, hermeneutics, and pastoral practice). But I have also shown the particular points and theories used by women in their thinking in accordance with the vision, interests, and desires for liberation of women who are oppressed. This has enabled me to identify the special features of this work done by women and outline what is particular to it, without abstracting it from its setting within liberation theology as a whole.

Throughout, I have pointed out certain provisional conclusions. I looked at the demands and challenges made from the perspective of women to theology, done by both men and women in Latin America. Certain omissions in the theologizing of women were presented more in terms of tasks and challenges than as limitations. Here I want to stress certain aspects I have tried to describe in this investigation and others that require further work.

Part 1 established the social and ecclesial context of a theological discourse, which is responding to the challenges presented by women's experiences of oppression and liberation. Although theology done by women sees itself as operating within liberation theology, it acquires certain particular features because of its own social position and hermeneutics: triply oppressed women in the process of liberation, interpreting their lives in the light of faith from their standpoint *as women*. Through their understanding of the faith, Christian women in Latin America are trying to describe Latin American and Caribbean women's age-old historical struggles, spiritual experiences, speech, and knowledge in order to contribute to the liberation of the suffering masses and their own liberation. The theology they do aims at gaining recognition as participants with full rights in the church and society.

Theology from the perspective of women incorporates what is *real* in the reality of human life into its thinking. Triply oppressed women are its starting point, and it uses the tools of feminist analysis to give an account of the situation of women. This has two important effects on theology. First, it criticizes and corrects liberation theology's initial androcentric and *machista* position; second, it generates a new way of thinking about faith starting from practical matters. In other words, it grants greater *realism* to theological discourse and returns basic honesty to what is *real*. Women's theological views deepen some of liberation theology's fundamental categories, such as praxis, oppression, liberation, poverty, life, faith, humanity, the earth, and its historical and eschatological becoming.

The theological perspective of women criticizes and demands the transformation of the present patriarchal structures in society, the church, and theology, as well as the mechanisms that cause the impoverishment and dehumanization of the oppressed masses under both present-day imperialist capitalism and white colonization. A theology that accompanies the struggles of the poor and oppressed cannot fail to point out the convergence and mutual reinforcement of these three systems today. Neither can it neglect or subsume women's expectations.

I paid special attention to Latin American women's awareness of causality. This awareness makes women see their whole lives and also the church's mission differently. Women want to create new ways of living together in society that enable both women and men to achieve human integrity. This awareness leads to a new, more inclusive behavior. It generates new theological ideas and theological discourse that are neither excluding nor reductionist, but equal and liberating. Women's contributions here have a strong effect on liberation theology, moving it away from its androcentric viewpoint, which splits up human life and relegates women to insignificance, toward a more all-embracing and relational view, which supports solidarity and justice among God, women, men, and the earth. Women's contributions affect both the method and the contents of current theology and show the possibilities that remain to be explored.

I stressed women's understanding of ourselves as *active participants* in history, the church, and theology. I discussed the relationship of our theology to traditional theology. Because traditional theology was created in the West and linked with the patriarchal system, this theology, from the perspective of women, is impositional, unilateral, one-voiced, and dualist; it stands with the conquistadors and colonists. Theology done by women has tried to overcome these failings and be more contextual and communitarian, in solidarity and relationship. It tries to be more all-embracing, plural and whole.

Part 2 focuses on the heart of my investigation. Here I explored and presented the methodology, presuppositions, and contents of liberation theology from the perspective of Latin American women. I described its characteristics and its special features in contrast to other theology. I paid special attention to what is new in its contribution to liberation theology in general.

Throughout I have noted matters that require more work and discussion between men and women and among women themselves. Various theological matters need to be reevaluated in our present context and reformulated so that theology can truly contribute to the abolition of the increasing suffering of the crucified peoples, among whom poor and oppressed women suffer most. The following points highlight certain questions still in need of attention.

• Some women theologians automatically affirm a quasi convergence between the vision of liberation of men and women theologians because both are doing liberation theology. Although they coincide in their option for the poor and in seeing the poor as primary for the understanding of faith in Latin America, they do not automatically agree in their view of women's situation *as women.* That is to say, the category *poor* does not *obviously* refer to the situation of triply oppressed women. The category *poor* often does not reveal the nature of women's oppression as women. Saying that women are included among the poor is too abstract to describe women's own oppression and leads to a partial and androcentric discourse. So the convergence of women and men doing liberation theology needs to be examined more carefully.

• Frequently the theological view of women gathers the experiences of women in various fields of activity in the church, politics, and society. But this merely describes the new things women are doing. These activities and commitments help to show how women have leaped from a naive individualistic view to a more critical and collective popular consciousness; the problem, however, lies in the failure to express these new activities explicitly in terms of new knowledge. So women's liberating activity acquires a fragmentary character, which does not contribute to theological reflection. Women's work for the survival of the poor and their own survival, their emancipatory activities in public and private, their commitment to justice and human integrity must be formalized theoretically in theological terms; that is, if women's activities are given epistemological value, they will become a constitutive part of theological knowledge.

This position requires us to recognize that today God's project also includes the lives and doings of women, and that this is the formal setting for theology from the perspective of women. By virtue of the essential relation between theory and practice, women themselves produce theology, create new content for it, and help to reformulate the theology that already exists. Therefore the perspective of women can be adopted by both men and women.

• The theology done by women is ambiguous in its formulation of women's interests and identity. The work of some women theologians makes use of androcentric categories because they base their work on traditional archetypes of the masculine and the feminine. This means that although they are clear about women's oppression through being poor, they lack the same clarity about their oppression *as women*. So there is a discrepancy between their discourse of equality when they are talking about class differences and a subordinationist discourse that maintains gender inequalities. The category of race presents fewer difficulties. This shows the increasing urgency of the need to incorporate feminist analysis into liberation theology. In the matter of reformulating gender characteristics, until now there has been recourse to the social sciences to answer questions about our identity as Latin American women. But the social sciences have their limitations, both in themselves and in the way they have been used in liberation theology. The social sciences look at global phenomena of social change and neglect personal and collective subjectivity. Here research into the field of Latin American liberation philosophy is useful because it engages with our own historical circumstances in connection with our ancestral cultures in order to clarify who we are and where we are going. This can be useful to our research because it has something in common with women's vision and goals, that is, the attainment of human integrity and our fulfillment as women.

• Anthropology has an important place in theology from the perspective of women. Although a dialogue with anthropology has begun, greater depth is necessary in order to establish more clearly our differences from the androcentric anthropological paradigm. For example, the changeover from a one-dimensional to a multidimensional anthropology has not been explained fully. The many dimensions of a person are not described in full, and therefore it is not possible to appreciate the process leading to a new way of looking at life. The field of theological anthropology offers great potential for the incursion of the perspective of women.

• Another important aspect that needs attention is the relationship of theology from the perspective of women to Latin American feminist movements. Although this theology grants priority to the experiences of the women in the base communities and the social movements (generally of mixed gender), it maintains an excessively critical distance from the feminist movements, which for the most part consist exclusively of women. Rather than weakening this theology's strength, greater involvement in these movements would certainly increase it. Encouraging membership in these movements does not have to be done in a naive way, but neither can women ignore them.

• In the field of biblical investigation, and christology in particular, I often find an extremely negative and sometimes simplistic view of the situation and activities of women in Jesus' time. While this emphasizes the liberating position Jesus adopted toward women, it diminishes the women's own initiatives and strength. Often rapid identifications are established between the situation of these women and that of women today due to the permanence of patriarchal structures, the imperialist power centers, and the historical continuity of women's subordinate position. This reduces the chance of establishing a link between feminist liberation thinking today and that found in the biblical context beyond the patriarchal texts. If today the struggle for liberation of oppressed women is the basis for liberation theology from the perspective of women, this same principle should be applied to biblical research and especially to christology. Hence the relation between Jesus and oppressed women can be reinterpreted and the great christological liberation themes reformulated.

• Finally, I should note the dialogue between theology from the perspective of women in Latin America and feminist liberation theology in the First World. I have already pointed out the characteristic attitude of dialogue, solidarity, and mutual support in women's theological work. As each represents a particular response to its own situation, in Latin America we prefer to speak of features or *particular traits* rather than convergences and divergences between the two theologies. The methodological and hermeneutic convergences are many and some are evident in this book. But the divergences are also enormous, beginning with our different historical and social reality and living conditions. In fact, this can lead us into an impasse, from which it is hard to see the way out, or to a sterile polarization, which makes dialogue impossible. Nevertheless, both theologies recognize their responsibility to the suffering of the poor and to the multiple oppression of women. They both want to contribute to the growth of the people of God and commit themselves to the attainment of justice, human integrity, and fulfillment for the whole of creation.

However, some first-world feminist positions disqualify liberation theology from the viewpoint of Latin American women because of "methodological weakness" and "limited feminist vision." According to these positions, the theology done by women in Latin America does not attain the systematic rigor required by all Christian theology. Consequently, it is no more than testimonial discourse, which may of course be listened to but which does not have credibility as *theology*. Two observations may be made about this view.

First, they cannot accuse feminist Latin American theology of methodological *under-development*, as its results clearly show otherwise. On the contrary, this theology demands a knowledge of its own channels to formulate an understanding of faith in terms of our own situation and as a response to it. Latin American women theologians are aware of the need to advance toward a way of thinking in line with women's vision. We recognize the gaps and realize that the internal methodological unity of our theology needs work, but we understand that this unity will not come as a result of intellectual activity alone. It is the fruit of a collective process of dialogue, consultation, and exchange among professional, pastoral, and popular theologians in order to agree about how to move forward. This process is slower than the process followed in the First World, which mainly advances in an academic environment. In the long run, however, it is much more effective because the feminist vision grows in breadth and depth.

Second, those who express these criticisms may articulate feminist epistemology coherently, but they are often ignorant of the global articulation of the social context. It seems their theology is barely affected by the enormity of women's triple oppression. They do not accept the theology done from the perspective of women in Latin America because it is not "sufficiently feminist." In this way they build walls that muffle the cries of poor women who refuse to lie down and die in the darkness of history. Furthermore, they fail to accompany the spiritual and intellectual development of their sisters, thereby vitiating the heart of their own position. Those doing feminist theology in the First World cannot deny the *causal* links for the impoverishment and inhumanity to which women in the Third World are condemned. The death and bare survival conditions these women suffer must affect them. Feminist liberation theology in the First World cannot relegate these realities outside its epistemological field or see them as irrelevant. It must incorporate them into its own work. Solidarity among *all* women on earth must activate all our physical and spiritual energies to anticipate today the gospel promises of fulfillment.

Consideration of these aspects, as well as others discussed in the body of this book, will give feminist liberation theology in Latin America greater power to accompany, illuminate, criticize, and activate the struggles of women for emancipation within the global liberation struggle. We know the present is hard, but the future belongs to us. Day by day we anticipate it in faith, with imagination and wisdom, from within the commitments we take to transform our present daily life.

Notes

1. The Irruption of History into Women's Life and Consciousness

1. For a long bibliography on the topic, see Pablo Richard, "The Theological Literature of Latin America," *Concilium* 199 (1988), pp. 76-89; see also an extensive bibliography in Juan José Tamayo-Acosta, *Para comprender la teología de la liberación* (Verbo Divino, Estella, Spain, 1989).

2. Gustavo Gutiérrez, *On Job: God-talk and the Suffering of the Innocent* (Orbis Books, Maryknoll, N.Y., 1987), p. xi; see also Gutiérrez, *A Theology of Liberation* (Orbis Books, Maryknoll, N.Y., 1988), pp. 9-10.

3. Gutiérrez, *On Job*, p. xiii.

4. Cf. Karl Rahner, *Foundations of Christian Faith* (Seabury Press, New York, 1978), pp. 119-20; Rahner particularly emphasizes God's self-communication, what the human creature's supreme action is directed toward, and the consummation of the individual's existence in God.

5. This principle is equally valid for a philosophy from the viewpoint of Latin America, according to Leopoldo Zea. See Zea, *Introducción a la filosofía*, 9th ed. (UNAM, Mexico, 1983), p. 13; Zea, *La filosofía americana como filosofía sin más* (Siglo XXI, Mexico, 1969).

6. M. C. L. Bingemer, "Third World Theologies," *Concilium* 199 (1988), p. 118.

7. Sergio Torres, "Dar-es-Salaam 1976," *Concilium* 199 (1988), p. 112.

8. Raúl Vidales, "Methodological Issues in Liberation Theology," *Frontiers of Theology in Latin America*, ed. Rosino Gibellini (Orbis Books, Maryknoll, N.Y., 1978), p. 38.

9. Ibid., p. 50.

10. Ibid.

11. I refer to persistent aggression in the economic, political, social, ideological, cultural, and religious spheres. See Leonardo Boff, "What Are Third World Theologies?," *Concilium* 199 (1988), pp. 3-4; Boff, *Faith on the Edge: Religion and Marginalized Existence* (Orbis Books, Maryknoll, N.Y., 1991), p. 16.

12. The lives of the impoverished believing masses are being sacrificed to the god capital. See Frei Betto, "The Prophetic Diaconia," *Concilium* 198 (1988), p. 58.

13. Gutiérrez, *A Theology of Liberation*, pp. 81 and 5-9. See also Leonardo Boff, *When Theology Listens to the Poor* (Harper & Row, San Francisco, 1988), pp. x and 10.

14. Henceforth I use the term "traditional theology" in the sense used by the Ecumenical Association of Third World Theologians (EATWOT).

199

"For the Third World this theology has been alienated and alienating. It has not provided the motivation for opposing the evils of racism, sexism, capitalism, colonialism, and neo-colonialism. . . . The tools and categories of traditional theology are inadequate for doing theology in context. They are still too wedded to Western culture and the capitalist system. . . . It has remained highly academic, speculative, and individualistic, without regard for the societal and structural aspects of sin. . . . It has generally failed to recognize worldviews that do not correspond to that of the West," from "Final Statement of the Fifth EATWOT Conference, New Delhi, August 17-29, 1981," *Irruption of the Third World: Challenge to Theology*, ed. Virginia Fabella and Sergio Torres (Orbis Books, Maryknoll, N.Y., 1983), p. 197. See also Evangelista Vilanova, *Historia de la teología cristiana* (Herder, Barcelona, 1984), pp. 385-96.

15. For what each level consists of, see Boff, "What Are Third World Theologies?," pp. 3-4; also his *When Theology Listens to the Poor*, pp. 13-14.

16. Carmen Lora, "Mujer: Víctima de opresión, portadora de liberación" in the collection, *Mujer: Víctima de opresión, portadora de liberación*, ed. Carmen Lora, Cecilia Barnechea, and Fryné Santisteban (Bartolomé de las Casas Institute, Lima, 1985), pp. 9-10.

17. For more about these aspects and their importance for liberation theology from the perspective of women, see the chapters that follow.

18. This is the point of Tamayo-Acosta's apt observation about liberation theology: "Liberation theology is neither static nor monolithic. It is not a closed doctrinal corpus or a system to which its adherents owe blind obedience. It is an open, plural, ongoing theological task" (*Para comprender la teología de la liberación*, p. 9). This observation appropriately makes room for the new contribution by women.

19. Otto Maduro, "Apuntes epistemológico-políticos para una historia de la teología en América Latina" in *Materiales para una historia de la teología en América Latina*, ed. Pablo Richard (CEHILA-DEI, San José, Costa Rica, 1981), pp. 19-20.

20. Carmen Lora, "Mujer latinoamericana: Historia de una rebeldía," in *Aportes para una teología desde la mujer*, ed. María Pilar Aquino (Biblia y Fe, Madrid, 1988), pp. 21-22; Jaime Wheelock, *Raíces indígenas de la lucha anti-colonialista en Nicaragua*, 7th ed. (Siglo XXI, Mexico, 1986).

21. Leonardo Boff, *Ecclesiogenesis: The Base Communities Reinvent the Church* (Orbis Books, Maryknoll, N.Y., 1986), pp. 76-77.

22. Juan Ginés de Sepúlveda's argument to justify the conquest and slavery. Quoted by Tamayo-Acosta (*Para comprender la teología de la liberación*, p. 28).

23. Leopoldo Zea, *Discurso desde la marginación y la barbarie* (Anthropos, Barcelona, 1988), p. 33. Vice versa, from the Indian viewpoint, and for women in particular, the conquistador is the barbarian. The indigenous chronicles in fact call them *popolocas*, that is, barbarians. "They took everything, grabbed everything, snatched everything for themselves, took possession of everything as if by right. And when they were taking the gold from everything, they gathered up everything else and piled it in the middle

of the yard. . . . As if they could all stay there like beasts, they were clapping each others' hands, their hearts were so happy. . . . They went everywhere and coveted everything for themselves, they were driven by greed. . . . The Mexicans did not dare go that way: as if there were a wild beast there, as if it were the weight of the night" (Miguel León Portilla, ed., *Crónicas indígenas: Visión de los vencidos*, vol. 6 [Historia 16, Madrid, 1985], pp. 95-103). The Mayan chronicles call them "puma of the peoples," "wild cat of the peoples," "bloodsuckers of poor Indians," "white sparrowhawks of the peoples," "cunning villains." See Miguel Rivera, ed., *Chilam Balam de Chumayel*, vol. 20 (Historia 16, Madrid, 1986), pp. 68 and 150.

24. Laurette Séjourné, *América Latina. Antiguas culturas precolombinas*, 19th ed. (Siglo XXI, Madrid, 1987), especially chapter 5; Jósefina O. de Coll, *La resistencia indígena ante la conquista*, 5th ed. (Siglo XXI, Mexico, 1986).

25. Lora describes these aspects more fully in "Mujer latinoamericana," pp. 23-25.

26. Indian women hid their faces to avoid abuse and persecution. See León-Portilla, *Crónicas indígenas*, pp. 161-62 and 141-42. See also the bibliography in Lora, "Mujer latinoamericana."

27. Some of the forms of struggle undertaken by women in defense of Tenochtitlan and Tlatelolco before their fall are described in León-Portilla, *Crónicas indígenas*, pp. 115, 155, 158. See also works cited in note 24.

28. C. Bustamante, "Intelectuales peruanas de la generación de J. C. Mariátegui," *Socialismo y Participación* 14 (Lima, 1981), quoted by Lora in "Mujer latinoamericana," p. 24; S. J. Stein and B. Stein, *La herencia colonial de América Latina*, 17th ed. (Siglo XXI, Mexico, 1986).

29. Lora, "Mujer latinoamericana," p. 25; Leonor Aída Concha, "Luchas y logros en el proceso de liberación de la mujer," in Aquino, *Aportes para una teología*, pp. 45-47. On the construction of equal and democratic models in the indigenous world, see María José Buxo I Rey, "El papel de la mujer indígena," in *Caminos de la democracia en América Latina*, 2nd ed. (Fundación Pablo Iglesias, Madrid, 1985), pp. 195-205.

30. Boff, "What Are Third World Theologies?," p. 4.

31. These are some of the characteristics of the so-called patriarchal society. Although I will return to this concept, I point out here that even though there are a number of theories, as Judith Astelarra indicates, "all coincide in pointing out that women's subordination does not originate from production relationships or in the area of production, but in the need for every human society to reproduce the species. . . . Sexuality and reproduction are biological facts but they are carried out in a social way that varies in every society and each historical period. Women's social situations have been historically determined by their role in the social system of human reproduction. This social regulation of reproduction means that biological sex becomes social gender, giving rise to a sex-gender system. When the relation between the sexes is unequal, that is, men can dominate women, we are dealing with a patriarchal society," ("Rasgos patriarcales en la sociedad y en la política" in *Caminos de democracia en América Latina*, pp. 154-55. On different conceptions of patriarchy see also Maruja González B.,

Qué es el feminismo? Breve historia y aproximaciones teórico-políticas, Series Pensamiento y Luchas 2 (EMAS, Mexico, 1989), pp. 24-27.

32. The situation for women in the dominant sectors is different. Although they are discriminated against as women, they have more leisure because of their privileged class situation. See "Mujer latinoamericana," pp. 26-27 and its source bibliography. For their domestic tasks they usually employ indigenous, black, or mestizo women in conditions close to slavery.

33. Ibid., p. 32.

34. These arguments wielded by liberal ideology from the end of the nineteenth and beginning of the twentieth centuries are echoed by the Catholic magisterium from Leo XIII's *Rerum Novarum* (15 May 1891), which affirms the supremacy of the patriarchal family (no. 9), to Pius XI's *Quadragesimo Anno* (15 May 1931), which calls upon women to return to their most important duties—home and family (no. 71). See David O'Brien and Thomas Shannon, eds., *Catholic Social Thought: The Documentary Heritage* (Orbis Books, Maryknoll, N.Y., 1992), pp. 8ff and 58ff.

35. One of the main challenges for Latin American women today is to recover the history of our struggles. Although there are several valuable works in existence, much still remains to be done. See Lora, "Mujer: víctima de opresión, portadora de liberación," p. 27. Also Lora, "Mujer latinoamericana," pp. 25-34; María Teresa Ruiz, *Racismo algo más que discriminación* (DEI, San José, Costa Rica, 1988); E. Tuñón Pablos, *También somos protagonistas de la historia de Mexico* I, II, III, Serie Pensamiento y Luchas 5, 6 and 7 (EMAS, Mexico, 1987). On this aspect see also other titles in the Pensamiento y Luchas series produced by the Women's Solidarity Action Team (EMAS), for example: *La lucha de las mujeres en América Latina y el Caribe* 3 and 4; *Feminismo y movimiento popular. Desencuentro o relación histórica?* 8; *La mujer en la lucha urbana y el Estado* 9; *De la casa a la calle Mujeres de la Plaza de Mayo, Argentina* 10; L. de Oyuela, *Notas sobre la evolución histórica de la mujer en Honduras*, Cuadernos para la mujer 5 (Guaymuras, Honduras, 1989).

36. Pablo Richard, "The Church of the Poor within the Popular Movement," *Concilium* 176 (1984), p. 10. Maruja González and Itziar Lozano give another description of the popular movement from a feminist point of view. They partly follow C. Camacho and R. Menjívar, but their description has the disadvantage of subordinating the interests, struggles, and objectives of women in the popular sectors to the hegemony of the working class and thus runs into the dead end of class reductionism. See González and Lozano, *Feminismo y movimiento popular* (Apuntes y Aportes, Cuaderno Pastoral 5, Mendoza, 1987), p. 10. This position is refined by the authors in subsequent works, which correct the reductionism we have noted here. See González, Loria, and Lozano, *Utopía y lucha feminista en América Latina y el Caribe* (EMAS-CIDHAL-GEM, Mexico, 1988), pp. 13-16. See also Ludolfo Paramio, "Feminismo y Socialismo: raíces de una relación infelíz," *Teoría* 6 (1981).

37. For an analysis of the Latin American context for the dependency theory, see Julio de Santa Ana, "The Situation of Latin American Theology (1982-1987)," *Concilium* 199 (1988), p. 49; Boff, "What Are Third World

Theologies?," pp. 4-6; Boff, "A Theological Examination of the Terms 'People of God' and 'Popular Church,' " *Concilium* 176 (1984), p. 93; Elsa Tamez and Saúl Trinidad, eds., *Capitalismo, violencia y anti-vida* I (DEI EDUCA, San José, Costa Rica, 1978).

38. Pedro Ribeiro de Oliveira, "An Analytical Exmination of the Term 'People,' " *Concilium* 176 (1984), pp. 82-88. See also Helio Gallardo's excellent work on the actors and political processes in Latin America: *Actores y procesos políticos latinoamericanos* (DEI, San José, Costa Rica, 1989).

39. González and Lozano, *Feminismo y movimiento popular*, pp. 11-12.

40. Ana Sojo, *Mujer y Política: Ensayo sobre el feminismo y el sujeto popular* (DEI, San José, Costa Rica, 1985), p. 30.

41. On the relevance of women's participation, see Lucía Ribeiro, *La relación entre mujeres profesionales y mujeres de sectores populares*, Pax Romana-MIIC International Seminar (Dar-es-Salaam, Tanzania, 1985), p. 103.

42. Ivone Gebara draws attention to the tendency of some intellectuals, theologians or social analysts to relegate, or even discount, the world of everyday struggle for survival facing the poor women of Latin America. I think this aspect is fundamental in order to overcome the reductionist view. See Gebara, "El Reino de Dios en la lucha por la supervivencia: Un aspecto de la lucha de las mujeres en Brasil," *Misiones Extranjeras* 108 (Madrid, 1988), pp. 369-79.

43. Fryné Santisteban, "Ser mujer en un contexto de opresión" in Lora, Barnachea and Santisteban, *Mujer: Víctima de opresión, portadora de liberación*, pp. 100-1. Living conditions include vital necessities and people's emotional and affective needs that allow for free and genuine participation in various human relationships and incoporation into creative activities (see note 6).

44. Lora, "Mujer latinoamericana," p. 39.

45. This radical change is mentioned by Karl Lehmann as one of the most important current signs of the times. See Lehmann, "La valoración de la mujer en el problema de la antropología," *Revista Católica Internacional Communio* IV/82 (Madrid, 1982), p. 237.

46. With the expression "the irruption of history into the lives of women" Ivone Gebara is reformulating Ezequiel Ander-Egg's expression "the irruption of women into history." Ander-Egg's position might lead one to think that women have only just started acting in history. The history of Latin American women's rebelliousness and resistance throughout the centuries forces us to recognize that women have not only just begun to claim their right to participate in history as actors and subjects. See Gebara, "Women Doing Theology in Latin America," in *Through Her Eyes: Women's Theology from Latin America*, ed. Tamez (Orbis Books, Maryknoll, N.Y., 1989), p. 43; Ander-Egg, *La mujer irrumpe en la historia* (Marisiega, Madrid, 1980), pp. 13-14 and 88.

47. Gebara, "Women Doing Theology," p. 43.

48. "Postura de la Mujer Latinoamericana frente a la Sociedad, la Iglesia y la Biblia, Encuentro Latinoamericano Comunidad de Mujeres y Hombres en la Iglesia," San José, Costa Rica, 1981, in Elsa Tamez et al., *Comunidad*

de mujeres y hombres en la iglesia (SEBILA, San José, Costa Rica, 1981), p. 19.

49. As well as the bibliography already mentioned, see Rosa Pardo, "Bajo el signo de la reproducción" *Misión Abierta* 3, p. 63; H. Hartmann, "Un matrimonio mal avenido: hacia una unión más progresiva entre marxismo y feminismo," *Zona Abierta* 24 (1980), pp. 109ff.

50. Lora, "Mujer latinoamericana," p. 38.

51. This is because the term "patriarchy" is ambiguous and does not wholly explain the many oppressions weighing on third-world women. It is also due to the lack of dialogue between theology and feminist social science.

52. The tendency of some social analysts and liberation theologians to see women's subordinate condition as a non-fundamental, partial, or non-central contradiction is following a dangerous subordinationist line, converging with the rigidity of Marxist analyses in the seventies that proposed the class struggle as the only focus of conflict. See Ludolfo Paramio, "Lo que todo marxista vulgar debe saber sobre feminismo," in *AAVV Nuevas perspectivas sobre la mujer, Actas de las Primeras Jornadas de Investigación Interdisciplinaria* vol. 2 (Universidad Autónoma de Madrid, 1982), pp. 11-19. In this article Paramio disputes the one-dimensional positions of Marxists (men and women), whose political analyses reduce all conflicts to the single one of class. Revolutionary feminist literature points out this same problem. See González and Lozano, *Utopía y lucha feminista en América Latina y el Caribe.*

53. Tamez, "Introducción a la problemática de la mujer en América Latina" in *Comunidad de mujeres y hombres en la iglesia*, pp. 34-38.

54. I return later to the theme of women as historical actors with full rights.

55. Tamez, "La mujer como sujeto histórico en la producción teológica" in *Mujer latinoamericana, iglesia y teología*, Mujeres para el Diálogo, eds. (MPD, Mexico, 1981), p. 111.

56. Ivone Gebara, "Option for the Poor as an Option for the Poor Woman," *Concilium* 194 (1987), p. 114.

2. Latin American Women's Discovery of Causality

1. For a good presentation of the socio-analytic contribution in liberation theology, from the pioneering works to the most recent, see Juan José Tamayo-Acosta, *Para comprender la teología de la liberación* (Verbo Divino, Estella, Spain, 1989), pp. 71-97; Ignacio Ellacuría, "Premisas socio-económicas implícitas y explícitas de la teología de la liberación," in *Implicaciones sociales y políticas de la teología de la liberación*, Tamayo-Acosta et al. (Instituto de Filosofía, University of Seville, Spain, 1989), pp. 135-46.

2. Leonardo Boff, *The Maternal Face of God* (Harper & Row, San Francisco, 1988), p. 3.

3. Gustavo Gutiérrez, *We Drink from Our Own Wells* (Orbis Books, Maryknoll, N.Y., 1984), p. 20; Ignacio Ellacuría, "La teología de la libera-

ción frente al cambio sociohistórico de América Latina" in *Implicaciones sociales y políticas de la teología de la liberación*, p. 69.

4. Ezequiel Ander-Egg, *La mujer irrumpe en la historia* (Marisiega, Madrid, 1980), p. 12.

5. Ivone Gebara, "Women Doing Theology in Latin America," in *Through Her Eyes, Women's Theology from Latin America*, ed. Elsa Tamez (Orbis Books, Maryknoll, N.Y., 1989), pp. 43-44.

6. Ivone Gebara, "Option for the Poor as an Option for the Poor Woman," *Concilium* 194 (1987), pp. 114-15. These contributions by Gebara are very important in indicating Latin American women's new situation as a protagonistic collective force, but they do not appear to question the exclusive assignment of domestic work to women or the use of women's biology to justify the assignment of social roles by sex.

7. Gebara, "Women Doing Theology in Latin America," p. 44.

8. Some of these characteristics are emphasized by María Josefa García Callado in the psychoanalytic field. See M. J. García Callado, "Automarginación femenina. Una aproximación desde el psicoanálisis" *Sal Terrae* 11 (1988), p. 759. The term *sentient* here indicates not only an affective-perceptual attitude, but carries the full philosophical meaning given to it by Xavier Zubiri as a particular way of understanding: "The Greeks always contrasted intelligence (*nous*) and feeling (*aisthesis*). Whatever the *doxa* of Parmenides, it is clear that Greek philosophy always ascribed the *doxa* to feeling. But what is feeling? It is the presentation of something that in one form or another has a moment of reality. But if this is so, there is never a structural opposition in human beings between intelligence and feeling. As knowing is apprehending the real, this means that if the real is already presented in and through the senses as real, then the act of intelligence itself already has a radically sentient character. So there is no opposition between intelligence and feeling, rather there is a structural unity: intelligence and feeling are just two moments in a single act: the act of apprehending reality" (*Inteligencia y Logos* [Alianza Editorial, Madrid, 1982], p. 51).

9. Ellacuría, "La teología de la liberación frente al cambio socio-histórico de América Latina," p. 191; Boff, "What Are Third World Theologies?," *Concilium* 199 (1988), p. 11; Jon Sobrino, *The True Church and the Poor* (Orbis Books, Maryknoll, N.Y., 1984), pp. 7-38.

10. Tamayo-Acosta, *Para comprender la teología de la liberación*, p. 73.

11. Teresita de Barbieri, *Mujeres y vida cotidiana* (SEP/80, Mexico, 1984), p. 14; see also Maruja González B., *Qué es el feminismo?: Breve historia y aproximaciones teórico-políticas* (EMAS, Mexico, 1989), which presents the different tendencies and positions in Latin American feminism.

12. Carmen Lora, "Mujer: víctima de opresión, portadora de liberación," in *Mujer: Víctima de opresión, portadora de liberación*, ed. Carmen Lora, Cecilia Barnechea, and Fryné Santisteban (Bartolomé de las Casas Institute, Lima, 1985), p. 21. The concept of patriarchy is not simple. It refers chiefly to male domination in every sphere of human life, although it is primarily focused on men's control of sexuality, reproduction, and women's work.

13. Ana Sojo, *Mujer y política: Ensayo sobre el feminismo y el sujeto popular* (DEI, San José, Costa Rica, 1985), p. 47.

14. Ibid.; Enrique Arnaz, "Discriminación de la mujer. Voz de colectivos feministas," *Misión Abierta* 3 (1980), p. 23.

15. Sojo, p. 48.

16. Santisteban, "Ser mujer en un contexto de opresión" in Lora, Barnachea and Santisteban, *Mujer: Víctima de opresión, portadora de liberación*, p. 95.

17. Ibid., pp. 98-99; Ander-Egg, "La mujer irrumpe en la historia," p. 37.

18. Santisteban, p. 98.

19. An analysis relevant to the women's liberation process in our countries must incorporate both aspects. As Maruja González emphasizes: "Although oppression and discrimination against women precede capitalism, as various studies have shown, it is fundamental to recognize that in the present capitalist phase the various forms and degress of daily violence against women and children become more acute," González, *Qué es el feminismo?*, p. 29. Likewise Elisabeth Schüssler Fiorenza points out: "An understanding of patriarchy solely in terms of male supremacy and misogynist sexism is not able to articulate the interaction of racism, classism and sexism in Western militarist societies" ("Breaking the Silence — Becoming Visible," *Concilium* 182 (1985), p. 5.

20. Sojo, *Mujer y política*, p. 49.

21. González, *Qué es el feminismo?*, p. 27.

22. Sojo, *Mujer y política*, p. 53. This author agrees with Judith Astelarra that the sex-gender system does not always imply inequality. In theory it could also be an equal system, in spite of its commonly unequal character in history.

23. This description of stereotypes is from Maite del Moral, "Lo femenino. Breve recorrido por la psicología y el mito," *Sal Terrae* 11 (1988), p. 750.

24. García Callado, "Automarginación femenina," p. 757; see also Arnaz, "Discriminación de la mujer," p. 32.

25. Sojo, *Mujer y política*, p. 54.

26. Ibid., p. 55.

27. Judith Astelarra, "Rasgos patriarcales en la sociedad y en la política" in Astelarra et al., *Caminos de democracia en América Latina* (Ed. Fundación Pablo Iglesias, Madrid, 1985), pp. 158-59.

28. Sojo, *Mujer y política*, p. 57.

29. Rosemary Radford Ruether, *New Woman, New Earth: Sexist Ideologies and Human Liberation* (Seabury Press, New York, 1975), p. 30.

30. Sojo, *Mujer y política*, p. 66.

31. On the importance of these three dimensions, see also Schüssler Fiozenza, "Toward a Feminist Biblical Hermeneutics: Biblical Interpretation and Liberation Theology" in *The Challenge of Liberation Theology*, 2nd ed., ed. Brian Mahan and L. Dale Richesin (Orbis Books, Maryknoll, N.Y. 1984), p. 92; M. Shawn Copeland, "The Interaction of Racism, Sexism and Classism in Women's Exploitation," *Concilium* 194 (1987), pp. 19-27; Anne

Carr, "Editorial Reflections on Women, Work and Poverty," *Concilium* 194 (1987), pp. 128-32.

32. B. M. Alves, *Ideología y feminismo: a lutta pelo voto no Brasil* (Vozes, Petrópolis, 1980), p. 35, cited by Lora, "Mujer: Víctima de opresión, portadora de liberación," p. 22.

33. Agnes Heller thinks that daily life involves the life of the *whole* human being, all of his or her senses, intellectual powers, skills, feelings, passions, ideas, ideologies, and so forth. Daily life is also the basis for understanding the movement of capital, the organization of classes, the structure of the state, ideologies and counter-ideologies, because they imply and express continuous forms of reproduction. See Heller, *Historia y vida cotidiana* (Grijalbo, Barcelona, 1972).

34. Sojo, *Mujer y política*, pp. 71-72.

35. Ibid., p. 71.

36. Ibid., p. 72.

37. Raúl Vidales, "Interview," *Against Machismo: Interviews* by Elsa Tamez (Meyer Stone Books, Oak Park, Il., 1987), p. 119.

38. Tamez, *Against Machismo*, p. 134.

39. Ibid., p. 135.

3. Women in the Church of the Poor

1. This is how Leonardo Boff understands the process of church renewal: "Herein resides what is specific to the church's mystery: the co-existence in one same reality—the church—of the two elements, the divine and the human. As Vatican II stresses: in the church, which is simultaneously visible and spiritual, the elements 'should not be considered as two things, but form one single complex reality, in which the human and the divine elements coalesce (*humano et divino coalescit element*: LG, no. 8)' " (*Y la Iglesia se hizo pueblo* [Paulinas, Bogotá, 1987], p. 32).

2. Pablo Richard, *La fuerza espiritual de la iglesia de los pobres* (DEI, San José, Costa Rica, 1987), p. 19. Richard states his fundamental thesis thus: "At present in Latin America there is a crisis of Christendom and the birth of the church of the poor. We cannot speak in the abstract of a crisis of the church, but of the crisis of one particular historical model of the church called Christendom, and the rise of another historical model of the church, which is the church of the poor" (p. 20). On the theological definition and christological foundation of the church of the poor, see Leonardo Boff, *When Theology Listens to the Poor* (Harper & Row, San Francisco, 1988); idem, *Church: Charism & Power: Liberation Theology and the Institutional Church* (Crossroad, New York, 1985); idem, *Y la iglesia se hizo pueblo*, pp. 41-61; Jon Sobrino, *The True Church and the Poor* (Orbis Books, Maryknoll, N.Y., 1984), pp. 84-227; Juan José Tamayo-Acosta, *Para comprender la teología de la liberación* (Verbo Divino, Estella, Spain, 1989), pp. 36-49; Richard, *La fuerza espiritual de la iglesia de los pobres*, pp. 20-42. See also the bibliographies cited by these authors.

3. On this point see the splendid work by Tamayo-Acosta, *Para comprender la teología de la liberación*, pp. 38-39.

4. On the viewpoint of the church as an equal participatory community, see Leonardo Boff, "The Terms 'People of God' and 'Popular Church,'" *Concilium* 176 (1984), pp. 92-93; on equal discipleship, see Elisabeth Schüssler Fiorenza, *In Memory of Her: A Feminist Theological Reconstruction of Christian Origins* (Crossroad, New York, 1983), pp. 105-159.

5. María Clara Bingemer, "De la teología del laicado a la teología del bautismo," *Páginas* 86 (1987), p. 9.

6. Ivone Gebara and María Clara Bingemer, *Mary, Mother of God, Mother of the Poor* (Orbis Books, Maryknoll, N.Y., 1989), p. 129.

7. Ibid.

8. F. de los Ríos, *Religión y Estado en la España del siglo XVI* (Mexico, 1957) p. 36; cited by Fernando Mires, *En el nombre de la cruz* (DEI, San José, Costa Rica, 1986), p. 29.

9. The historian J. M. G. Le Clezio expresses the drama of the situation in these words: "Empires destroyed, princes murdered, the priests destitute, the indigenous culture, religion and social order reduced to silence, over this annihilated world Spanish peace reigned. . . . The silence of the Indian world is certainly one of humanity's greatest tragedies. . . . It is a tragedy whose consequences we have not yet finished with today. A double tragedy because when they destroyed the Amerindian cultures, the Conquistadors were destroying part of themselves, a part that can never be recovered" (*Le rêve mexicain ou la pensée interrompue* [Gallimard, Mesnil-sur-l'Estrée, 1988], pp. 211-13. See also Ronald Muñoz, *La Iglesia en el pueblo* (CEP, Lima, 1983), pp. 85-92.

10. Carmen Lora, "Mujer latinoamericana: historia de una rebeldía" in *Aportes para une teología desde la mujer*, María Pilar Aquino, ed. (Biblia y Fe, Madrid, 1988), p. 21.

11. Cited by Mires, *La colonización de las almas* (DEI, San José, Costa Rica, 1987), p. 137.

12. Mires, *En nombre de la cruz*, p. 140.

13. Ibid., pp. 152ff. See also Lora, "Mujer latinoamericana," p. 21; Raúl Vidales and Tokhiro Kudó, *Práctica religiosa y proyecto histórico* (CEP, Lima, 1977).

14. "It was under the sign of the cross that the Iberian colonization of Latin America promoted the genocide of the Indians and the sacking of its natural wealth—with the complicity of the Catholic church. More than ten million blacks were brought from Africa as slaves for our continent with the connivance of our Christian churches" (Frei Betto, *Fe, política e ideología* [Prague, 21 June 1988, xerox]).

15. Bartolomé de las Casas, *Tratados*, vol. 1 (Mexico, 1955), quoted by Mires, *La colonización de las almas*, p. 141.

16. Mires, *En nombre de la cruz*, p. 95. "Evidently many patriarchal elements taken from the Western and Eastern culture in which Christianity developed were transmitted together with its message" (Lora, "Mujer latinoamericana," p. 21).

17. Mires, *En nombre de la Cruz*, pp. 93-94; see also *La colonización de las almas*, pp. 220-21.

18. Mires, *En nombre de la Cruz*, p. 46. The Indian account gathered by

Miguel León-Portilla is suggestive here. It concerns the first exchanges between the envoys of Moctezuma and Hernán Cortés, which took place on the Spanish ship. The envoys came to offer gifts as a sign of friendship and welcome to the strangers. When they arrived "the Captain [Cortés] gave orders; so they were bound [the Indians]; they put chains on their feet and round their necks. When they had done this they fired the great canon. And at this moment the envoys lost their reason, they were dismayed. They fell down, they crumpled and were no longer themselves. Then the Spaniards lifted them up, gave them wine, and then they gave them food to eat, they made them eat. With this they recovered their courage and were comforted. Then the captain said to them: 'Listen, I have heard, it has reached my ears, it is said the Mexicans are very strong, very warlike, that they are very terrifying. So that a single Mexican can easily put to flight, force to retreat, conquer and overcome even ten or twenty warriors. Well now, my heart wants to be convinced: I am going to see, I am going to test how strong you are, how manly! So then he gave them leather shields, swords and lances. So let's see who will fall to the floor!' They replied to the captain: 'It may be that this is not what Motecuhzoma, your lieutentant orders! We have come with a single commision to give rest and repose we have come, so that we may greet each other. What your lordship wants is not in our brief' " (*Crónicas indígenas*, pp. 68-69). Clearly the indigenous envoys had not come to give a demonstration of their *machismo*.

19. F. de Armas Medina, *Cristianización del Peru* (Seville, 1953), p. 336, cited by Mires, *La colonización de las almas*, p. 90.

20. Ignacio Ellacuría, "Premisas socio-ecónomicas implícitas y explícitas de la teología de la liberación," in *Implicaciones sociales y políticas de la teología de la liberación* (Instituto de Filosofía, University of Seville, 1989), p. 137.

21. Lora, "Mujer latinoamericana," p. 42.

22. Boff, *Y la Iglesia se hizo pueblo*, p. 68; on the dimensions of the church proclaiming the gospel, witnessing, celebrating, and transforming action, see Jon Sobrino, *The True Church and the Poor*, pp. 265ff.

23. Tereza Cavalcanti, "Sobre la participación de las mujeres en el VI Encuentro Intereclesial de los CEB" in Aquino, *Aportes para una teología desde la mujer*, p. 128.

24. On the characteristics of the church of the poor and women's participation, see Richard, *La fuerza espiritual de la iglesia de los pobres*, pp. 171-72.

25. For this part my inspiration is Boff, *Y la Iglesia se hizo pueblo*, pp. 68ff; Sobrino, *The True Church and the Poor*, pp. 280ff. Although these fields of action are not exclusive to women, women are the majority in the actual communities and they do most of the work. See note 29 below.

26. Karl Rahner, "Do Not Stifle the Spirit," in *Theological Investigations*, vol. 7 (Seabury, New York, 1977), p. 81.

27. Richard, *La fuerza espiritual de la iglesia de los pobres*, p. 86.

28. Boff, *Church: Charism and Power*, p. 131.

29. This is the result arrived at by Luis Evelio Cardona Velásquez in a recent doctoral thesis defended and approved in the Pontifical University

of Salamanca on the church base communities in Colombia. I am taking the liberty of extending it to the majority of Latin American countries. See Cardona Velásquez, *Comunidades ecclesiales de base: Una experiencia de solidaridad*, doctoral thesis (Pontifical University of Salamanca, Madrid, June 1988), pp. 515ff.

30. Sobrino, *The True Church and the Poor*, p. 93.

31. Cavalcanti, "Sobre la participación de las mujeres en el VI Encuentro Intereclesial de las CEB," p. 141.

32. Cardona Velásquez, *Comunidades ecclesiales de base*, p. 516.

33. Boff, *Church: Charism and Power*, p. 127.

34. Ibid., p. 128.

35. Boff, *Y la Iglesia se hizo pueblo*, pp. 98-99.

36. Cavalcanti, "Sobre la participación de las mujeres en el VI Encuentro Intereclesial de las CEB," pp. 129-30; Cardona Velásquez, *Comunidades ecclesiales de base*, p. 516.

37. Ibid., pp. 140-41.

38. Richard, *La fuerza espiritual de la iglesia de los pobres*, p. 89.

39. "You rarely find the 'rich' celebrating a liturgy and spontaneously inviting the poor. The converse does, however, occur. A liturgical celebration held because of something that has happened in the Church of the poor—a martyrdom, a peasant celebration—has the power to draw other Christians who in social terms are not poor" (Sobrino, *The True Church and the Poor*, p. 104).

40. Cavalcanti, "Sobre la participación de las mujeres en el VI Encuentro Intereclesial de los CEB," p. 132.

41. Ibid.

42. Ibid., p. 133.

43. Ibid., p. 134.

44. Richard, *La fuerza espiritual de la iglesia de los pobres*, p. 84; Boff, *Y la Iglesia se hizo pueblo*, pp. 106-7.

45. Cavalcanti, "Sobre la participación de las mujeres en el VI Encuentro Intereclesial de los CEB," p. 134.

46. Thomas Aquinas, *Summa Teologiae*, Ia. 92, I. Blackfriars, New York, 1964, pp. 35 and 37.

47. On the role of historical memory, see H. Cox, *The Seduction of the Spirit: The Use and Misuse of People's Religion* (Simon & Schuster, New York, 1973), pp. 146-154.

48. Cavalcanti, "Sobre la participación de las mujeres en el VI Encuentro Intereclesial de los CEB," p. 135.

49. This current is stressed by Schüssler Fiorenza in her proposal—which I broadly share—for a critical feminist hermeneutic of liberation. See Schüssler Fiorenza, "Toward a Feminist Biblical Hermeneutics," in *The Challenge of Liberation Theology*, 2nd ed., ed. Brian Mahan and L. Dale Richesin (Orbis Books, Maryknoll, N.Y., 1981), pp. 102ff.

50. Cavalcanti, "Sobre la participación de las mujeres en el VI Encuentro Intereclesial de los CEB," p. 135.

51. Ibid., pp. 136-37. Hugo Assman approaches the theme of the poor's resistance in terms of the common sense and daily lives of the oppressed,

as manifested in popular religious practice, from a Gramscian viewpoint. See Assman, "CEBs, Quando la vivencia da fe remeixe o senso comum dos pobres," *REB* 46/183 (1986), p. 566.

52. Cavalcanti, "Sobre la participación de las mujeres en el VI Encuentro Intereclesial de las CEB," p. 138. From numerous testimonies I give one cited by Uriel Molina: "A little while ago a mother asked me to say a mass for her son who had died in combat. Seeing her weeping, I said: 'Losing him has caused you much grief, hasn't it?' 'Yes, father,' she answered, 'but the cause for which he died was greater than my womb.' All this helps us to understand the extent of the love felt for the people's cause (*la causa del pueblo*). So it was when a rocket destroyed the body of Lupita Montiel's son. Risking the heavy bombardment, Lupita collected her son's remains to give them Christian burial. They asked me to perform the funeral ceremony. The mother bent over her lifeless son in a posture of grief. I could not bring myself to uncover the body, but she invited me to do so, saying in a loud voice: 'I am proud to have borne a Sandinista son' "(Molina, "How a People's Christian Community (*Comunidad Cristiana Popular*) Is Structured and How It Functions," *Concilium* 176 (1984), p. 8.

53. Sobrino, *The True Church and the Poor*, p. 103; Boff, *Y la Iglesia se hizo pueblo*, p. 162.

54. Karl Rahner, *The Shape of the Church To Come* (Seabury Press, New York, 1974), pp. 51 and 62.

55. Cavalcanti, "Sobre la participación de las mujeres en el VI Encuentro Intereclesial de los CEB," pp. 138-39.

56. Elsa Tamez, "Meditación bíblica sobre la mujer en Centroamérica," *Vida y Pensamiento* 6, no. 2 (1986).

57. Cavalcanti, "Sobre la participación de las mujeres en el VI Encuentro Intereclesial de los CEB," p. 139; Bingemer, "Reflections on the Trinity," in Tamez, *Through Her Eyes: Women's Theology from Latin America* (Orbis Books, Maryknoll, N.Y., 1989), pp. 61-62.

58. Cavalcanti, "Sobre la participación de las mujeres en el VI Encuentro Intereclesial de los CEB," p. 140; Boff, *Church: Charism and Power*, pp. 129-30.

59. Most popular religious expressions relate both to the Christian mystery and to daily life; for example, "Religious pictures of the crucifixion portray a self-possessed Mary bearing the cup of suffering as she stands at the foot of the cross. This strong woman is an example of so many others who, weighed down by children and pain, also bear the cross of the poor, and helps them on their way. In this shared Calvary, women stay strong and inspire strength in their fellow travelers" (Carmen del Prado, "I Sense God in Another Way," in Tamez, *Through Her Eyes*, p. 143.

60. A good exploration of the female tone or character of popular religiosity is to be found in Luis Maldonado, *Introducción a la religiosidad popular* (Sal Terrae, Santander, 1985). It is noteworthy to point out that popular celebrations like the Christmas festivities, in spite of being articulated by a predominantly female-centered symbol system, do not relate to women's situation and their experience of oppression-liberation.

61. Del Prado, "I Sense God in Another Way," p. 147.
62. Richard, *La fuerza espiritual de la iglesia de los pobres*, p. 89.

4. The Understanding of Faith from the Perspective of Women

1. Gustavo Gutiérrez, *On Job: God-Talk and the Suffering of the Innocent* (Orbis Books, Maryknoll, N.Y., 1987), p. xiv. "If theology is faith seeking understanding, then feminist theology is the reflection on Christian faith-experiences in the struggle against patriarchal oppression" (Elisabeth Schüssler Fiorenza, "Editorial," *Concilium* 182 [1985], p. x).

2. Ivone Gebara, "Option for the Poor as an Option for the Poor Woman," *Concilium* 194 (1987), p. 111.

3. Elsa Tamez, "La mujer como sujeto histórico en la producción teológica" in *Mujer Latinoamericana, iglesia y teología* (MPD, Mexico, 1981), p. 110. On the other hand, the split I am alluding to is also related to the ways of understanding and doing politics. "Feminism has transformed the way of understanding and doing politics. One of its fundamental contributions is restoring the political dimension to daily life. In saying the personal is political, it puts its finger on the spot with respect to problems relegated in traditional political struggle, because they are considered secondary and because a comfortable and unquestioned separation is maintained between the *private* and the *public, private* life and *public* life. For feminism *both* lives are required to change and this does not depend only on women but also on men and the rest of society" (Maruja González B., *¿Qué es el feminismo? Breve historia y aproximaciones teórico-políticas* [EMAS-Pensamiento y Luchas 2, 1989], p. 80).

4. Although not in the same terms, Tamez suggests this observation. See Tamez, "La mujer como sujeto histórico en la producción teológica," pp. 109 and 111.

5. Jon Sobrino, "Como hacer teología? La teología como *intellectus amoris*," *Sal Terrae* 5 (1989), pp. 397-417. Leonardo Boff and Clodovis Boff, *Introducing Liberation Theology* (Orbis Books, Maryknoll, N.Y., 1987), pp. 28-30.

6. Julio de Santa Ana, "The Situation of Latin American Theology (1982-1987)," *Concilium* 199 (1988), p. 51.

7. María Clara Bingemer, "Third World Theologies: Conversion to Others," *Concilium* 199 (1988), p. 121.

8. I say this situation is improving because in recent years both male and female theologians have shown a clear interest in the situation of women. The bibliography cited in this work offers an opportunity to verify this point.

9. "There is obvious oppression of women (both nuns and laywomen) in the church, and there is also an absence of women in theology ... so much so that in order for this situation to change we are obliged to speak of a new church and a new theology, both liberating" (Tamez, "Introducción a la problemática de la mujer en América Latina," in *Comunidad de mujeres y hombres en la iglesia* , p. 38). Schüssler Fiorenza, "Breaking the Silence:

Becoming Visible," *Concilium* 182 (1985), pp. 3-4.

10. "Previously, there was never any mention of sexual difference with regard to those who wrote theology, since this was obvious that the task was something proper to men" (Gebara, "Option for the Poor as an Option for the Poor Woman," p. 37).

11. Tamez, "Introducción a la problemática de la mujer en América Latina," p. 40; Catherina Halkes, "Feminist Theology: An Interim Assessment," *Concilium* 134 (1980), p. 110.

12. Ibid. Schüssler Fiorenza is also against a "theology of women" because it "theologically legitimates the existing economic structures of patriarchal exploitaton as well as the cultural gender role division and socialization for feminine behavior which internalize and maintain such exploitation" (Schüssler Fiorenza, "The Endless Day," *Concilium* 194 (1987), p. xix. Although theological reflection from the perspective of women in Latin America does not describe itself as *feminist theology*, as it is called in the First World, there are important convergences with the works of significant North American and European women theologians; these should not be underestimated. These perspectives are aware of the different contexts, but their presuppositions, starting point, methods, and objectives bring them within liberation theology. Thus there are no serious reasons for not speaking of a *feminist liberation theology from Latin America*.

13. María Clara Bingemer, "Chairete: Alegrai-vos (Lk 15:8-10) ou a Mulher no futuro da Teología da Libertaçao" *REB* 48/191 (1988), p. 566. Likewise Schüssler Fiorenza: "In short my thesis is: the silence and invisibility is generated by the patriarchal structures of the Church and maintained by androcentric, i.e., male-defined theology" ("Breaking the Silence," p. 4.

14. Bingemer, "Chairete: Alegrai-vos," p. 567.

15. Ibid. Also see Gebara, "Option for the Poor as an Option for the Poor Woman," p. 37.

16. I return to the theme of theological anthropology in part 2 of this work.

17. Bingemer, "Chairete: Alegrai-vos."

18. On this line of reflection on theology as a need, a duty, and a right for the poor and oppressed, I am indebted to the Peruvian theologian Luis F. Crespo. This viewpoint was constantly expressed in the various meetings I had with young people in a number of Mexican dioceses during the summer of 1983. Without doubt, these meetings and my conversations with the MIEC-JECI comrades in Mexico and Lima have had an effect on my own theological options and on the writing of this book.

19. Nelly Ritchie points out these features in the context of her reflection on women and christology, but they are valid also in the context of doing theology from women's viewpoint. See Ritchie, "Women and Christology," in Tamez, *Through Her Eyes: Women's Theology from Latin America* (Orbis Books, Maryknoll, N.Y., 1989), p. 83.

20. Ritchie, "Women and Christology," pp. 83-84.

21. Tamez, "Introduction: The Power of the Naked," *Through Her Eyes*, p. 8.

22. Ibid.

23. Ibid., p. 13.

24. For a selection of the most recent works (1988-1990) see the bibliography to Chapter 1, note 1. Likewise Julio de Santa Ana, "The Situation of Latin American Theology (1982-1987)" and especially Bingemer, "Chairete: Alegrai-vos," pp. 565-87; Juan José Tamayo-Acosta, *Para comprender la teología de la liberación* (Verbo Divino, Estella, 1989).

25. Bingemer, "Chairete: Alegrai-vos," p. 165.

26. With the expression *traditional or classical theology* I refer to the dominant Western theological discourse, which in general has been white, male, clerical, racist, and sexist—theology done from the centers of power, which found it difficult to embrace the periphery, the suffering, and pain of the masses in the third world. It is clear, from what I have said up till now, that I recognize the existence of liberating theologies elaborated by prophetic minorities in the first world and I welcome them with a profound sense of solidarity. Among these are feminist liberation theology and black theology. See Chapter 1, note 14.

27. Tamez, "Introduction: The Power of the Naked," p. 5.

28. This is one of the most serious and painful factors that emerged during the Women's Conference on Women's Situation in Latin America, which took place in the Ecumenical Department of Investigations (DEI) in San José, Costa Rica in July 1989. Reflection by women who did not have formal academic theological training was regarded as lacking credibility by the hierarchy, some theologians, and even by some of the women themselves.

29. Tamayo-Acosta, *Para comprender la teología de la liberación*, p. 131; Bingemer, "Chairete: Alegrai-vos," pp. 565-66.

30. See the observations made by Karl Rahner on the situation of current theology (*Foundations of Christian Faith*, pp. 1-14). His observations hint at a certain distaste for the division of current theology into an endless series of particular disciplines, each with immense material and a very different and difficult methodology, which often makes it impossible to get through it all. For Latin America this theology is moving further and further away from the requirements and hopes of the poor and oppressed.

31. "The Irruption of the Third World: Challenge to Theology. Final Statement of the Fifth EATWOT Conference, New Delhi, August 17-29, 1981," in *Irruption of the Third World: Challenge to Theology*, Virginia Fabella and Sergio Torres, eds. (Orbis Books, Maryknoll, N.Y., 1983), p. 197.

32. Ibid.

33. Tamez, "The Power of the Naked."

34. "Theology Was Not Universal But European," Sergio Torres, "Dar-es-Salaam 1976," *Concilium* 199 (1988), p. 111.

35. Tamez, "The Power of the Naked," p. 4; Tamayo-Acosta, *Para comprender la teología de la liberación*, p. 131.

5. Methodological Premises for Theology from the Perspective of Women

1. Elisabeth Schüssler Fiorenza, *In Memory of Her. A Feminist Theological Reconstruction of Christian Origins* (Crossroad, New York, 1985), p. xviii.

2. See Juan José Tamayo-Acosta, *Para comprender la teología de la liberación* (Verbo Divino, Estella, Spain, 1989), p. 13.

3. Georges Casalis, in Tamayo-Acosta, *Para comprender la teología de la liberación*.

4. Otto Maduro, "Apuntes epistemológicos-políticos para una historia de la teología en América Latina" in Enrique Dussel et al., *Materiales para una historia de la teología en América Latina* (CEHILA-DEI, San José, Costa Rica, 1981), pp. 19-38.

5. Tamayo-Acosta, *Para comprender la teología de la liberación*, p. 53.

6. Schüssler Fiorenza, *In Memory of Her*, p. xx.

7. Ivone Gebara and María Clara Bingemer, *Mary, Mother of God, Mother of the Poor* (Orbis Books, Maryknoll, NY, 1989), p. 9. The outlines of an egalitarian anthropology I present here are taken from this book. Even though the first two chapters of this book aim to set the anthropological bases for a Marian theology from the Latin American viewpoint, I believe that its anthropological premises are also valid for Latin American women's theology. So I take them as premises for women's theological work.

8. Ibid., p. 30.

9. Karl Rahner, *Foundations of Christian Faith: An Introduction to the Idea of Christianity* (Crossroad, New York, 1987), pp. 25ff.

10. Gebara and Bingemer, *Mary, Mother of God, Mother of the Poor*, pp. 16-17.

11. When I speak of women's fulfillment as persons with full rights, I do not see this as a process isolated from peoples' struggle as a whole. In Latin America women also work for men's liberation, even though here I emphasize women's liberation, given the many forms of their oppression and the general androcentric tendency of anthropological projects today.

12. Karl Lehmann, "La valoración de la mujer, el problema de la antropología teológica," *Revista Católica Internacional Communio* IV/82 (1982), p. 232.

13. Lehmann, "La valoración de la mujer."

14. Ibid., pp. 243-44.

15. Gebara and Bingemer, *Mary, Mother of God, Mother of the Poor*, p. 30.

16. Ibid., p. 2.

17. One of the negative aspects of this legacy is the anthropological dualism that was assimilated by scholastic theology. For Karl Rahner, this Greek anthropological dualism is not Christian. See Rahner, *Foundations of Christian Faith*, p. 30.

18. The best study to date on the anthropology of St. Augustine and Thomas Aquinas is the rigorous work by Kary E. Børresen, *Subordination et Equivalence* (Oslo, 1968).

19. Ibid., p. 259.

20. Kary E. Børresen, "Fundamentos antropológicos de la relación entre el hombre y la mujer en la teología clasica," *Concilium* 111 (1976), p. 25.

21. An example of this statement is the recent book by Juan L. Ruíz de la Peña, *Imagen de Dios: Antropología teológica fundamental* (Sal Terrae, Santander, 1988). It is noteworthy, for example, that whereas for Børresen

Augustinian thought is clearly dualistic and androcentric, for Ruíz de la Peña St. Augustine's anthropology only displays "a certain dualist propensity" (in De la Peña, *Imagen de Dios: Antropología teológica fundamental*, p. 99) and its androcentrism is not even mentioned.

22. Børresen, *Subordination et Equivalence*, pp. 141-45 and 255.

23. Ibid., pp. 250-51.

24. Ibid., p. 240.

25. Ana Sojo, *Mujer y Política. Ensayo sobre el feminismo y el sujeto popular* (DEI, San José, Costa Rica, 1985) , p. 47.

26. Elsa Tamez. "Introducción a la problemática de la mujer en América Latina," in Elsa Tamez et al., *Comunidad de mujeres y hoombres en la iglesia* (SEBILA, San José, Costa Rica, 1981), p. 37.

27. Here I am following the outline proposed by Gebara and Bingemer described in Chapter 5, note 7 above.

28. Gebara and Bingemer, *Mary, Mother of God, Mother of the Poor*, p. 11.

29. Ibid., pp. 3-4.

30. Ibid., p. 4.

31. Ibid., pp. 4-5.

32. Ibid., p. 5.

33. Ibid., p. 6.

34. Ibid.

35. Ibid., p. 7.

36. Ibid., p. 8.

37. Ibid., p. 9.

38. Ibid., p. 10.

39. Ibid.

40. Ibid., p. 11.

41. Ibid., p. 17.

42. See the spirituality of the liberated body in Pablo Richard, "Espiritualidad para tiempos de revolución," *Espiritualidad y liberación en América Latina*, ed., Eduardo Bonnín (DEI, San José, Costa Rica, 1982), pp. 87-101.

43. Juan L. Ruíz de la Peña, *Imagen de Dios: Antropología teológica fundamental*, p. 130.

44. Gebara and Bingemer, *Mary, Mother of God, Mother of the Poor*, p. 12.

45. These questions are always asked by those marginalized by Western European culture and civilization, which imposed an external identity upon the colonized peoples, one which did not arise from our own self-awareness. Cf. Leopoldo Zea, *Discurso desde la marginación y la barbarie* (Ed. Anthropos, Barcelona, 1988), p. 34.

46. The same process can be seen among marginalized peoples when they pose the problem of their identity: "The Western European is gradually becoming aware of its other face, that of the other which it has refused to see and insisted on describing as barbarian, savage, uncivilized. In their supposed barbarism these others speak a language which the supposedly civilized find difficult to understand and repeat with equal clarity, so that

when they speak a language that is not their own they become the barbarians. The marginalized and so-called barbarian peoples have posed the problem of their identity; they want to know what they are in their world." Zea, *Discurso desde la marginación y la barbarie*, p. 270.

47. Ana María Tepedino, "Jesús e a recuperação do ser humano mulher," *REB* 48/190 (1988), pp. 275-6; María Clara L. Bingemer, "E a mulher rompeu o silêncio," *Perspectiva Teológica*, 46 (1986) pp. 373 ff.

48. Tepedino, "Jesús e a recuperação do ser humano mulher," p. 278.

49. The documents prepared for the Commission on Women and Theology during the meeting on the Situation of Women in Latin America (DEI, San José, Costa Rica, 1989) repeatedly make this point.

50. Cf. Elsa Tamez, *Contra toda condena. La justificación por la fe desde los excluidos* (DEI, San José, Costa Rica, 1991). One of Tamez's key points is the affirmation of the poor and women as full persons and active subjects through divine right.

51. Carmen Lora, "Mujer, víctima de opresión, portadora de liberación" in Lora et al., *Mujer, víctima de opresión, portadora de liberación* (Bartolomé de las Casas, Lima, 1985), pp. 23-24.

52. This insensitivity to the word of oppressed women is similar to the devaluation of the word of the poor by Western culture. Cf. L. Zea, *La filosofía americana como filosofía sin más* (Siglo XXI, Mexico, 1969) pp. 10-11.

53. Carmen Lora, *Implicaciones teológicas en la experiencia de las organizaciones femeninas en el ámbito de la vida cotidiana*, paper presented at the Maryknoll School of Theology, January 1987 (photocopied).

54. On this question see Zea, *La filosofía américana como filosofía sin más*. Efforts to colonize Latin America are particularly virulent today. José María Arguedas reports a North American anthropologist as saying that "our culture is cruel but it is advancing and no one can hold it back." Arguedas continues, "I think I am not saying anything subversive, let alone new or original, when I say that Latin America is being fought over by the great world powers and in the more or less stable carve-up made and agreed between the East and West, we belong to the sphere of influence of the USA and Western Europe. . . . The powers that dominate the weaker countries economically and politically are trying to consolidate their rule through a process of cultural colonization. . . . This great enterprise has important and powerful helpers in the Latin American branches of the large businesses . . . who are identified with the interests, lifestyle, preferences, and ideas of the new colonizers" (*Formación de una cultura nacional indoamericana*, 3d ed. [Siglo XXI, Mexico, 1981], pp. 183-88).

Nevertheless, Latin American countries with a strong ancient indigenous tradition, like Mexico, Peru, Bolivia, Guatemala, and Ecuador, not only resist such projects but have managed to foster their own genuinely original thinking (ibid., p. 187).

55. On this matter see the recent book by Gustavo Gutiérrez, *Dios o el oro en las indias* (Sígueme, Salamanca, 1989).

56. Ibid., pp. 13 and 155.

57. Francisco Javier González Carrión, "Filosofía de la historia lati-

noamericana según Leopoldo Zea," *Anthropos* 13 (1986), p. 43.

58. As Fernando Miró Quesada reminds us, we cannot ignore the fact that "our reality is *ab initio* a reality split in two, one small, light, and full of sonorous words and the other immense, dark, and silent" (*El Perú como doctrina en la antología de la filosofía americana contemporánea* [Mexico, 1968], p. 193, quoted by Zea, *La filosofía américana como filosofía sin más*, p. 55).

59. This appears to be suggested in Juan Luis Segundo's commentaries, although these refer primarily to first-world bourgeois feminism. See Elsa Tamez, *Against Machismo* (Meyer-Stone, Oak Park, Illinois, 1987), p. 4. During the meeting on the situation of women in Latin America (DEI, San José, Costa Rica, 1989) some male theologians present said that women should speak of *reciprocity* rather than *equality*.

60. Zea, *Discurso desde la marginación y la barbarie*, p. 24.

61. This position tries to embrace the interests of the whole society, especially the masses who are excluded and marginalized. It shares the fate of the exploited who are struggling for their liberation. Cf. Leopoldo Zea, *Dialéctica de la conciencia americana* (Biblioteca Iberoamericana, Mexico, 1976), pp. 318-26.

62. María José Rosado Nuñez recently expressed this concern. See Rosado Nuñez, "Interview," in Elsa Tamez, *La mujeres toman la palabra* (DEI, San José, Costa Rica, 1989), p. 44. Her question is: Can we construct a theological discourse in which women are recognized as persons?

63. It is highly significant that the claim by oppressed peoples, despised races, marginalized cultures, and oppressed women to be actors in history, and considered in their human integrity is a constant in the theological thinking of Gustavo Gutiérrez. I need mention only a few of his works: *We Drink From Our Own Wells*, "Liberation and the Poor: The Puebla Perspective" in *The Power of the Poor in History* (Orbis Books, Maryknoll, N.Y., 1983), "The Task of Theology and Ecclesial Experience" *Concilium* 176 (1984), pp. 61-64.

64. On this subject see Luis Fernando Crespo, "Método teológico. Notas sobre la reflexión teológica en América Latina" (*CAM-Serie Iglesia y Religión* 18 (1983), pp. 1-19.

65. On consciousness that eliminates prejudices and liberating consciousness, cf. Zea, *La filosofía américana como filosofía sin más*, pp. 159-60.

66. A lot of this influence is due to the longevity of the Christianity whose theological-anthropological support lay in St. Augustine and Thomas Aquinas (cf. Børresen, *Subordination et Equivalence*). This phenomenon is not exclusive to the Christian tradition; it is shared by the Eastern cultures. We need only remind ourselves of women's excessive submission in Islam and Buddhism.

67. A. Kosnik, ed., *Human Sexuality: New Directions in American Catholic Thought* (Paulist Press, New York, 1977), p. 1 (italics are mine). Cf. Rosemary Radford Ruether, *Contemporary Roman Catholicism: Crises and Challenges* (Sheed & Ward, Kansas City, 1987), pp. 24-45.

68. "Sexual difference and relationship are intrinsically human, good, and fruitful. ... According to Genesis 1 and 2, then, humanity, the two

sexes, and sexuality are created good and are designed for a harmonious and productive existence" (Lisa Sowle Cahill, *Between the Sexes: Foundations for a Christian Ethics of Sexuality* [Fortress Press, Philadelphia, 1985], pp. 52 and 55).

69. Ibid., p. 99.

70. This is what is meant by the category "gender," which I noted in the first chapter. "We are born with biological characteristics of a man or woman, with anatomical differences between the sexes, but socially each person will behave in accordance with the totality of norms and prescriptions laid down by society and culture about what is masculine and feminine behavior. But although the roles change in accordance with the culture and the historical moment, a basic division remains: the feminine gender is in charge of the private sphere and the masculine of the public sphere. The problem is that the structuring of gender is so strong that it comes to be thought of as something *natural*" (Maruja González B., *¿Qué es el feminismo? Breve historia y aproximaciones teóricas-políticas*, Serie Pensamiento y Luchas 2 (EMAS, Mexico, 1989), p. 27).

71. Benjamín Forcano, *Nueva ética sexual*, 3d ed. (Paulinas, Madrid, 1981), p. 40.

72. Virginia Vargas et al., "Educación popular y construcción de la identidad de género," *Tejiendo nuestra red* 2 (1989), pp. 15-17.

73. The Women's Legal Office of the Luisa Amanda Espinoza Association of Nicaraguan Women (AMNLAE) in Nicaragua took the initiative to combat abuse and violence against women, given its high level in the country. See *Aporte al maltrato en la relación de pareja* (AMNLAE Nacional, Managua, 1986). See also the investigations on daily life and violence against women carried out by the Women's Solidarity Action Team (EMAS, Coyoacán, Mexico, 1989).

74. Cf. Lory Heise, *Crimes of Gender* (Worldwatch Institute, Washington, D.C., March-April 1989), p. 14. The most irrational instance of violence against women is the mutilation of their genital organs in infancy (clitoris, labia minora, labia majora) in some African countries (Sudan, Senegal, Ghana, Kenya, Gambia, Guinea, Sierra Leone, and Somalia among others), particularly among Muslim and Islamic people. This also occurs in Middle Eastern countries, the Arabian peninsula, the Persian Gulf, Malaysia and the Island of Java. According to the World Health Organization, more than eighty million women have suffered this mutiliation. Its origin lies in the control exercised by men over women's sexuality and pleasure, and its aim is to ensure the woman's virginity until marriage (ibid., pp. 18ff). This inhuman practice must be denounced and rejected by women all over the world.

75. Lora, *Mujer, víctima de opresión, portadora de liberación*, p. 34.

76. Ibid.

77. González, *¿Qué es el feminismo?*, p. 8.

78. "We believe it is necessary to assume the process of women's liberation as a whole. A proposal for change that took no account of oppression at the sexual level would not wholly liberate women. At the same time the demand for women's liberation, which lays excessive stress on the sexual question, does not tackle the problem as a whole or go to its roots. So it

cannot produce total liberation either" (Cecilia Barnechea, "Sexualidad, vivencias y actitudes de la mujer popular" in *Mujer, víctima de opresión, portadora de liberación*, p. 86).

79. Kosnik, ed., *Human Sexuality: New Directions in American Catholic Thought*, p. 108; Cahill, *Between the Sexes: Foundations for a Christian Ethics of Sexuality*, p. 56; Ruether, *Contemporary Roman Catholicism: Crises and Challenges*, pp. 33-34.

80. The logic of death belongs to the current international economic order. See Elsa Tamez, "Justicia y justificación en ocasión de la deuda externa de América Latina," *Pasos* 22 (1989), pp. 11-13.

81. Ivone Gebara, "Option for the Poor as an Option for the Poor Woman," *Concilium* 194 (1987), pp. 113-114.

82. Ibid., p. 114.

83. Ibid., pp. 114-115.

84. In recent years there has been an unusual growth in feminist research centers and publications, which is a sign of hope. For example: Women's Network of the Adult Education Council for Latin America (CEAAL); Maria Quilla Center for Research and Education on the Women's Condition (Ecuador); Luisa Amanda Espinoza Association of Nicaraguan Women (AMNLAE, Nicaragua); Women for Dialogue (MPD, Mexico); Women's Solidarity Action Team (EMAS, Mexico); Flora Tristán Peruvian Women's Center (Peru); Research Center for Women's Action (CIPAF, Dominican Republic); Women's Action Center (Ecuador); Association of Salvadorean Women (AMS, El Salvador); Gregoria Apaza Center for the Promotion of Women (Bolivia); Barrancabermeja Popular Women's Organization (OFP, Colombia), and others.

85. What I call *heartfelt solidarity* is concerned with the profound ancestral community spirit of our peoples. See Francisco Javier González Carrión, "Identidad del hombre latinoamericano según Leopoldo Zea," *Anthropos* 14 (1987), pp. 9-11; Laurette Séjourné, *América Latina, antigüas culturas precolombinas*, 19th ed. (Siglo XXI, Mexico, 1987); Miguel León-Portilla, *Crónicas indígenas. Visión de los vencidos*, vol. 6, *Historia 16*, (Madrid, 1985); S. Ramírez Mercado, *El pensamiento vivo de Sandino* (Nueva Nicaragua, Managua, 1981) V. Gómez, "Perspectivas de la mujer andina," in Irene Foulkes, *Teología desde la mujer en Centroamérica* (SEBILA, San José, 1989), p. 78. See, for example, the songs full of love, longing, and tenderness in the indigenous chronicles. Their community feeling is clear, since "we have come here to know each other, the earth is only lent to us. So let us live in peace, let us live in harmony. . . . Through God's commandment we love each other. . . . I recall God's design and we must cease our disturbance. Here are your flowers" (Miguel León-Portilla, ed., *Cantos y crónicas del México antigüo* (Historia 24, Madrid, 1986), pp. 142-43. We find a similar spirit in the account of Chilam Balam. See Miguel de Rivera, ed., *Chilam Balam de Chumayel* (Historia 20, Madrid, 1986).

86. Raúl Vidales, "La insurgencia de las etnias-utopía de los pueblos profundos," in *La esperanza en el presente de América Latina*, Raúl Vidales and Luis Rivera Pagán, eds. (DEI, San José, 1983), pp. 257-74. "When you hear the testimony of the brave Nicaraguan women who fought against the

Somoza dictatorship and who are now giving their lives to rebuild the country and defend the revolution, or the testimony of the Salvadorean and Guatemalan women who keep on with the struggle, we other women in Latin America are dumbfounded for a while in respect and admiration; many of us offer our arms, feet, and heads in material and spiritual solidarity with the arms, feet, and heads of the Central American women" (Elsa Tamez, "Mujer y varón llamados a la vida: Un acercamiento bíblico-teológico," in *La esperanza en el presente de América Latina*, p. 289.

87. Cf. González Carrión, "Identidad del hombre latinoamericano según Leopoldo Zea." See also Carmen Lora, *Implicaciones teológicas en la experiencia de las organizaciones femeninas en el ámbito de la vida cotidiana*, pp. 7-14. Although not much is written about it we find the dimension of solidarity, friendship, and simple spontaneous affection is a feature of the different local national or Latin American women's meetings. This creates more spiritual strength, and often it is this solidarity that enables many women to persist in various projects of work or research lasting a long time in difficult places, including conditions of loneliness, isolation, and deprivation. Whatever the physical place Latin American women committed to the liberation of the poor and themselves feel bound together in this network of heartfelt solidarity. Generally, Latin American communal behavior is different from the cold, individualistic, and closed relations in the reigning system and more in accord with the gospel ethic. On the community praxis inherent in Christian experience, refer to Enrique Dussel, *Ethics and Community* (Orbis Books, Maryknoll, N.Y., 1988), pp. 78-87.

88. Gebara, "Option for the Poor as an Option for the Poor Woman," p. 115.

89. Ibid., p. 115-16.

90. Ibid., p. 116.

91. Ibid., p. 117.

6. Women's Contribution to Theology in Latin America

1. We understand that both locations must be articulated and at the same time maintain their relative autonomy. "The unity of these two locations also requires their autonomy, because while the epistemological location guarantees methodological coherence, the social one provides the themes to be analyzed. This is most important, because in the very act of choosing a topic and rejecting others you are saying where this theme comes from. ... Of course the social location occupied by philsophers [women theologians, in our case] is no guarantee of the internal quality of their discourse. But it does constitute the necessary condition for this same philsophical theory [theological in this case] to choose a particular theoretical object and present a style appropriate for its communication. So both locations need one another and complement each other: one contributes the theme, the other the method" (J. Francisco Gómez Hinojosa, *Intelectuales y pueblo. Un acercamiento a la luz de Antonio Gramsci* [DEI, San José, Costa Rica, 1987], pp. 225-26).

2. María Clara Bingemer, "Chairete: Alegrai-vos a mulher no futuro da teología da liberção," *REB* 48/191 (1988), p. 571.

3. Elsa Tamez, "Introduction: The Power of the Naked," in *Through Her Eyes: Women's Theology from Latin America* (Orbis Books, Maryknoll, N.Y., 1989), p. 4.

4. Bingemer, "Chairete," p. 572.

5. "The time of silence is the time of living encounter with God and of prayer and commitment; it is a time of 'staying with him' (John 1:39). As the experience of human love shows us, in this kind of encounter we enter depths and regions that are ineffable. When words do not suffice, when they are incapable of communicating what is experienced at the affective level, then we are fully engaged in loving. And when words are incapable of showing forth our experience, we fall back on symbols, which are another way of remaining silent. For when we use a symbol, we do not speak; we let an object or gesture speak for us. . . . This is why images of human love are so often used in the Bible in speaking of the relations between God and the people of God" (Gustavo Gutiérrez, *On Job: God-Talk and the Suffering of the Innocent* [Orbis Books, Maryknoll, N.Y., 1987], p. xiv).

6. Bingemer, "Chairete."

7. Ibid., p. 573.

8. Ibid.

9. Ibid., p. 574. Everyday poetic and playful language is used by the Spanish biblical scholar Dolores Aleixandre in her writing (see Dolores Aleixandre, "María cómplice de nuestra espera, ruega por nosotros," *Sal Terrae* 11 (1984), pp. 785-91; "La arcilla y el tesoro (con minúsculas, por favor . . .)," *Sal Terrae* 10 (1987), pp. 719-30; "La estatua de Nabucodonosor y otros sueños," *Sal Terrae* 11 (1988), pp. 785-92; "Profetas alcanzados y alterados por Dios," *Sal Terrae* 2 (1990), pp. 93-106.

10. Bingemer, "Chairete."

11. Ibid., p. 575.

12. Bingemer, "Chairete."

13. The oppression suffered by women is a profound oppression, incomparably worse than that suffered by the poor man (Gustavo Gutiérrez in Elsa Tamez, *Against Machismo: Interviews* [Meyer-Stone Books, Oak Park, Illinois, 1987], p. 40).

14. Hence Ivone Gebara's contribution, "Option for the Poor as an Option for the Poor Woman," *Concilium* 194 (1987), p. 113.

15. For the articulation of the locations in the dialectic between theory and practice, see Gómez Hinojosa, note 1 above.

16. Gebara, "Option for the Poor as an Option for the Poor Woman," p. 113.

17. Ibid., pp. 111-12.

18. Ibid.

19. Ibid., pp. 112-13.

20. Ibid., pp. 116-17.

21. Ana María Tepedino, "Feminist Theology as the Fruit of Passion and Compassion," *With Passion and Compassion: Third World Women Doing*

Theology, Virginia Fabella and Mercy Oduyoye, eds. (Orbis Books, Maryknoll, N.Y., 1988), p. 165.

22. Ibid., p. 166.

23. Gebara, "Women Doing Theology in Latin America," in *With Passion and Compassion: Third World Women Doing Theology,* p. 133.

24. Ibid., p. 132; Elsa Tamez, "The Power of the Naked" in *Through Her Eyes: Women's Theology from Latin America,* Elsa Tamez, ed. (Orbis Books, Maryknoll, N.Y., 1989), p. 5.

25. Gebara, "Women Doing Theology in Latin America," p. 132.

26. María José Rosado Nuñez, Interview in Elsa Tamez, *Las mujeres toman la palabra* (DEI, San José, 1989), p. 41.

27. Ibid.

28. Ibid.

29. Ibid.

30. As João B. Libanio and María Clara Bingemer write: "The reign of God will not come ostentatiously. You will not be able to say: 'It is here or it is there' (Lk. 17:20-21). So there is no transparency in a liberation movement that enables us to see, so to speak, in its waters the clear and perfect image of God's reign. This would be an audacity and human presumption. But, on the other hand, from the criteria of charity, justice, freedom, love for the poor and others offered us by the gospel we can hope that God is near in these movements. And in that hope and faith we approach them, either to analyze them theoretically or commit ourselves politically with them. And with that hope we trust those who die in them to God" (*Escatología cristiana* [Paulinas, Madrid, 1985], pp. 132-33).

31. Tepedino, "Feminist Theology as the Fruit of Passion and Compassion," p. 166.

32. Ibid.

33. Leonardo Boff, *Faith on the Edge: Religion and Marginalized Existence* (Orbis Books, Maryknoll, N.Y., 1991), p. 63; Juan José Tamayo-Acosta, *La teología de la liberación. Implicaciones sociales y políticas* (Ediciones de Cultura Hispanica, Madrid, 1990); Elisabeth Schüssler Fiorenza, "Editorial," *Concilium* 182 (1985), p. 14.

34. Cf. Gebara, "Women Doing Theology in Latin America," p. 131; Elisabeth Schüssler Fiorenza, *In Memory of Her: A Feminist Theological Reconstruction of Christian Origins* (Crossroad, New York, 1983), pp. xv-xvi.

35. Cf. Tepedino, "Feminist Theology as the Fruit of Passion and Compassion," p. 167; Schüssler Fiorenza, "Breaking the Silence — Becoming Visible," *Concilium* 182 (1985), p. 14.

36. Gebara, "Women Doing Theology in Latin America," p. 132; see also Tamayo-Acosta, *Para comprender la teología de la liberación,* p. 13; Schüssler Fiorenza, *In Memory of Her,* pp. 48-49.

37. Tereza Cavalcanti, "Sobre la participación de las mujeres in el VI Encuentro Intereclesial de las CEB" in María Pilar Aquino (ed.), *Aportes para una teología desde la mujer* (Biblia y Fe, Madrid, 1988), p. 135; Schüssler Fiorenza, *In Memory of Her,* pp. 30-34.

38. On this point see Tereza Cavalcanti, "Produzindo teología no Feminino plural: A propósito do III Encontro Nacional de Teología na per-

spectiva da mulher," *Perspectiva Teológica* 20 (1988), pp. 362ff.

39. Boff, *Faith on the Edge: Religion and Marginalized Existence*, pp. 62-63; Tamayo-Acosta, *La teología de la liberación. Implicaciones sociales y políticas*.

40. Cf. "Final Document: Intercontinental Women's Conference (Oaxtepec, Mexico, Dec. 1-6, 1986,) in *With Passion and Compassion: Third World Women Doing Theology*, pp. 184-90.

41. In Tamez, *Through Her Eyes: Women's Theology from Latin America*, p. 151.

42. Ibid., pp. 151-52.

43. Rosado Nuñez, in Tamez, *Las mujeres toman la palabra*, p. 46.

44. As often happens in theology and pastoral studies, many of the works are collective. In general, the writings gather the procedure, contents, results, and commitments reached by the communities. See, for example, *Mulher-Comunidade: a nova mulher*, in *Pastoral da Mulher pobre* (Vozes, Petrópolis, 1988), pp. 65-108; L. Ferreira, "La vocación pastoral de la mujer según la biblia," in Jorge Pixley, *La mujer en la construcción de la Iglesia* (DEI, San José, 1986), pp. 55-106; Raquel Rodríguez, "Esperanza contra esperanza: Perspectivas bíblico-teológicas de la pobreza desde la mujer latinoamericana," *Pasos* 20 (1988), pp. 1-9; idem, "La mujer y su autoridad en la Nueva Creación," *Vida y Pensamiento* 6/2 (1986), pp. 33-41; Ana María Tepedino, "Jesús e a recuperação do ser human o mulher," *REB* 48/190 (1988), pp. 273-82; idem, *Mulheres discípulas nos Evangelhos-discipulado de iguais*, master's thesis, Pontifical Catholic University of Rio de Janeiro, April, 1987; M. V. González Apaza, *Leer el evangelio desde la mujer* (Quelco, Oruro, 1988), pp. 103-18; R. M. Figur Messer, *A historia de Tamar com Judá*, photocopied text, 1986; I. Rodríguez Caldeira, *A revelação de um Deus partidario*, photocopied text, 1985; Tereza Cavalcanti, "The Prophetic Ministry of Women in the Hebrew Bible," in Elsa Tamez, *Through Her Eyes*, pp. 118-39; María Teresa Porcile, "El derecho a la belleza en América Latina," in *El rostro femenino de la teología* (DEI, San José, 1986), pp. 85-107; V. Moreira da Silva, "La mujer en la teología: Reflexión bíblico-teológica" in *Mujer latinoamericana, iglesia y teología* (MPD, Mexico, 1981), pp. 140-66; Elsa Tamez, "Meditación bíblica sobre la mujer en Centroamérica," *Vida y Pensamiento* 6/2 (1986), pp. 53-57; idem, "Justicia y justificación en ocasión de la deuda externa en América Latina," *Vida y Pensamiento* 6/2 (1986), pp. 11-13; "The Woman Who Complicated the History of Salvation," *Cross Currents* 20 (1986), pp. 129-39; idem, "Women's Rereading of the Bible," in Virginia Fabella and Mercy Oduyoye, *With Passion and Compassion*, pp. 173-83; María Pilar Aquino, "Praxis ministerial hoy: La respuesta del Tercer Mundo," *Revista de Teología Bíblica* 46 (1990), pp. 116-39; idem, "Beinaventurados los perseguidos por causa de la justicia y los que buscan la paz," *Sal Terrae* 12 (1989), pp. 895-907.

45. Ivone Gebara and María Clara Bingemer, *Mary, Mother of God, Mother of the Poor* (Orbis Books, Maryknoll, N.Y., 1990), p. 27.

46. Ibid., pp. 28-29.

47. Ibid., p. 29.

48. "Final Document," in *The Challenge of Basic Christian Communites*.

Papers from the International Ecumenical Congress of Theology, February 20-March 2, São Paulo, Brazil, Sergio Torres and John Eagleson, eds. (Orbis Books, Maryknoll, N.Y., 1981), p. 235.

49. Cf. Encuentro Latinoamericano sobre la Situación de la mujer en América Latina (DEI, San José, 1989). This criterion must be methodologically incorporated into the task of biblical interpretation. It also serves as a norm for evaluating the traditions, texts, and interpretations of the Bible as well as for reformulating the principle of biblical authority.

50. Gebara and Bingemer, *Mary, Mother of God, Mother of the Poor,* p. 31. Biblical reflection in Latin America "tries to be sensitive to the questions that are welling up in a Church whose place among the poor demands a faithful, and at the same time renewed, rereading of the scriptures," Tereza Cavalcanti, "The Prophetic Ministry of Women in the Hebrew Bible," p. 119.

51. Cavalcanti, "Sobre la participación de las mujeres en el VI Encuentro Intereclesial de las CEB," pp. 131-32.

52. Ibid., p. 131.

53. Within the limits of this book it is not possible to describe all the works on rereading the Bible written by women in Latin America. But here I describe the sort of rereading of the Bible that is being done in terms of the daily experience of women in the base communities and the popular social movements. See note 44 above.

54. Gebara, "Women Doing Theology in Latin America," p. 126. Such dialogue is characteristic of women doing theology.

55. Cavalcanti, "Sobre la participación de las mujeres en el VI Encuentro Intereclesial de las CEB," pp. 131-32.

56. Ibid., p. 132.

57. Many women have to face *machismo* from their husbands, who see women's new awareness as incompatible with the "proper" tasks of a wife and mother in the home. On the other hand, when husbands join in the base communities. they gradually acquire an attitude of more solidarity.

58. Final Statement of Women's Theological Congress ("Mujer Latinoamericana: Iglesia y Teología") in Cora Ferro et al., *Mujer latinoamericana: Iglesia y Teología* (MPD, Mexico, 1981), p. 214.

59. Tamez, "Women's Rereading of the Bible," p. 174.

60. Ibid. For a view of the whole of biblical hermeneutics in liberation theology with an extensive bibliography, see Tamayo-Acosta, *Para comprender la teología de la liberación,* pp. 98-114.

61. Tamez, "Women's Rereading of the Bible," p. 174.

62. Ibid.

63. Ibid., p. 175.

64. Ibid., p. 176.

65. Ibid.

66. Ibid.

67. Ibid.

68. Ibid.

69. Ibid., p. 177.

70. For the different hermeneutic models or paradigms used up till now

by biblical research, see Elisabeth Schüssler Fiorenza, "Toward a Feminist Biblical Hermeneutics: Biblical Interpretation and Liberation Theology," in *The Challenge of Liberation Theology*, ed. Brian Mahan and L. Dale Richesin (Orbis Books, Maryknoll, N.Y., 1984), pp. 91-112.

71. The term was first used by Tamez in *Against Machismo: Interviews*, pp. 143-47.

72. Tamez, "Women's Rereading of the Bible," p. 178.

73. Ibid.

74. Ibid.

75. In the Latin American context we cannot avoid the significance of death and life. It is a key theme to all liberating thought on biblical theology. In fact, there is no Latin American country that is not in turmoil. The long history of crimes in El Salvador against imnnumerable unknown men and women goes on day after day, although sometimes public opinion is aroused by a particular outrage such as the massacre on November 16, 1989, of two women and six Jesuit priests. Thousands fall defending life against systems of death that oppress, impoverish, and kill. I want to stress this point to serve as a reference for what it means to speak about life and death and Latin America. These facts call for justice and collective solidarity, so that God may be seen *really* to be the God of Life and on the side of the oppressed.

76. Tamez, "Women's Rereading of the Bible," p. 179.

77. Ibid.

78. Ibid., p. 180.

79. Schüssler Fiorenza, *In Memory of Her*. See also her *Bread not Stone: The Challenge of Feminist Biblical Interpretation* (Beacon Press, Boston, 1984); and "Toward a Feminist Biblical Hermeneutics: Biblical Interpretation and Liberation Theology."

80. María Clara Bingemer, "Reflections on the Trinity," in Tamez, *Through Her Eyes: Women's Theology from Latin America*, (Orbis Books, Maryknoll, N.Y., 1989), p. 56.

81. I am referring here to theological language, not strictly to grammar, although this is included.

82. Cf. Luz Beatríz Arellano, "Women's Experience of God in Emerging Spirituality," in *With Passion and Compassion: Third World Women Doing Theology*, pp. 135-36.

83. Ineke Bakker, "Si Dios es todopoderoso ¿por qué tenemos que sufrir tanto?" in *Teología desde la mujer en Centroamérica*, I. Foulkes, ed. (SEBILA, San José, 1989), pp. 81-104; Arellano, "Women's Experience of God in Emerging Spirituality," p. 136. These questions become more acute in situations of aggression, hardship, and unceasing threat against Latin American countries, especially Central America, by the big capitalist countries, particularly North America.

84. Gebara, "Women Doing Theology in Latin America," p. 44.

85. Arellano, "Women's Experience of God in Emerging Spirituality," pp. 113-14.

86. Tepedino, "Feminist Theology as the Fruit of Passion and Compassion," p. 167.

87. Arellano, "Women's Experience of God in Emerging Spirituality," p. 137.

88. Aurora Lapiedra, "Religiosidad popular y mujer andina" in Tamez, *El rostro femenino de la teología*, pp. 56 and 72.

89. Tepedino, "Feminist Theology as the Fruit of Passion and Compassion," p. 167.

90. Cavalcanti, "The Prophetic Ministry of Women in the Hebrew Bible," pp. 118-39.

91. Ibid., 138-39.

92. Bingemer, "Reflections on the Trinity," pp. 56-80.

93. Ibid., p. 56.

94. Ibid., pp. 61-62.

95. Ibid., p. 66.

96. Ibid., p. 67.

97. Ibid.

98. Ibid.

99. Ibid., p. 74.

100. Bingemer, "Chairete: Alegrai-vos a mulher no futuro da teología da liberção," pp. 581-84.

101. Bingemer, "Reflections on the Trinity," p. 67.

102. Tamez, *Against Machismo: Interviews*, p. 147.

103. Cavalcanti, "Sobre la participación de las mujeres in el VI Encuentro Intereclesial de las CEB," pp. 139-40.

104. Inquiry among women participating in the *Encuentro* on the Situation of Women in Latin America (DEI, San José, July 1989), in the archives.

105. Bakker, "Si Dios es todopoderoso ¿por qué tenemos que sufrir tanto?" p. 100.

106. Tamez, *Against Machismo: Interviews*, p. 147.

107. Elisabeth Moltmann-Wendell, *A Land Flowing with Milk and Honey: Perspectives on Feminist Theology* (Crossroad, New York, 1986), p. 82; Schüssler Fiorenza, *In Memory of Her*, pp. 316-23.

108. Tepedino, "Feminist Theology as the Fruit of Passion and Compassion," p. 170. See also Schüssler Fiorenza, *In Memory of Her*, pp. 323-33.

109. Nelly Ritchie, "Women and Christology," in *Through Her Eyes*, p. 82.

110. Ibid., p. 84.

111. The most relevant christological works in Latin America are: Jon Sobrino, *Cristology at the Crossroads* (Orbis Books, Maryknoll, N.Y., 1976); Leonardo Boff, *Jesus Christ Liberator* (Orbis Books, Maryknoll, New York, 1978); Juan Luis Segundo, *Jesus of Nazareth: Yesterday and Today*, 5 vols. (Orbis Books, Maryknoll, N.Y., 1985-1988); Hugo Echegaray, *The Practice of Jesus* (Orbis Books, Maryknoll, N.Y., 1984).

112. Echegaray, *The Practice of Jesus*, p. 82.

113. Thus the Final Statement of the Encuentro Comunidad de Mujeres y Hombres en la Iglesia declares, "We see in Jesus' historical activity the guidelines by which we should read the whole Bible" (Tamez et al., *Comu-*

nidad de mujeres y hombres en la iglesia, p. 24). This is because Jesus' practice does not exclude women. For my methodological observations I have followed Julio Lois, *Jesucristo Liberador* (AA.VV., Pontifical University of Salamanca, 1988), pp. 41-43.

114. Ritchie, "Women and Christology," p. 91.

115. For the reign of God as eschatological gift and human task, see Echegaray, *The Practice of Jesus*, pp. 79-81.

116. María Clara Bingemer, "Mujer y Cristología: Jesucristo y la salvación de la mujer" in Aquino, *Aportes para una teología desde la mujer* (Biblia y Fe, Madrid, 1988), pp. 80-93. From Rosemary Radford Ruether's works, I list the following: *To Change the World: Christology and Cultural Criticism* (Crossroad, New York, 1983); *Sexism and God Talk* (Beacon Press, Boston, 1983). Elisabeth Moltmann-Wendell also acknowledges a debt to Rosemary Radford Ruether in her research on the subject. Cf. Moltmann-Wendell, *A Land Flowing with Milk and Honey: Perspectives on Feminist Theology*, p. 117.

117. Bingemer, "Mujer y Cristología: Jesuscristo y la salvación de la mujer," pp. 82-85.

118. Ibid., p. 84.

119. Ibid., p. 85.

120. Cora Ferro et al., *Mujer latinoamericana: Iglesia y teología* (MPD, Mexico, 1981), p. 216.

121. For a detailed investigation of the socio-religious movements in Jesus' time see, Echegaray, *The Practice of Jesus*, pp. 39-67. On research into whether women participated in these movements or not, see Schüssler Fiorenza, *In Memory of Her*, pp. 110-18.

122. Schüssler Fiorenza, *In Memory of Her*, pp. 113 and 110-18; Echegaray, *The Practice of Jesus*, pp. 79-88.

123. Tamez et al., *Comunidad de mujeres y hombres en la iglesia*, p. 24.

124. Bingemer, "Mujer y Cristología," pp. 86-87.

125. Ibid., p. 87.

126. Moltmann-Wendell, *A Land Flowing with Milk and Honey*, p. 129.

127. Schüssler Fiorenza, *In Memory of Her*, pp. 129 and 140.

128. Bingemer, "Mujer y Cristología," pp. 86-87.

129. Tepedino, "Jesús e a recuperação do ser humano mulher," p. 274.

130. The commentaries on the biblical texts are found in Tepedino, "Jesús e a recuperação do ser humano mulher," pp. 273-82.

131. Schüssler Fiorenza, *In Memory of Her*, p. 138; also quoted by Tepedino in "Jesús e a recuperação do ser humano mulher."

132. The features I point out from here onward are those mentioned by Nelly Ritchie, "Women and Christology," in Tamez, *Through Her Eyes*, pp. 81-95.

133. Bingemer, "Mujer y Cristología," p. 90.

134. Ibid.

135. I have pointed out this aspect elsewhere. Cf. Aquino, "Praxis ministerial hoy: La respuesta del Tercer Mundo," *Revista de Teología Bíblica* 46 (1990), pp. 116-39.

136. Arellano, "Women's Experience of God in Emerging Spirituality," p. 135.

137. Consuelo del Prado, "I Sense God in Another Way," in Tamez, *Through Her Eyes*, p. 140.

138. Cavalcanti, "Produzindo teología no Feminino plural: A propósito do III Encontro Nacional de Teología na perspectiva da mulher," *Perpsectiva Teológica* 20 (1988), p. 366.

139. Del Prado, "I Sense God in Another Way," p. 140.

140. Ibid.

141. Cavalcanti, "Produzindo teología no Feminino plural."

142. Ibid., pp. 366-67.

143. Schüssler Fiorenza, *In Memory of Her*, p. 346.

144. Arellano, "Women's Experience of God in Emerging Spirituality," p. 201.

145. Ibid.

146. Moltmann-Wendell, *A Land Flowing with Milk and H*, p. 99.

147. Schüssler Fiorenza, *In Memory of Her*, p. 188; Bingemer, "Reflections on the Trinity," pp. 65-66; Bingemer only mentions this point; she does not develop it fully.

148. Schüssler Fiorenza, *In Memory of Her*, p. 186.

149. Ibid., p. 199.

150. Arellano, "Women's Experience of God in Emerging Spirituality," p. 203.

151. Ibid., p. 124.

152. Leonardo Boff and Clodovis Boff, *Introducing Liberation Theology* (Orbis Books, Maryknoll, N.Y., 1987), p. 56.

153. For Segundo Galilea, "having a spirituality of liberation means creating a dynamism in which death (conflicts, frustration, failure) acquires meaning in relation to a new life, a new man, a new society. ... The goal of man and societies, according to the gospel, is to create true brotherhood. Jesus will die 'to gather together all God's scattered sons' divided by hatred, exploitation and sin. Christian brotherhood ... is the fruit of following Christ, who transforms us from selfish people into brothers. This leads to a community of brothers where no one unjustly dominates anyone else. It is based on the God's fatherhood of all, Jesus as everyone's brother and the key to all brotherhood, and Mary as the mother of men" (*El camino de la espiritualidad* [Paulinas, Bogotá, 1987], pp. 47 and 50). Some chapters of this book, including the one from which this passage is cited, were not included in the English edition entitled *The Way of Living Faith: A Spirituality of Liberation*, trans. J. Diercksmeier (Harper and Row, San Francisco, 1980). Sexist language was eliminated by the English-language publisher and not by the author.

The androcentric perspective of all Segundo's work is explicit. The same may be said about Leonardo and Clodovis Boff when they describe the "society of the free" producing the "new man" (see *Introducing Liberation Theology*, pp. 92-93). We find the same emphasis in Jon Sobrino, *Spirituality of Liberation*, trans. R. Barr (Orbis Books, Maryknoll, N.Y., 1988). Again, the publisher of the English-language editions has eliminated sexist language.

154. Rosemary Radford Ruether, *New Woman, New Earth* (Seabury Press, New York, 1975), p. xiii.

155. Arellano, "Women's Experience of God in Emerging Spirituality," p. 205. Although this work refers specifically to Nicaraguan women, its observations can be extended to other Latin American countries.

156. Cavalcanti, "Produzindo teología no Feminino plural," pp. 368-69.

157. Del Prado, "I Sense God in Another Way," pp. 148-49. For the author our teachers are the women of the people; and Mary, also a woman of the people, a believer, and mother, is the paradigm of our prayer.

158. Ibid., p. 141.

159. Ibid., p. 142.

160. Arellano, "Women's Experience of God in Emerging Spirituality," p. 207.

161. Del Prado, "I Sense God in Another Way," p. 143.

162. Ibid.

163. On these aspects see Del Prado, "I Sense God in Another Way," pp. 143-44; Arellano, "Women's Experience of God in Emerging Spirituality," p. 145.

164. Del Prado, "I Sense God in Another Way," pp. 44-45.

165. Arellano, "Women's Experience of God in Emerging Spirituality," p. 208.

166. Schüssler Fiorenza, *In Memory of Her*, p. 350.

167. Cavalcanti, interview in Tamez, *Las mujeres toman la palabra*, p. 25.

168. Schüssler Fiorenza, *In Memory of Her*, p. 350.

169. Arellano, "Women's Experience of God in Emerging Spirituality," pp. 144-45.

170. Schüssler Fiorenza, *In Memory of Her*, p. 349.

171. Arellano, "Women's Experience of God in Emerging Spirituality," p. 210.

172. Del Prado, "I Sense God in Another Way," p. 143.

173. Ibid., p. 148.

174. Ibid.

175. María Clara Bingemer, "De la teología del laicado a la teología del bautismo," *Páginas* 218 (1987), p. 9.

176. Elisabeth Schüssler Fiorenza, " 'Waiting at Table': A Critical Feminist Theological Reflection on Diakonia," *Concilium* 198 (1988) pp. 84-94; Schüssler Fiorenza, "Breaking the Silence—Becoming Visible," *Concilium* 182 (1985).

177. This agrees with the summons made by Paul VI, saying that "it is necessary for the Church to liberate itself from historical structures that have now revealed themselves to be deformations of its evangelical character and its apostolic mission. We must make a criticial historical and ethical examination in order to give the Church its genuine form, in which the present generation wants to recognize the figure of Christ" (*Insegnamenti di Paolo VI*, vol. 8, Rome, 1970, quoted by Leonardo Boff, *Y la iglesia se hizo pueblo* [Paulinas, Bogotá, 1987], p. 30).

178. Nelly Ritchie, "Women's Participation in the Church," *With Passion and Compassion*, p. 152.

179. Aracely de Rocchietti "Women and the People of God," *Through Her Eyes*, pp. 97-98.

180. Bingemer, "De la teología del laicado a la teología del bautismo," p. 5.

181. Antonio José de Almeida, "Modelos eclesiológicos y ministérios eclesiais," *REB* 48/190 (1983), pp. 311-12.

182. Bingemer, "Mujer y Cristología," p. 84.

183. "Such a patriarchalization of the church is not yet found in the first century" (Schüssler Fiorenza, *In Memory of Her*, p. 278).

184. De Almeida, "Modelos eclesiológicos y ministérios eclesiais," p. 314.

185. H.-M. Legrand, quoted in de Almeida, "Modelos eclesiológicos y ministérios eclesiais," p. 326.

186. De Almeida, "Modelos eclesiológicos y ministérios eclesiais."

187. Bingemer, "De la teología del laicado a la teología del bautismo," p. 5.

188. Ibid., pp. 5-6.

189. De Rocchietti "Women and the People of God," p. 102.

190. Leonardo Boff, *Y la iglesia se hizo pueblo*, pp. 30-31; see also Juan Luis Segundo, *The Community Called Church* (Orbis Books, Maryknoll, New York, 1973), pp. 9-11.

191. De Rocchietti "Women and the People of God," p. 103.

192. Ritchie, "Women's Participation in the Church," in Fabella and Oduyoye, *With Passion and Compassion*, p. 152.

193. Ibid., p. 153.

194. Boff, *Y la iglesia se hizo pueblo*, p. 33.

195. Ritchie, "Women's Participation in the Church," p. 153.

196. Ibid., p. 152.

197. Ibid., p. 154.

198. Bingemer, "De la teología del laicado a la teología del bautismo," p. 6.

199. Schüssler Fiorenza, *In Memory of Her*, p. 142. "We must not oppose Jesus' 'concern for the Poor' to 'emancipation from patriarchal structures.' The Jesus traditions show both his stance on behalf of the poor as well as his concern for women. . . . " (ibid.)

200. Ritchie, "Women's Participation in the Church," p. 154; De Rocchietti, "Women and the People of God," pp. 107-8.

201. Schüssler Fiorenza, *In Memory of Her*, p. 286.

202. Rosemary Radford Ruether, "Misogynism and Virginal Feminism in the Fathers of the Church," in *Religion and Sexism* (Simon and Schuster, New York, 1974), pp. 150-83. The Fathers of the church combine a misogynist attitude with the elevation of the virginal woman as a result of their cosmic-anthrolopological dualism and their patriarchal theological monism.

203. Schüssler Fiorenza, *In Memory of Her*, p. 277; Rosemary Radford Ruether, "La mujer y el ministerio en una perspectiva historica y sociologica", *Concilium* 111 (1976), pp. 47ff.

204. Kari Vogt, " 'Becoming Male': One Aspect of an Early Christian Anthropology," *Concilium* 182 (1985), pp. 73-74.

205. Schüssler Fiorenza, *In Memory of Her*, p. 286-87 and 341 and 335-37.

206. Bingemer, "De la teología del laicado a la teología del bautismo," p. 7.

207. Rafael Aguirre, *Del movimiento de Jesús a la iglesia cristiana* (Desclée de Brouwer, Bilbao, 1987), p. 173.

208. Ritchie, "Women's Participation in the Church," pp. 152-53; Bingemer, "De la teología del laicado a la teología del bautismo."

209. Bingemer, "De la teología del laicado a la teología del bautismo," p. 6.

210. Gustavo Gutiérrez, *The Power of the Poor in History* (Orbis Books, Maryknoll, N.Y., 1983), p. 211.

211. Jon Sobrino, *The True Church and the Poor* (Orbis Books, Maryknoll, N.Y., 1984), pp. 84-124.

212. Leonardo Boff, *Ecclesiogenesis: The Base Communities Reinvent the Church* (Orbis Books, Maryknoll, N.Y., 1986).

213. Bingemer, "De la teología del laicado a la teología del bautismo," p. 4.

214. Ibid., p. 6; De Almeida, "Modelos eclesiológicos y ministérios eclesiais," p. 348.

215. Bingemer, "De la teología del laicado a la teología del bautismo," p. 6.

216. Ibid.

217. De Almeida, "Modelos eclesiológicos y ministérios eclesiais," pp. 348-49.

218. Bingemer, "De la teología del laicado a la teología del bautismo," p. 7.

219. Ritchie, "Women's Participation in the Church," p. 155.

220. Gebara and Bingemer, *Mary: Mother of God, Mother of the Poor*, p. 37.

221. Tereza Cavalcanti, "O culto a María. Tradição e renovação," *Grande Sinal* 40 (1986), p. 276.

222. This is observable in the texts by Latin American women theologians that I quote here. Nevertheless, the one who best expresses this trend is Leonardo Boff in his book *The Maternal Face of God*. There are serious criticisms of this book, perhaps the most pertinent in Kary E. Børresen, "Mary in Catholic Theology," *Concilium* 168 (1983), pp. 54-55. Rosemary Radford Ruether writes, "The liberation of women, as well as men, from sexist hierarchicalism cannot happen as long as this symbolism of masculinity and feminity remains. ... Mariology cannot be a symbol for women as long as it preserves this meaning of feminity that is the complementary underside of masculine domination. Mariology becomes a liberating symbol for women only when it is seen as a radical symbol of a new humanity freed from hierarchical power relations, including that of God and humanity" (Ruether, *New Woman, New Earth*, pp. 57-58).

223. Bingemer, "Chairete: Alegrai-vos a mulher no futuro da teología da liberção," pp. 580-81.

224. Cavalcanti, "O culto a María. Tradição e renovação," p. 274.

225. On the patriarchal and androcentric character of traditional Catholic mariology, cf. Kary E. Børresen, "Mary and Catholic theology," pp. 48-56; see also Gebara and Bingemer, *Mary, Mother of God, Mother of the Poor*, pp. 3-19.

226. Gebara and Bingemer, *Mary, Mother of God, Mother of the Poor*, p. 2.

227. For example, see the theological lines suggested by the Final Document of the Encuentro Latinoamericano sobre La mujer, la praxis y la Teología de la Liberación (Mexico, 1979) in Cora Ferro et al., *Mujer latinoamericana, iglesia y teología* (MPD, Mexico, 1981), pp. 216-17.

228. Bingemer, "Chairete: Alegrai-vos a mulher no futuro da teología da liberção," p. 580.

229. Gebara and Bingemer, *Mary, Mother of God, Mother of the Poor*, p. 161.

230. Børresen, "Mary and Catholic Theology," p. 55.

231. Cavalcanti, "O culto a María. Tradição e renovação," p. 273.

232. Ibid., p. 274.

233. Gebara and Bingemer, *Mary, Mother of God, Mother of the Poor*, 54.

234. Cf. Bingemer, "María a que soube dizer 'não,'" pp. 245-56.

235. Gebara and Bingemer, *Mary, Mother of God, Mother of the Poor*, p. 32.

236. Ibid., p. 37.

237. Ibid., p. 32.

238. Ibid., pp. 33 and 35.

239. Ibid., pp. 163-64.

240. Margarida Luiza Brandao, "María e a espiritualidade femenina," *Grande Sinal* 40 (1986), pp. 260-61.

241. Bingemer, "María a que soube dizer 'não,'" p. 255.

242. Gebara and Bingemer, *Mary, Mother of God, Mother of the Poor*, p. 122.

243. Ibid., 151.

7. Other Themes in Latin American Feminist Theology

1. María Clara Bingemer has begun a dialogue about the eucharistic dimension of the female body. See Bingemer, "Chairete: Alegrai-vos (Lc 15, 8-10) ou a mulher no futuro da teología de libertação," *REB* 48 (1988), pp. 584-86.

2. The Instituto de Pastoral Andina in Cuzco (Peru) has taken up this matter and promoted research on the subject. Among others, especially important are the works of Aurora Lapiedra on the religious experience of women of the Andes. See Lapiedra, "Roles y valores de la mujer andina," *Allpanchis* 25 (1985), pp. 43-63; and "Religiosidad popular y mujer andina" in Elsa Tamez, *El rostro femenino de la teología* (DEI, San José, 1986), pp. 49-72.

3. On various theories of popular religiosity we already have the following classic studies: Raúl Vidales and T. Kudó, *Práctica religiosa y proyecto histórico. Hipótesis para un estudio de la religiosidad popular en América Latina* (CEP, Lima, 1975); T. Kudo, *Práctica religiosa y proyecto histórico II* (CEP, Lima, 1980); D. Irarrázabal, *Religión del pobre y liberación en Chimbote* (CEP, Lima, 1978); José Luis González, "Apuntes para la observación de la religiosidad popular," *CAM Serie Iglesia y Religión* 19, (1984), pp. 7-21 and "Teología de la Liberación y religiosidad popular," *Páginas* 49-50 (1982); further bibliography given by the authors.

4. González, "Apuntes para la observación de la religiosidad popular," p. 15.

5. Lapiedra, "Religiosidad popular y mujer andina," pp. 49-50.

6. Ibid.

7. In the religion of the Andes there exists the *Roal*, the creator spirit who rules the forces of nature and maintains the balance between them, and the *Pachamama*, the origin of things, specially concerned with agriculture, who has her own powers; see ibid., p. 50. Similar personages are found in the Náhuatl, Maya, and in other Latin American cultures.

8. Lapiedra, "Religiosidad popular y mujer andina," p. 71.

9. Most of these features are presented by Aurora Lapiedra. Ibid., pp. 57-58 and 69-72.

10. González, "Apuntes para la observación de la religiosidad popular," p. 18.

11. These aspects were discussed at length during the Meeting on the Situation of Latin American Women (DEI, San José, Costa Rica, 1989). We noted the difficulty women had in integrating these aspects, especially when they work in a field where men are in the majority. In theological circles, male theologians in general expect women theologians not to be emotional but conceptual, precise, and rational in argument, research, and writing. The androcentric way of seeing the task of theology—for both men and women—tends not to empower women but to intimidate them. On this point, see also Elisabeth Moltmann-Wendell, *A Land Flowing with Milk and Honey: Perspectives on Feminist Theology* (Crossroad, New York, 1986), pp. 157-60.

12. María Teresa Porcile, "El derecho a la belleza en América Latina," in Tamez, *El rostro femenino de la teología*, p. 85.

13. Janet W. May, "Desde la debilidad hacia la fuerza: El proceso educativo en la pastoral de la mujer," *Vida y Pensamiento* 8/2 (1988), p. 105.

14. Porcile, "El derecho a la belleza en América Latina," p. 88.

15. Ibid., p. 86.

16. Working papers. Meeting on the Situation of Women (DEI, San José, Costa Rica, 1989).

17. Ibid. See also Working groups: Diagnostic, Methodology, and Strategies.

18. Moltmann-Wendell, *A Land Flowing with Milk and Honey: Perspectives on Feminist Theology*, p. 154.

19. Porcile, "El derecho a la belleza en América Latina," p. 89.

20. Ibid., p. 92.

21. See Porcile's biblical study on beauty, ibid., pp. 93-104.

22. Ibid., p. 90.

23. Ibid., p. 105.

24. Elsa Tamez, "Prayer of Iztaccíhuatl" (unpublished).

25. Irma Janis Jordan, *A libertação da mulher hoje, na igreja e na socie-dade: uma aproximação teológico-moral*, paper presented at the National Meeting of Professors of Moral Theology, Brasilia, 1985 (photocopied), pp. 2-3.

26. Beatríz Melano-Couch, "El Reino de Dios y la ética," in Ivone Gebara et al., *Apuntes y aportes de la mujer ecuménica*, Cuaderno Pastoral 5 (APE-FEC, Mendoza, Argentina, 1987), p. 104.

27. Jordan, "A libertação de mulher hoje, na igreja e no sociedade,", p. 6.

28. This is also one of the tasks facing liberation ethics in general. Cf. Enrique Dussel, *Ethics and Community* (Orbis Books, Maryknoll, N.Y., 1988), p. 242.

29. Ibid., p. 31.

30. Theologian and economist Franz Hinkelammert has worked on these aspects, which I merely mention here. See Franz Hinkelammert, *The Ideological Weapons of Death* (Orbis Books, Maryknoll, N.Y., 1985); also *Crítica a la razón utópica* (DEI, San José, 1984) and *La deuda externa en América Latina* (DEI, San José, 1988). In this latter book see especially chapter 7, "Algunas aspectos teológicos sobre el cobro de la deuda," pp. 61-65.

31. Ignacio Ellacuría, "Diez Afirmaciones sobre Utopía y Profetismo desde América Latina," *Sal Terrae*, 12 (1988), p. 889.

32. Maruja González B., "¿Qué es el feminismo? Breve historia y aproximaciones teórico-políticas," *Pensamiento y Luchas 8* (1989), p. 31.

33. Ibid., pp. 29-30. "The division of labor by sexes, which obliges women to be housewives, is fundamental for capitalism. Within the individual family the workforce is privately reproduced, which involves a mass of ongoing daily tasks done by women, which are not socially recognized but whose fruits are appropriated by capital" (ibid. p. 29).

34. Ibid., pp. 30-31.

35. Ibid.

36. Melano-Couch, "El Reino de Dios y la ética," p. 104.

37. Ibid., p. 106.

38. Dussel, *Ethics and Community*, p. 16.

39. Melano-Couch, "El Reino de Dios y la ética," p. 110.

40. Ellacuría, *Diez Afirmaciones sobre Utopía y profetismo desde América Latina*, p. 254. Ellacuría bore witness to this conviction by his death.

Bibliography

Publications marked by a bullet (•) are written by Latin American women.

ABRAHAM, K. C., ed. *Third World Theologies: Commonalities & Divergences* (Maryknoll, N.Y.: Orbis Books, 1990).

AGUIRRE, Rafael. *Del movimiento de Jesús a la iglesia cristiana* (Bilbao: Desclée de Brouwer, 1987).

ALEIXANDRE, Dolores. "La arcilla y el tesoro (con minúsculas, por favor . . .)," *Sal Terrae* 10 (1987): 719-730.

———. "La estatua de Nabucodonosor y otros sueños," *Sal Terrae* 11 (1988): 785-792.

———. "María, cómplice de nuestra espera, ruega por nosotros," *Sal Terrae* 11 (1984): 785-791.

———. "Profetas alcanzados y alterados por Dios," *Sal Terrae* 2 (1990): 93-106.

AMNLAE-Nacional Asociación de Mujeres Nicaragüenses Luisa Amanda Espinoza, "Aporte al maltrato en la relación de pareja," *Study on Violence Against Women*, (Managua, Nicaragüa: AMNLAE, 1986).

AMOROS, Celia, Maite DEL MORAL et al. "Mujer y cristianismo," *Iglesia Viva* 126 (1986).

ANDER-EGG, Ezequiel. *La mujer irrumpe en la historia* (Madrid: Marisiega, 1980).

• AQUINO, María Pilar, ed. *Aportes para una teología desde la mujer* (Madrid: Biblia y Fe, 1988).

• ———. "Bienaventurados los perseguidos por causa de la justicia y los que buscan la paz," *Sal Terrae* 12 (1989): 895-907.

• ———. "Mujer y praxis ministerial hoy: la respuesta del Tercer Mundo," *Revista de Teología Bíblica* 46/XVI (1990): 116-139.

• ———. "Qué es hacer teología desde la perspectiva de la mujer, in IX Congreso de Teología, Asociación de Teólogos Juan XXIII, in Hugo Assman et al., *Iglesia y Derechos Humanos* (Madrid: Evangelio y Liberación, 1989).

• ———. "Women's Participation in the Church. A Catholic Perspective," in Virginia Fabella and Mercy Amba Oduyoye, ed., *With Passion and Compassion: Third World Women Doing Theology* (Maryknoll, N.Y.: Orbis Books, 1988).

• ARELLANO, Luz Beatríz. "Women's Experience of God in Emerging Spirituality," in Virginia Fabella and Mercy Amba Oduyoye, ed., *With Passion and Compassion: Third World Women Doing Theology* (Maryknoll, N.Y.: Orbis Books, 1988), pp. 135-150.

ARGUEDAS, José María. *Formación de una cultura nacional indoamericana*, 3th. ed., (Mexico: Siglo XXI, 1981).

ARNAZ, E. "Discriminación de la mujer. Voz de colectivos feministas," *Misión Abierta* 3 (1980): 9-52.

ASSMANN, Hugo. "CEBs: Quando la vivencia da fe remeixe o senso comum dos pobres," *Revista Eclesiástica Brasileira* 46/183 (1986).

ASTELARRA, Judith. *El feminismo como perspectiva teórica y como práctica política: Teoría feminista* (Dominican Republic: CIPAF, 1984).

———. "Rasgos patriarcales en la sociedad y en la política," in María José Buxo I Rey et al., *Caminos de democracia en América Latina*, 2nd. ed. (Madrid: Fundación Pablo Iglesias, 1985).

• BAKKER, Ineke. "Si Dios es todopoderoso ¿por qué tenemos que sufrir tanto?" in Irene Foulkes, ed., *Teología desde la mujer en Centroamérica* (San José, Costa Rica: SEBILA, 1989).

• BARNACHEA, Cecilia. "Sexualidad, vivencias y actitudes de la mujer popular," in Carmen Lora, Cecilia Barnachea, and Fryné Santisteban, ed., *Mujer: víctima de opresión, portadora de liberación* (Lima: Instituto Bartolomé de las Casas, 1985).

BETTO, Frei. "Diaconía profética," *Concilium* 218 (1988): 79-87.

———. *Fe, política e ideología*, Praga, June, 1988 (Photocopied).

• BINGEMER, María Clara. "Chairete: Alegrai-vos (Lc 15, 8-10) ou a mulher no futuro da teología da libertação," *REB* 48/191 (1988): 565-587.

• ———. "De la teología del laicado a la teología del bautismo," *Páginas* 86 (1987): 2-10.

• ———. "E a mulher rompeu o silêncio," *Perspectiva Teológica* 46 (1986): 272-380.

• ———. "María, a que soube dizer «não»," *Grande Sinal* 40 (1986): 245-256.

• ———. "Mujer y Cristología. Jesucristo y la salvación de la mujer," in María Pilar Aquino, ed., *Aportes para una teología desde la mujer* (Madrid: Biblia y Fe, 1988).

• ———. "Preface: Third World Theologies: Conversion to Others," in K. C. Abraham, ed., *Third World Theologies: Commonalities & Divergences* (Maryknoll, N.Y.: Orbis Books, 1990).

• ———. "Reflections on the Trinity," in Elsa Tamez, ed., *Through Her Eyes: Women's Theology from Latin America* (Maryknoll, N.Y.: Orbis Books, 1989).

• ———, and Ivone GEBARA. *Mary Mother of God, Mother of the Poor* (Maryknoll, N.Y.: Orbis Books, 1989).

BOFF, Leonardo. "Masculino y femenino: ¿Qué es?" Medellín, *Instituto Pastoral del CELAM* 4 (1975): 501-514.

———. *Church: Charism & Power* (New York: Crossroad, 1985).

———. *Ecclesiogenesis: The Base Communities Reinvent the Church* (Maryknoll, N.Y.: Orbis Books, 1986).

———. *Faith on the Edge: Religion & Marginalized Existence* (Maryknoll, N.Y.: Orbis Books, 1989).

———. *Iglesia, carisma y poder* (Santander: Sal Terrae, 1984).

———. *The Maternal Face of God: The Feminine and its Religious Expressions* (San Francisco: Harper & Row, 1987).

———. "Qué son las teologías del Tercer Mundo," *Concilium* 219 (1988): 181-194.

———. "Significado teológico de Pueblo de Dios e Iglesia Popular," *Concilium* 196 (1984): 441-454.

———. *Teología desde el lugar del pobre* (Santander: Sal Terrae, 1986).

———. *When Theology Listens to the Poor* (San Francisco: Harper Row, 1984).

———. *Y la iglesia se hizo pueblo* (Bogotá: Paulinas, 1987).

BOFF, Leonardo and Clodovis BOFF. *Introducing Liberation Theology* (New York, Orbis Books, 1990).

BONIN, Eduardo, ed. *Espiritualidad y liberación en América Latina* (San José, Costa Rica: DEI, 1982).

BØRRESEN, Kary E. "Fundamentos antropológicos de la relación entre el hombre y la mujer en la teología clásica," *Concilium* 111 (1976): 24-40.

———. "Mary in Catholic Theology," *Concilium* 168 (1983): 48-56.

———. *Subordination et Equivalence: Nature et rôle de la femme d'après Augustin et Thomas d'Aquin* (Oslo: Paris, 1968).

• BRANDAO, Margarida Luiza. "María e a espiritualidade feminina," *Grande Sinal* 40 (1986): 257-266.

BUXO I REY, María José. "El papel de la mujer indígena," in Judith Astelarra et al., *Caminos de democracia en América Latina*, 2nd. ed. (Madrid: Fundación Pablo Iglesias, 1985).

CADY, Susan A. *Sophia: The Future of Feminist Spirituality* (New York: Harper & Row, 1986).

CARDONA VELAZQUEZ, Luis Evelio. *Comunidades eclesiales de base. Una experiencia de solidaridad*, doctoral thesis, Universidad Pontificia de Salamanca, Madrid, 1988.

CARR, Anne E. "Editorial Reflections," *Concilium* 194 (1987): 128-132.

———. *Transforming Grace. Christian Tradition and Women's Experience* (San Francisco: Harper & Row, 1988).

• CAVALCANTI, Tereza. "O culto a María: Tradição e renovação," *Grande Sinal* 40 (1986): 267-278.

• ———. "Produzindo teologia no feminino plural. A propósito do III Encontro Nacional de Teología na perspectiva da mulher," *Perspectiva Teológica* 20 (1988): 359-370.

• ———. "The Prophetic Ministry of Women in the Hebrew Bible," in Elsa Tamez, ed., *Through Her Eyes. Women's Theology from Latin America* (Maryknoll, N.Y.: Orbis Books, 1989).

• ———. "Sobre la participación de las mujeres en el VI Encuentro Intereclesial de las CEB," in María Pilar Aquino, ed., *Aportes para una teología desde la mujer* (Madrid: Biblia y Fe, 1988).

• CHRISTIAN, A. Luceta. "La mujer negra centroamericana," in Irene Foulkes, ed., *Teología desde la mujer en Centroamérica* (San José, Costa Rica: SEBILA, 1989).

• CONCHA, Leonor Aída. "Luchas y logros en el proceso de liberación de la mujer," in María Pilar Aquino, ed., *Aportes para una teología desde la mujer* (Madrid: Biblia y Fe, 1988).

COPELAND, Mary Shawn. "The interaction of Racism, Sexism and Classism in Women's Exploitation," *Concilium* 194 (1987): 19-27.

COX, Harvey. *The Seduction of the Spirit: The Use and Misuse of People's Religion* (New York: Simon and Schuster, 1973).

CRESPO, Luis Fernando. "Método teológico: Notas sobre la reflexión teológica en América Latina," *CAM-Serie Iglesia y Religión* 18 (1983): 1-19.

DE ALMEIDA, Antonio José. "Modelos eclesiológicos e ministérios eclesiais," *Revista Eclesiástica Brasileira* 48/190 (1988): 310-352.

• DE BARBIERI, Teresita. *Mujeres y vida cotidiana* (Mexico: SEP/80, 1984).

DE COLL, Josefina O. *La resistencia indígena ante la conquista*, 5th. ed., (Mexico: Siglo XXI, 1986).

DEL MORAL, Maite. "Lo femenino. Breve recorrido por la psicología y el mito," *Sal Terrae* 11 (1988): 747-756.

• DEL PRADO, Consuelo. "I Sense God in Another Way," in Elsa Tamez, ed., *Through Her Eyes. Women's Theology from Latin America* (Maryknoll, N.Y.: Orbis Books, 1989).

DE RIVERA, Miguel, ed. *Chilam Balam de Chumayel*, vol. 20, (Madrid: Historia 16, 1986).

• DE ROCCHIETTI, Araceli. "Women and the People of God," in Elsa Tamez, ed., *Through Her Eyes. Women's Theology from Latin America* (Maryknoll, N.Y.: Orbis Books, 1989).

DE SANTA ANA, Julio. *Ecumenismo y liberación* (Madrid: Paulinas, 1987).

———. "The Situation of Latin American Theology (1982-1987)," *Concilium* 199 (1988): 231-241.

DUMAIS, Monique. "Must a Theology of Service for Women make Them into Second Class Citizens?" *Concilium* 194 (1987): 102-109.

DUSSEL, Enrique. *Ethics and Community* (Maryknoll, N.Y.: Orbis Books, 1988).

ECHEGARAY, Hugo. *La práctica de Jesús*, 3rd. ed. (Lima: CEP, 1989).

———. "Educación popular y construcción de la identidad de género," *Tejiendo nuestra red* 2 (1989).

ELLACURIA, Ignacio. "Diez Afirmaciones sobre Utopía y Profetismo," *Sal Terrae* 12 (1989): 889-893.

———. "Hacia una fundamentación filosófica del método teológico latinoamericano," in Raúl Vidales, Jon Sobrino, Gustavo Gutiérrez et al., *Liberación y Cautiverio* (Mexico, 1976).

———. "Premisas socio-económicas implícitas y explícitas de la teología de la liberación," in Ignacio Ellacuría, Juan José Tamayo-Acosta, et al., *Implicaciones sociales y políticas de la Teología de la Liberación* (Instituto de Filosofía, Universidad de Sevilla, 1989).

———. "La teología de la liberación frente al cambio sociohistórico de América Latina," in Ignacio Ellacuría and Juan José Tamayo-Acosta et al., *Implicaciones sociales y políticas de la teología de la liberación* (Instituto de Filosofía, Universidad de Sevilla: 1989).

FABELLA, Virginia and Mercy Amba ODUYOYE, eds. *With Passion and Compassion: Third World Women Doing theology* (Maryknoll, N.Y.: Orbis Books, 1988).

• FERRO, Cora, Elsa TAMEZ, María Pilar AQUINO et al. *Mujer Latinoamericana, Iglesia y Teología* (Mexico: MPD, 1981).

FORCANO, Benjamín. *Nueva ética sexual*, 3rd. ed., (Madrid: Paulinas, 1981).

• FOULKES, Irene, ed. *Teología desde la mujer en Centroamérica* (San José, Costa Rica: SEBILA, 1989).

GALILEA, Segundo. *El camino de la espiritualidad*, 3rd. ed. (Bogotá: Paulinas, 1987).

GALLARDO, Helio. *Actores y procesos políticos latinoamericanos* (San José, Costa Rica: DEI, 1989).

GARCIA CALLADO, María Josefa. "Automarginación femenina: Una aproximación desde el psicoanálisis," *Sal Terrae* 11 (1988): 757-762.

―――. "Comentario global a los capítulos II, III y IV del libro de L. Boff, *El rostro materno de Dios*," Photocopied personal notes, Madrid, 1989.

―――, Maite DEL MORAL et al. "La mujer: Novedad de un antiguo proyecto," *Sal Terrae* 11 (1988).

• GEBARA, Ivone. "Option for the Poor as an Option for the Poor Woman," *Concilium* 194 (1987): 110-117.

• ―――. "El reino de Dios en la lucha por la sobrevivencia. Un aspecto de la lucha de las mujeres en el Brasil," *Misiones Extranjeras* 108 (1988): 369-379.

• ―――. "Women Doing Theology in Latin America," in Elsa Tamez, ed., *Through Her Eyes: Women's Theology from Latin America* (Maryknoll, N.Y.: Orbis Books, 1989).

• ――― and María Clara BINGEMER. *Mary, Mother of God, Mother of the Poor* (Maryknoll, N.Y.: Orbis Books, 1989).

• ―――, Maruja GONZALEZ B., Beatríz MELANO-COUCH et al. *Apuntes y Aportes de la mujer ecuménica* (APE-FEC, Mendoza, Argentina, Cuaderno Pastoral 4-6, 1986-1987).

• ―――, Elsa TAMEZ, María Clara BINGEMER et al., *El rostro femenino de la teología* (San José, Costa Rica: DEI, 1986).

GIBELLINI, Rosino. "Feminismo y Teología," *Iglesia Viva* 121 (1986): 49-66.

―――, ed. *Frontiers of Theology in Latin America* (Maryknoll, N.Y.: Orbis Books, 1979).

GOMEZ HINOJOSA, J. Francisco. *Intelectuales y pueblo. Un acercamiento a la luz de Antonio Gramsci* (San José, Costa Rica: DEI, 1987).

GOMEZ TRETO, Raúl. *The Church and Socialism in Cuba* (Maryknoll, N.Y.: Orbis Books, 1988).

GONZALEZ, José Luis. "Apuntes para la observación de la religiosidad popular," *CAM Serie Iglesia y Religión* 19 (1984): 7-21.

• GONZALEZ B., Maruja. *¿Qué es el feminismo? Breve historia y aproximaciones teórico-políticas* (EMAS, Serie Pensamiento y Luchas 2, Mexico, 1989).

• ―――. "La situación de la mujer en América Latina," in Itziar Lozano,

Maruja González B. et al., *La mujer, taller de la vida: Constructora de la nueva sociedad* (Habana, Cuba: CCP-LAC, 1984).

• ———, Carmen LORIA, and Itziar LOZANO. *Utopía y lucha feminista en América Latina y el Caribe* (Mexico: EMAS-CIDHAL-GEM, 1988).

• ———, and Itziar LOZANO. *Feminismo y movimiento popular en América Latina*, (Mexico: EMAS-CIDHAL, Serie Pensamiento y Luchas 8, 1986).

• ———, Itziar LOZANO et al. *La mujer, taller de la vida: Constructora de la nueva sociedad* (Habana, Cuba: CCP-LAC, 1984).

GONZALEZ CARRION, Francisco Javier. "Filosofía de la historia latinoamericana según Leopoldo Zea," *Anthropos* 13 (1986): 43-61.

———. "Identidad del hombre latinoamericano según Leopoldo Zea," *Anthropos* 14 (1987): 5-14.

GUTIERREZ, Gustavo. *Dios o el oro en las indias* (Salamanca: Sígueme, 1989).

———. *On Job: God-Talk and the Suffering of the Innocent* (Maryknoll, N.Y.: Orbis Books, 1987).

———. "Un lenguaje sobre Dios," *Concilium* 191 (1984): 53-61.

———. *The Power of the Poor in History* (Maryknoll, N.Y.: Orbis Books, 1983).

———. *Teología desde el reverso de la historia* (Lima: CEP, 1977).

———. "Theology and the Social Sciences," in *The Truth Shall Make You Free* (Maryknoll, N.Y.: Orbis Books, 1990).

———. *A Theology of Liberation* (Maryknoll, N.Y.: Orbis Books, 1988).

———. *We Drink from Our Own Wells: The Spiritual Journey of a People* (Maryknoll, N.Y.: Orbis Books, 1984).

HALKES, Catharina. "The Rape of Mother Earth: Ecology and Patriarchy," *Concilium* 206 (1989): 91-100.

———. "Feminist Theology: An Interim Assessment," *Concilium* 134 (1980): 110-123.

HARTMANN, Heidi. "Un matrimonio mal avenido: hacia una unión más progresiva entre marxismo y feminismo," *Zona Abierta* 24 (1980): 105-116.

HEISE, Lory. *Crimes of Gender: Documented Prevalence of Violence against Women* (Worldwatch Institute, March/April 1989).

HELLER, Agnes. *Historia y vida cotidiana* (Barcelona: Grijalbo, 1972).

HINKELAMMERT, Franz. *Crítica a la razón utópica* (San José, Costa Rica: DEI, 1984).

———. *La deuda externa en América Latina* (San José, Costa Rica; DEI, 1988).

———. *The Ideological Weapons of Death: A Theological Critique of Capitalism* (Maryknoll, N.Y.: Orbis Books, 1986).

• JORDAN, Irma Janis. *A libertação da mulher hoje, na igreja e na sociedade: uma aproximação teológico-moral*. Report presented to the National Meeting of Professors of Moral Theology, Brasilia, 1985 (photocopied).

KELLER, Miguel Angel. *Evangelización y liberación. El desafío de Puebla* (Madrid: Biblia y Fe, 1987).

KOSNIK, A. *Human Sexuality: New Directions in American Catholic Thought* (New York: Paulist Press, 1977).

• LAPIEDRA, Aurora. "Religiosidad popular y mujer andina," in Elsa Tamez, ed. *El rostro femenino de la teología* (San José, Costa Rica: DEI, 1986).

• ———. "Roles y valores de la mujer andina," *Allpanchis* 25 (1985): 43-63.

LE CLEZIO, J.M.G. *Le rêve mexicain ou la pensée interrompue* (Mesnil-sur-l'Estrée: Gallimard, 1988).

LEGRAND, H.-M. "Ministerios de la iglesia local," in *Iniciación a la práctica de la teología*, vol. III, (Madrid: Cristiandad, 1984).

LEHMANN, Karl. "La valoración de la mujer en el problema de la antropología," *Revista Católica Internacional Communio* IV/82, Madrid (1982): 237-245.

LEON-PORTILLA, Miguel, ed. *Cantos y crónicas del Mexico antiguo*, vol. 23, (Madrid: Historia 16, 1986).

———. *Crónicas indígenas: Visión de los vencidos*, vol. 6, (Madrid: Historia 16, 1985).

———. *El reverso de la Conquista: Relaciones aztecas, mayas e incas*, 7th. ed. (Mexico: Joaquín Mortiz, 1980).

LIBANIO, J. B. and María Clara BINGEMER. *Escatología cristiana* (Madrid: Paulinas, 1985).

LOIS, Julio. "Jesucristo liberador," *AA.VV.*, Universidad Pontificia de Salamanca (1988): 37-67.

———. *Teología de la liberación. Opción por los pobres* (San José, Costa Rica: DEI, 1988).

• LORA, Carmen. *Implicancias teológicas en la experiencia de las organizaciones femeninas en el ámbito de la vida cotidiana*. Report presented to the Maryknoll School of Theology, April, 1987 (photocopied).

• ———. "Mujer latinoamericana, historia de una rebeldía," in María Pilar Aquino, ed., *Aportes para una teología desde la mujer* (Madrid: Biblia y Fe, 1988).

• ———. "Mujer: víctima de opresión, portadora de liberación," in Carmen Lora et al., *Mujer: víctima de opresión, portadora de liberación* (Lima: Instituto Bartolomé de las Casas, 1985).

• ———, Cecilia BARNACHEA, and Fryné SANTISTEBAN, eds. *Mujer: Víctima de opresión, portadora de liberación* (Lima: Instituto Bartolomé de las Casas, 1985).

• LOZANO, Itziar. *Feminismo y movimiento popular en América Latina* (Mexico: EMAS-CIHDAL, Serie Pensamiento y Luchas 8, 1986).

MADURO, Otto. "Apuntes epistemológico-políticos para una historia de la teología en América Latina," in Pablo Richard et al., *Materiales para una historia de la teología en América Latina* (San José, Costa Rica: CEHILA-DEI, 1981).

MALDONADO, Luis. *Introducción a la religiosidad popular* (Santander: Sal Terrae, 1985).

• MAY, W. Janet. "Desde la debilidad hacia la fuerza: El proceso educativo en la pastoral de la mujer," *Vida y Pensamiento* 8/2 (1988): 105-109.

MEJIA, Jorge Julio. "La coyuntura de la iglesia católica en América Latina," *Pasos* 19 (1988): 1-7.

• MELANO-COUCH, Beatríz. "El Reino de Dios y la ética," in Ivone Gebara et al., *Apuntes y Aportes de la mujer ecuménica* 5 (Mendoza, Argentina: APE-FEC, 1987).

MIRES, Fernando. *La colonización de las almas* (San José, Costa Rica: DEI, 1987).

————. *En nombre de la cruz* (San José, Costa Rica: DEI, 1986).

MOLINA, Uriel. "Estructura y funcionamiento de una comunidad cristiana popular," *Concilium* 196 (1984): 321-330.

MOLTMANN-WENDEL, Elisabeth. *A Land Flowing with Milk and Honey: Perspectives on Feminist Theology* (New York: Crossroad, 1986).

MUÑOZ, Ronaldo. *La Iglesia en el pueblo* (Lima: CEP, 1983).

PACHECO, Juan Manuel. "La evangelización en Colombia," in Enrique Dussel, ed., *Historia general de la Iglesia en América Latina*, vol. VII, (Salamanca: Sígueme, 1981).

PARAMIO, Ludolfo. "Feminismo y socialismo: raíces de una relación infelíz," *Teoría* 6, April-June (1981).

————. *Lo que todo marxista vulgar debe saber sobre feminismo: Nuevas perspectivas sobre la mujer*, (Madrid: Universidad Autónoma de Madrid, 1982).

PARDO, Rosa. "Bajo el signo de la reproducción," *Misión Abierta* 3 (1980): 62-69.

PINTOS, Margarita. *Aportación de la mujer a las iglesias de América Latina*. University of Munich, Faculty of Sociology, 1989 (photocopied).

————. *La Mujer en la Iglesia* (Madrid: Paulinas, 1990).

————. *Recogiendo la antorcha de Débora*. Report presented to the XVIII Congreso de Teología-Asociación de Teólogos Juan XXIII, Madrid, 1988 (photocopied).

PINTOS M. Margarita, Felisa ELIZONDO et al. *La mujer, realidad y promesa* (Madrid: PS, 1989).

PIXLEY, Jorge, ed. *La mujer en la construcción de la iglesia* (San José, Costa Rica: DEI, 1986).

• PORCILE, María Teresa. "El derecho a la belleza en América Latina," in Elsa Tamez, ed. *El rostro femenino de la teología* (San José, Costa Rica: DEI, 1986).

RAHNER, Karl. "Do Not Stifle the Spirit," *Theological Investigations*, Vol. VII (New York: Seabury Press, 1977).

————. *Foundations of Christian Faith: An Introduction to the Idea of Christianity* (New York: Crossroad, 1987).

————. *The Shape of the Church To Come* (New York: Crossroad, 1983).

RAMING, Ida. "From the Freedom of the Gospel to the Petrified 'Men's Church': The Rise and Development of Male Domination in the Church," *Concilium* 134 (1980): 3-13.

• RIBEIRO, Lucía. "La relación entre mujeres profesionales y mujeres de los sectores populares," International Seminar PAX ROMANA-MIIC, Dar-es-Salam, Tanzania, 1985.

RIBEIRO DE OLIVEIRA, P. "¿Qué significa analíticamente pueblo?," *Concilium* 196 (1984): 433-441.

RICHARD, Pablo. "Década de los noventa: una esperanza para el Tercer Mundo," *Pasos* 27 (1990): 1-6.

———. "Espiritualidad para tiempos de revolución: Teología espiritual a la luz de San Pablo," in Eduardo Bonín, ed., *Espiritualidad y liberación en América Latina* (San José, Costa Rica: DEI, 1982).

———. *La fuerza espiritual de la iglesia de los pobres* (San José, Costa Rica: DEI, 1987).

———. "La iglesia de los pobres en el movimiento popular," *Concilium* 196 (1984): 331-340.

———. *La iglesia latinoamericana entre el temor y la esperanza* (San José, Costa Rica: DEI, 1980).

———. "Literatura teológica de América Latina," *Concilium* 219 (1988): 277-287.

RICHARD Pablo, Otto MADURO et al. *Materiales para una historia de la teología en América Latina* (San. José, Costa Rica: DEI, 1981).

• RITCHIE, Nelly. "Women and Christology," in Elsa Tamez, ed., *Through Her Eyes. Women's Theology from Latin America* (Maryknoll, N.Y.: Orbis Books, 1989).

• ———. "Women's Participation in the Church. A Protestant Perspective," in Virginia Fabella and Mercy Amba Oduyoye, ed., *With Passion and Compassion. Third World Women Doing Theology* (Maryknoll, N.Y.: Orbis Books, 1988).

• RODRIGUEZ, Marcia. *Haití: Un pueblo rebelado 1915-1981,* (Mexico: Macció, 1982).

• RODRIGUEZ, Raquel. "La mujer y su autoridad en la nueva creación," *Vida y Pensamiento* 6/2 (1986): 33-41.

• ———. "Esperanza contra esperanza: Perspectivas bíblico-teológicas de la pobreza desde la mujer latinoamericana," *Pasos* 20 (1988): 1-9.

• ROSADO NUÑEZ, María José. "Entrevista," en Elsa Tamez, *Las mujeres toman la palabra* (San José, Costa Rica: DEI, 1989).

RUETHER, Rosemary Radford. *Contemporary Roman Catholicism. Crises and Challenges* (Kansas City: Sheed & Ward, 1987).

———. "Misogynism and Virginal Feminism in the Fathers of the Church," in Rosemary Radford Ruether, ed., *Religion and Sexism. Images of Woman in the Jewish and Christian Traditions* (New York: Simon & Schuster, 1974).

———. "La mujer y el ministerio en una perspectiva histórica y socioló-gica," *Concilium* 111 (1976): 41-53.

———. *New Woman New Earth. Sexist Ideologies & Human Liberation* (San Francisco: Harper & Row, 1975).

———. *Sexism and God Talk* (Boston: Beacon Press, 1983).

———. *To Change the World: Christology and Cultural Criticism* (New York: Crossroad, 1983).

• RUIZ, María Teresa. *Racismo algo más que discriminación* (San José, Costa Rica: DEI, 1988).

RUIZ DE LA PEÑA, Juan L. *Imagen de Dios. Antropología teológica fundamental* (Santander: Sal Terrae, 1988).

• SANTISTEBAN, Fryné. "Mujeres profesionales y mujeres pobres," Inter-

national Seminar Pax Romana-MIIC, Dar-es-Salam, Tanzania, 1985.
• ———— and Lucía RIBEIRO. "Participación de las mujeres profesionales en el desarrollo y en el cambio de la sociedad: Papel actual y potencial," International Seminar Pax Romana-MIIC, Dar-es-Salam, Tanzania, 1985.

SAUQUILLO, Francisca, Rosino GIBELLINI et al. "Mujeres en un mundo masculino," *Iglesia Viva* 121 (1986).

SCHÜSSLER FIORENZA, Elisabeth. *Bread Not Stone: The Challenge of Feminist Biblical Interpretation* (Boston: Bacon Press, 1984).

————. "Breaking the Silence — Becoming Visible," *Concilium* 182 (1985): 3-16.

————. "The Endless Day: Introduction," *Concilium* 194 (1987): xvii-xxiii.

————. "Editorial," *Concilium* 182 (1985): ix-xiii.

————. *In Memory of Her: A Feminist Theological Reconstruction of Christian Origins* (New York: Crossroad, 1985).

————. "Remembering the Past in Creating the Future: Historical-Critical Scholarship and Feminist Biblical Interpretation," in A. Yarbro Collins, ed., *Feminist Perspectives on Biblical Scholarship* (Chico, California: Scholars Press, 1985).

————. "Toward a Feminist Biblical Hermeneutics: Biblical Interpretation and Liberation Theology," in B. Mahan and L. Dale Richesin, ed., *The Challenge of Liberation Theology* (Maryknoll, N.Y.: Orbis Books, 1984).

————. " 'Waiting at Table': A Critical Feminist Theological Reflection on Diakonia," *Concilium* 198 (1988): 84-94.

SEGUNDO, Juan Luis. *The Liberation of Theology* (Maryknoll, N.Y.: Orbis Books, 1976).

————. *Teología abierta para el laico adulto*, vol. I, (Buenos Aires: Lohlé, 1972).

SERRANO, Augusto. *Los caminos de la ciencia: Una introducción a la epistemología* (San José, Costa Rica: DEI, 1988).

SOBRINO, Jon. "¿Cómo hacer teología? La teología como intellectus amoris," *Sal Terrae* 5 (1989): 397-417.

————. *Spirituality of Liberation. Toward Political Holiness* (Maryknoll, N.Y.: Orbis Books, 1988).

————. "Teología de la liberación y teología europea progresista," in *Desafíos Cristianos-Misión Abierta* (Madrid: Loguez, 1988).

————. *The True Church and the Poor* (Maryknoll, N.Y.: Orbis Books, 1984).

————. "El Vaticano II y la iglesia en América Latina," in Casiano Floristán and Juan José Tamayo-Acosta, ed., *El Vaticano II veinte años después* (Madrid: Cristiandad, 1985).

SÉJOURNÉ, Laurette. *América Latina: Antiguas culturas precolombinas*, 19th. ed. (Mexico: Siglo XXI, 1987).

• SOJO, Ana. *Mujer y política: Ensayo sobre el feminismo y el sujeto popular* (San José, Costa Rica: DEI, 1985).

SOWLE CAHILL, Lisa. *Between the Sexes. Foundations for a Christian Ethics of Sexuality* (Philadelphia: Fortress Press; New York: Paulist Press, 1985).

STEIN, S. J. y B. H. *La herencia colonial en América Latina*, 17th. ed. (Mexico: Siglo XXI, 1986).

TAMAYO-ACOSTA, Juan José. "Claves para comprender la Teología de la Liberación," in Juan José Tamayo-Acosta, ed., *La Teología de la Liberación: Implicaciones Sociales y Políticas* (Madrid: Ediciones de Cultura Hispánica, 1990).

———. *Para Comprender la Teología de la Liberación* (Estella, Navarra: Verbo Divino, 1989).

———, ed., *La teología de la liberación: implicaciones sociales y políticas* (Madrid: Ediciones de Cultura Hispánica, 1990).

• TAMEZ, Elsa. *Against Machismo: Interviews* (Oak Park: Meyer-Stone Books, 1987).

• ———. *Contra toda condena. La justificación por la fe desde los excluídos* (San José, Costa Rica: DEI, 1991).

• ———. *Introducción a la problemática de la mujer en América Latina*, in Elsa Tamez et al., *Comunidad de mujeres y hombres en la iglesia* (San José, Costa Rica: SEBILA, 1981), pp. 33-41.

• ———. "Introduction: The Power of the Naked," in Elsa Tamez, ed., *Through Her Eyes. Women's Theology from Latin America* (Maryknoll, N.Y.: Orbis Books, 1989).

• ———. "Justicia y justificación con ocasión de la deuda externa en América Latina," *Pasos* 22 (1989): 11-13.

• ———. "Meditación bíblica sobre la mujer en Centroamérica," *Vida y Pensamiento* 6/2 (1986): 53-57.

• ———. "La mujer como sujeto histórico en la producción teológica," in Cora Ferro et al., *Mujer Latinoamericana, Iglesia y Teología* (Mexico: MPD, 1981).

• ———. "Mujer y varón llamados a la vida. Un acercamiento bíblico-teológico," in Raúl Vidales and Luis Rivera Pagán, ed., *La esperanza en el presente de América Latina* (San José, Costa Rica: DEI, 1983).

• ———. *Las mujeres toman la palabra* (San José, Costa Rica: DEI, 1989).

• ———. "Ser madre en un contexto de opresión," in Carmen Lora et al., *Mujer: víctima de opresión, portadora de liberación* (Lima: Instituto Bartolomé de las Casas, 1985).

• ———. "The Woman Who Complicated the History of Salvation," *Cross Currents* 20 (1986) 129-139.

• ———. "Women's Rereading of the Bible," in Virginia Fabella and Mercy Amba Oduyoye, ed., *With Passion and Compassion: Third World Women Doing Theology* (Maryknoll, N.Y.: Orbis Books, 1988).

• ———. ed., *Through Her Eyes: Women's Theology from Latin America* (Maryknoll, N.Y.: Orbis Books, 1989).

• ——— et al. *Comunidad de mujeres y hombres en la iglesia* (San José, Costa Rica: SEBILA, 1981).

• ——— et al. "La mujer, Biblia y Teología," *Vida y Pensamiento* 6 (1986).

• ——— and Saúl TRINIDAD, eds. *Capitalismo, violencia y anti-vida* I (San José, Costa Rica: DEI-EDUCA, 1978).

• TEPEDINO, Ana María. "Feminist Theology as the Fruit of Passion and

Compassion," in Virginia Fabella and Mercy Amba Oduyoye, ed., *With Passion and Compassion: Third World Women Doing Theology* (Maryknoll, N.Y.: Orbis Books, 1988).

• ———. "Jesús e a recuperação do ser humano mulher," *Revista Eclesiástica Brasileira* 48/190 (1988): 273-282.

• ———. "Mujer y misión," *Misiones Extranjeras* 108 (1988): 361-367.

TOLBERT, Mary Ann. "Defining the Problem: The Bible and Feminist Hermeneutics," *Semeia* 28 (1983): 113-126.

TORRES, Sergio. "Dar-es-Salam, 1976," *Concilium* 219 (1988): 295-304.

TUÑON PABLOS, E. *También somos protagonistas de la historia de Mexico* I,II,III (Mexico: EMAS, Serie Pensamiento y Luchas 5, 6 y 7, 1987-1988).

VIDALES, Raúl. *Desde la tradición de los pobres* (Mexico: CRT, 1978).

———. "La insurgencia de las etnias: Utopía de los pueblos profundos," in Raúl Vidales and Luis Rivera Pagán, ed., *La esperanza en el presente de América Latina* (San José, Costa Rica: DEI, 1983).

———. "Methodological Issues in Liberation Theology," in Rosino Gibellini, ed., *Frontiers of Liberation Theology* (Maryknoll, N.Y.: Orbis Books, 1979).

——— and Tokhiro KUDO. *Práctica religiosa y proyecto histórico* (Lima: CEP, 1977).

VILANOVA, Evangelista. *Historia de la teología cristiana*, vol. I, (Barcelona: Herder, 1984).

• VILCHIS REYES, Laura. *Vida cotidiana y violencia hacia las mujeres.* Report presented to the Encuentro Latinoamericano sobre la Situación de la Mujer en América Latina (San José, Costa Rica: DEI, 1989) (Photocopied).

VOGT, Kary. "«Becoming Male»: One Aspect of an Early Christian Anthropology," *Concilium* 182 (1985): 72-83.

WEELOCK, R. Jaime. *Raíces indígenas de la lucha anticolonialista en Nicaragua*, 7th. ed. (Mexico: Siglo XXI, 1986).

YARBRO COLLINS, Adela, ed. *Feminist Perspectives on Biblical Scholarship* (Chico, California: Scholars Press, 1985).

ZEA, Leopoldo. *Dialéctica de la conciencia americana* (Mexico: Biblioteca Iberoamericana, 1976).

———. *Discurso desde la marginación y la barbarie* (Barcelona: Anthropos, 1988).

———. *La filosofía americana como filosofía sin más* (Mexico: Siglo XXI, 1969).

———. *Introducción a la filosofía. La conciencia del hombre en la filosofía*, 9th. ed. (Mexico: UNAM, 1983).

ZUBIRI, Xavier. *Inteligencia y Logos* (Madrid: Alianza Editorial, 1982).

Church Documents

The Documents of Vatican II, Walter M. Abbott, S.J., ed. (New York: American Press, 1966).

Final Document of the Second General Conference of Latin American Bishops, The Medellín Conclusions II, 2nd. ed., Division for Latin America USCC, Washington, D.C., 1973.

Final Document of the Third General Conference of Latin American Bishops, The Puebla Conclusions, Secretariat for Latin America NCCB, Washington, D.C., 1979.

Quadragesimo Anno and *Rerum Novarum*, in David J. O'Brien and Thomas A. Shannon, ed. *Catholic Social Thought: The Documentary Heritage* (Maryknoll, N.Y.: Orbis Books, 1992).

Final Documents of Theological Congresses

"Final Document" in Sergio Torres and John Eagleson, ed. *The Challenge of Basic Christian Communities: Papers from the International Ecumenical Congress of Theology, February 20-March 2, 1980, São Paulo, Brazil* (Maryknoll, N.Y.: Orbis Books, 1981).

"Intercontinental Women's Conference, Oaxtepec, Mexico, December 16, 1986," in Virginia Fabella and Mercy Amba Oduyoye, ed. *With Passion and Compassion: Third World Women Doing Theology* (Maryknoll, N.Y.: Orbis Books, 1988).

"The Irruption of the Third World: Challenge to Theology, Fifth Ecumenical Association of Third World Theologians Conference, New Delhi, August 17-29, 1981," in Virginia Fabella and Sergio Torres, eds., *Irruption of the Third World: Challenge to Theology* (Maryknoll, N.Y.: Orbis Books, 1983).

"La mujer latinoamericana, la praxis y la teología de la liberación, Encuentro Latinoamericano sobre Mujer, Iglesia y Teología," México, 1979, in Cora Ferro et al., *Mujer Latinoamericana, Iglesia y Teología* (Mexico: MPD, 1981).

"Postura de la Mujer Latinoamericana frente a la Sociedad, la Iglesia y la Biblia, Encuentro Latinoamericano Comunidad de Mujeres y Hombres en la Iglesia," San José, Costa Rica, 1981, in Elsa Tamez, Irene Foulkes et al., *Comunidad de Mujeres y Hombres en la Iglesia* (San José, Costa Rica: SEBILA, 1981).

"Theology from the Perspective of Women. Latin American Conference, Buenos Aires, Argentina, Oct. 30-Nov. 3, 1985," in Elsa Tamez, ed., *Through Her Eyes. Women's Theology from Latin America* (Maryknoll, N.Y.: Orbis Books, 1989).

Index